MW01518809

THE EXPERIENCE OF
POVERTY

THE EXPERIENCE OF POVERTY

Fighting for respect and resources in village India

TONY BECK

INTERMEDIATE TECHNOLOGY PUBLICATIONS 1994

Intermediate Technology Publications Ltd
103/105 Southampton Row, London WC1B 4HH, UK

© Intermediate Technology Publications 1994

A CIP catalogue record for this book is available from the British Library

ISBN 1 85339 218 9

Typeset by Dorwyn Ltd, Rowlands Castle, Hants
Printed by BPC Wheatons, Exeter

Contents

Acknowledgements

As the Russian proverb goes, to live one's life is not as simple as crossing a field, and neither, so I discovered, is writing a book. Fortunately I was helped by many people.

My family managed to maintain good humour during what at times may have appeared an extended eccentric exercise – a notable achievement. In India, I have to thank Maitraye Devi, who unfortunately died before this book could be published, for her unstinting hospitality and friendship; and Samar Bagchi, for his willingness to make time in an overbusy schedule for friends over many years. The children and staff at *Khelaghar* in West Bengal, where I worked for two and a half years, were a continual source of inspiration; apologies to two of the children (now grown up) for naming two of the villages in this book after them. Drs Sunil Sengupta, Madan Ghosh and C.R. Pathak gave intellectual and moral support.

At field level several people assisted with interviews, including Maya Rani Lodh, Kalipodo Pal, Electron Mukherjee, and villagers from the three study villages. Niranjan Ghosh of the Government of West Bengal Forest Department assisted in many ways to make the stay in Midnapore successful and enjoyable. The officers of the Land Revenue Office in Barasat were also very helpful in directing me to land records.

My thanks also go to Larry Becker, Tirthankar Bose, Bob Bradnock, Graham Chapman, Edward Clay, Benny Farmer, Barbara Harriss and Barrie Morrison who read and commented on one or more chapters, or related work. Numerous conversations with the peripatetic Steve Jones provided many insights. I am grateful in particular to Robert Chambers who suggested I turn what was a content PhD thesis into a book.

Cathy Nesmith drew the maps, and read and commented on the whole of the text, improving its intellectual content and restraining its more garish impulses. Thanks to her for seeing it through thin and thick, and much more.

Glossary

Adibhashi	Tribal (literally: indigenous dweller)
Aman	The late monsoon agricultural season, or paddy grown in that season
Aus	The early monsoon agricultural season, or paddy grown in that season
Bargadar	Sharecropper
Basta	60 kg (literally: a sack)
Boro	The dry agricultural season, or paddy grown in that season
Bhadoi	The early monsoon season
Bhadralok	Gentleman
Bigha	Measure of land, equivalent to 0.33 decimals in 24 Parganas District, and 0.62 decimals in Midnapore District
Dacoit	Robber, bandit
Dadan	Agricultural contract system where credit is repaid with labour
Danga Dahi	High, usually poor-quality land
Dhan	Paddy
Dheki	Machine for dehusking rice
Dhoti	Men's garment
Goondah	Criminal, usually belonging to a gang
Hat	Measure, about 45 cm
Jhinghe	*Luffa acuntangula*
Jotedar	Rich peasant, and/or rent receiver
Kaccha	Made of natural materials; poorly made (literally: unripe)
Kaloo	Black
Kattah	Land measure, equal to one-twentieth of a *bigha*
Khas	Land vested in the government under a land reform programme
Khathah	Sown quilt
Lal	Red
Lathial	Henchman of *zamindar*
Maund	Weight, equivalent to 40 kg
Mouza	Village-level administrative boundary, roughly equivalent to one village and the fields and land associated with it
Panchayat	Village-level government body
Panchayat Samiti	Block-level government body
Par Routi	Leavened bread
Para	Sub-section of a village
Prahdhan	Leader
Purdah	System of seclusion of women (literally: curtain)
Robi	The dry agricultural season
Sal	*Shorea robusta*
Sali	Lower-lying paddy land
Shottuck	Land measure, equivalent to one decimal
Zamindar	Traditional rent collectors in Bengal, made into landlords by the British Permanent Settlement
Zilla Parishad	District-level government body

Acronyms

BFTW	Bread for the World
CPM	Communist Party of India (Marxist)
CPR	Common Property Resource
DRDA	District Rural Development Authority
HYV	High Yielding Variety
IRDP	Integrated Rural Development Programme
MV	Modern Variety
NSS	National Sample Survey
RDC	Rural Development Consortium, Calcutta
STW	Shallow Tubewell
USKS	*Udayan Samaj Kalyan Samity*
WBEAA	West Bengal Estates Acquisition Act

1 Poor people love to eat fish

LET ME START with a story. I have heard different renditions of this story in my travels over West Bengal and Bangladesh. The latest version I heard was in north-east Bangladesh, in the middle of the monsoon season, August 1992. I was holding a meeting with fifteen farmers and two Bangladeshi government officials in a village near Maulvi Bazaar in Sylhet District, in connection with an aid project there. These were not poor farmers. They were all wearing wristwatches, and some of them were also wearing western clothes. From the look of them, some must have been substantial landowners locally, and one was a village-level political representative who also, so I heard, had significant landholdings. As it was the middle of the monsoon, we had a very dramatic backdrop. There was a thunderstorm close by. During the meeting rain came beating down on the roof of the small shed we were sitting in, which eased the mid-afternoon heat, and lightning lit up the darkening paddy fields. The monsoon rains can be very beautiful.

I was asking the farmers about the local farming systems and crops that they grew and we got on to the subject of agricultural labourers and their daily wages. These wages were very low at that time of year because there is little work for labourers to do. I asked the farmers about the price of rice, which was seasonally high, and then, doing some simple calculations out loud, I asked them how the poor got by when they weren't even earning enough to buy rice for their families. The reply from the local political representative, who did much of the talking, was this: 'This happens every year at this time of year and the poor have got used to it. They are used to eating less and it doesn't bother them.' Then someone else chipped in in a more sinister fashion: 'They have to be used to it, they don't have any choice.' We then moved on to development projects in the area and I asked if there were any projects for the poor locally. The reply to this was: 'It is pointless setting up projects to try and help the poor. There was an NGO locally that lent some money to some poor women, but rather than buying a cow as they were meant to, they spent all the money in three days stuffing themselves with fish.' This response touched a vein and elicited laughter from the other farmers. Here was a familiar and comforting note – 'Poor people love to eat fish.'

I have heard this story about how irresponsible the poor are many times from different farmers and officials throughout West Bengal and Bangladesh, and there is always the same punch line – poor people spend any loans in three days because they can't control their greed and can't plan for the future. I'm not, of course, trying to suggest that it is only the rich who spend money irresponsibly – no doubt many poor people do so as

1

well. But the representation of the poor in these stories is a clear one – they are greedy, irresponsible, or lazy. They are used to their poverty and it doesn't bother them, and even if it did bother them they have to get used to it, because they don't have any choice in the matter.

One of the main arguments of this book will concern the representation of the poor. I will argue that the way in which the poor are represented, in discussions on aid, in development documents and discourse, and in everyday conversations, affects the way in which anti-poverty development programmes are made. This might seem obvious once spelled out in this fashion, but has not been sufficiently recognized in the past. If the poor are represented as passive, irresponsible or lazy, then external intervention will probably take a top-down approach where benefits are 'targeted' at the poor. If, on the other hand, the poor are viewed as active contributors to the making of their societies, external intervention may take a quite different approach.

Most contemporary studies of poverty concentrate on weaknesses of the poor. They look at how hungry or weak the poor are, how many of them die or are sick, how many of them can't read, or simply count the numbers who are poor. Similarly, most evaluations of development programmes look at the way the poor have been excluded from these programmes, rather than at how the poor have succeeded in making demands on the state or the village élite. From one perspective, this makes good sense, because illness, death and hunger, and the denial of crucial resources are so closely related to poverty. But from another perspective the representation that we get from these studies is overwhelmingly a negative one. I will turn the standard approach to the poor and poverty upside down and focus not on their weaknesses but on their strengths. The book will consider how poor people in rural India experience poverty in its many forms, and what they attempt to do about it; in other words, how they themselves go about improving their quality of life and standard of living. It is best to say from the start that the opportunities the poor have to do this are extremely limited, constrained as they are by the exploitation to which they are subjected by the élite in their villages with whom they must co-exist to survive at all. The poor are subordinated within the iron vices of class, caste and patriarchy. How poor women and men fight against these constraints is explored throughout this book.

This book is a study of how poor people gain respect and resources in three villages of West Bengal in eastern India, but to come to an understanding of what the experience of these poor people means, I take a long route. The book begins, in chapter two, with an examination of the development of poverty measurement, now the main means of conceptualizing poverty worldwide, tracing its origins to nineteenth-century Britain, and the influence this British heritage has had on the way that the poor are represented in India today. The narrowness and political objectives of the

2

dominant statistical paradigm of poverty measurement is called into question, and linked in turn to other negative representations of the poor in mainstream political science writing on India.

The tradition of poverty measurement is contrasted with a radically different tradition in chapter three. Here I examine work that has been broadly sympathetic to the plight of the poor. In particular I analyse the writings of E.P. Thompson and the people's history school, and their attention to poor people's agency and experience. While such a focus brings us closer to what poverty is and means, I argue that 'experience' and 'agency' remain difficult terms, and the approach of the authors I discuss remains problematic in that they fail to delineate adequately the socio-economic and political constraints in which the agency and experience of the poor need to be situated. Nevertheless, the contribution made by Thompson and others who approach poverty from a similar perspective remains the best theoretical tool that I have come across to understand the interactions of poverty and power, particularly given their ability to link theory and practice in their analysis. The chapter then goes on to consider writing on the experience of the modern-day poor in South Asia and what can be learnt from this.

The next three chapters analyse socio-economic and power structures at regional and local levels, and in doing so contextualize the experience of the poor at village level. Chapter four provides background to the case study areas, 24 Parganas and Midnapore districts in West Bengal, and includes an analysis of the West Bengal government's anti-poverty programmes since 1977. Chapter five describes how the study came to be carried out, how it was done, and gives background information on the three villages that were chosen as the focus of the study, noting in particular structural features of village life, who controls village resources, and power relations. An attempt is then made to categorize village households so that relations of power can be more clearly understood.

Chapter six examines the structural features of the rural economies of the study villages in more detail by evaluating two rural development programmes, both supported by the state government. In the 24 Parganas District study village, an irrigation scheme is assessed over three seasons to discover its effects on village socio-economic structures and on the poor. This allows a contribution to an ongoing debate on the equity effects of the 'green revolution' in India. In the two study villages from Midnapore District, I evaluate the government land reform programme. Both of these programmes are seen to reinforce existing socio-economic structures, but with some uneven benefits accruing to the poor.

Chapters seven and eight move to the short- and long-term coping strategies that are used by the poor, and particularly poor women, as they struggle, negotiate and bargain for respect and village resources. Chapter seven looks at a number of strategies, from use of common property resources to

3

management of livestock and assets, paying close attention to the relations between poor and rich involved with the use of each of these strategies. Chapter eight turns directly to the question of power, how the poor resist oppression and violence, and their views on the rich and their fellow poor. In both of these chapters I look for areas of strengths of the poor that could be built upon through external intervention by policymakers. Chapter nine ends the fieldwork study on a sombre note, looking at how three poor villagers died and why their coping strategies broke down.

Two themes run persistently through the book. The first is that, as outsiders, we should look to the strengths of the poor, but also that these strengths have to be viewed as interacting with the enormous constraints that the poor face. To overstress the strengths of the poor would be to romanticize their abilities; they certainly are capable and often ingenious, but this does not mean that they can solve all of their problems without outside help. On the other hand, to overstress constraints they face would be to negate the abilities they do have. This in turn is related to my emphasis on experience as an organizing feature. I wanted to know what oppression, exploitation, powerlessness, hunger, survival and initiative mean to the poor themselves. But I argue as well that focusing on experience is complicated by issues of limited vision of individuals and complex identities that poor people may hold. I have addressed these problems by locating and attempting to understand the experience of the poor in the overall context of poor people's lives.

A second theme of the book is that understanding the experience of poverty can help us see why poverty continues to exist, and what it is feasible to do about it, not from the perspective of the outsider but from that of those who have most knowledge of poverty. All too often policy seems to be made on the basis of conceptualizations such as 'poor people love to eat fish' or 'poor farmers are risk adverse'. Focusing on strengths of the poor can have two important consequences. The first is to contribute to the theoretical meta-debate about the characteristics of the poor and argue against the representation of the poor as particularly passive or irresponsible. Policymakers and politicians are going to be making development programmes for the foreseeable future, and influencing the way that they think about the poor will have an input into the kinds of programmes that are made. The second consequence is that what poor people already do, from within unequal power structures, to improve the quality of their lives, may act as a base for development programmes to build on. If poor people have learnt how to get more respect or resources from the village élite, to manipulate village power structures to their benefit, no matter how small, don't we have something to learn from that ourselves? The message is a simple one – build on the strengths of the poor before attempting anti-poverty development programmes such as those considered in chapter six that may be irrelevant (or worse) as far as the poor are concerned.

4

This book, like much of the work it criticizes, still involves a labelling of the poor, but in this case the labelling will be a positive one. I have decided that this is the best level at which to answer critics of the poor, as it is at this level that much of the debate on poverty is conducted. However, this book is written to be constructive rather than negative. While I am critical of some approaches, I believe that the academic 'community' needs to join together to find something that works as far as eliminating poverty is concerned. So far we have not had much success.

2 'Beyond enumeration': The construction of poverty in nineteenth-century Britain and twentieth-century India

Introduction

How have the poor been perceived historically, and how does this affect policy-making? This chapter will answer this question using nineteenth-century Britain and twentieth-century India as case studies. It will argue that the way in which poverty is constructed as a concept is a crucial factor in determining how society reacts to the poor.

Poverty has been defined and explained in various ways. The most important contemporary method of discussing poverty is through its measurement. Despite this, there is little understanding of the origins of poverty measurement, or the connection between choice of this particular technique and policy-making. I therefore examine how methods of poverty measurement originated in nineteenth- and early twentieth-century Britain, and how authors on poverty measurement drew on contemporary views of the poor in developing these methods. I argue that the view taken of the poor in early studies of poverty measurement is integrally connected to regulatory policy for dealing with poverty.

Measurement of poverty as developed in Britain has been a central influence on poverty measurement in India. I show that the methods of measuring poverty in pre- and post-Independent India, and the preoccupations of the measurers, remain those of the British originators of the poverty line. As poverty measurement is considered by planners and academics as the most important method of conceptualizing poverty in India, I argue in these three sections that it can be considered a dominant paradigm. I then extend the discussion by reviewing the work of selected contemporary political scientists writing on India, and point out how their methods of conceptualizing the poor remains within the same dominant paradigm.

An understanding of the history and political nature of poverty measurement makes it clear that mainstream debates concerning poverty conducted in India today operate within a sterile statistical paradigm which has developed out of a tradition that sees poverty as the responsibility of the poor and the solution to poverty as social control. I argue in this chapter that if the poor are viewed simply as statistics, figures and ciphers, then the policy that is formulated to alleviate poverty will, in all likelihood, follow suit and be more relevant to the manipulation of statistics than to the needs of people.

The construction of poverty in nineteenth-century Britain

'Absolute' poverty, now prevalent as a means of conceptualizing poverty in India and most other countries, is usually traced back to the work of the two British social reformers, Charles Booth and Seebohm Rowntree (see for example Sen, 1982; Townsend, 1979). The concept of absolute poverty can be equated with the 'head count' measure; that is, it involves the setting of a 'poverty line' by estimating the minimum level at which an individual or household can subsist. In developing countries, poverty lines are often set dependent on the amount of money considered necessary to purchase an adequate number of calories. The number counted below this subsistence level or poverty line are said to be in poverty (hence the term 'head count'). Absolute poverty is usually contrasted to 'relative' poverty, which compares the relative living standards of different groups or individuals and considers those with lower living standards to be in poverty (see Townsend, 1979).

The purpose of this section is to examine the writings of Booth and Rowntree and the origins of and background to the formation of the concept of absolute poverty measurement, discussing the nineteenth-century tradition of debates on poverty in Britain on which these two men drew. In addition, this section will examine the underlying or structural features of the poverty measurement paradigm, and the construction of the poor within it. To make my argument I will exploit the various meanings of the word 'measure'. According to the 1989 edition of the Oxford English Dictionary, measure has three meanings. The everyday meaning or most common usage is: 'to estimate the amount, duration, value, etc. of (an immaterial thing) by comparison with some standard'. The second meaning, which is less commonly used, is: 'to form an opinion or opinions . . . to weigh or gauge the abilities or character of (a person), with a view to what one is to expect from him'. An example of this meaning would be: 'When she came into room to start the speech, we took her measure'. The third meaning, now rarely used (but resurrected for the purposes of this chapter) is: 'to regulate, moderate, restrain'. An example of this meaning would be: 'He walked forward at a measured pace'. This section will show that, with regards to poverty measurement, measure in its normal usage – that is, 'to estimate the amount', cannot be separated from its other two meanings, concerning character and regulation.[1]

---

[1] The moral or ethical and the mathematical are often closely connected in the English language. For example, one can estimate a person's character as well as estimate an amount, or weigh up a character as well as weigh an object. 'Worth' is a similar term – for example, a person's contribution can be considered worthless. Terms of affection, such as 'dear' or 'precious', also have the same double meaning (an item can be dear, or people may use the term as one of affection). This connection is probably related to the mercantile base of British society.

Contemporary views of the poor informed poverty measurement when it first moved to a more 'scientific' and mathematical basis at the end of the nineteenth century in Britain. One set of such views stemmed from the nature of nineteenth-century British society. As Hobsbawm put it (1975: 219): 'Inequality of life and expectation was built into the system'. The 'bourgeois' view of society was thus: 'Since success was due to personal merit, failure was due to personal lack of merit. The traditional bourgeois ethic, puritan or secular, had ascribed this to moral or spiritual feebleness rather than lack of intellect . . .' (ibid.: 246).

Much of the work of authors on poverty in Britain in the eighteenth and nineteenth centuries embraced this 'bourgeois' ethic. Their 'opinions' were sensitive to the sufferings of the poor, but they also took a stance of moral superiority. Frederick Eden, who provided 'parochial reports' on the state of the poor from parishes throughout Britain in the 1790s, presented a view that was the forerunner to many others, and representative of one way the rich thought about the poor in the nineteenth century (1928: 100):

> There seems to be just reason to conclude that the miseries of the labouring Poor arose less from the scantiness of their income (however much the philanthropist might wish it to be increased) than from their own improvidence and unthriftiness . . .

Eden makes a connection between poverty and morality ('improvidence and unthriftiness') that was to be made again and again throughout the nineteenth century (for examples, see Thompson, 1986). Associated with this view of the poor as improvident came a criticism of their unwise eating habits (Eden 1928: 106):

> The aversion to broths and soups composed of barley meal or oatmeal is in many parts of the South almost insuperable. Instances occurred during last winter [1794] when the poor were extremely distressed by the high price of provision; of their rejecting soup which was served at a gentleman's table.[2]

The 'general ignorance of the poor in cooking', to quote the title of one of the chapters of Alexis Soyer's cookery book *A Shilling Cookery For The People* (Soyer, 1855), remained a common theme into the early twentieth century. The poor were considered ignorant not only in cooking but also in most other areas of their lives (see Mennell, 1985; and Snell, 1985 on the nineteenth-century rural labourer).[3] It is unsurprising to see a constant

---

[2] See also Thompson (1986: 347–51) and the Hammonds (1948: 119) on attempts to change the diet of the poor at the beginning of the nineteenth century.

[3] Various bodies proselytized improved eating habits for the poor. Two of these were the Universal Cookery and Food Association (Cookery Annual, 1908: 121), and the influential Charity Organisation Society (Bosanquet, 1898; Dendy, 1895).

connection made in the nineteenth century between poverty, the eating habits of the poor, and hunger, as hunger plays such a large part in poor people's lives and what the non-poor think poverty is like. Many studies of poverty in the contemporary Third World have continued this tradition (now almost an obsession) of focusing on the eating habits of the poor to the exclusion of a consideration of other aspects of their lives.

This view of the poor as irresponsible is further documented in the report of the House of Commons Inter-Departmental Committee on Physical Deterioration of 1904, to which Booth and Rowntree made presentations. The Committee was set up to examine the poor physical status of recruits for the army intended for the war in South Africa. The ability of the state to maintain a fighting force to protect colonial interests depended on the physical status of the poor, which in turn rested on what and how the poor ate. Here is the contemporary view of the poor (Inter-Departmental Committee 1904: 15):

> . . . in large classes of the community there has not been developed a desire for improvement commensurate with the opportunities offered to them. Laziness, want of thrift, ignorance of household management, and particularly to the choice and preparation of food, filth, indifference to parental obligations, drunkenness, infect adults of both sexes, and press with terrible severity on their offspring.

Such comments might of course be made about other more literate and richer members of society, but were and are usually reserved for the poor. Nor have such views disappeared from modern-day political discourse on poverty; for example, the front page of the British *Guardian* newspaper reported in June 1991 that a British social security minister had said: 'People in Britain only go hungry because they buy the wrong food'.

Such views of the poor in nineteenth and early twentieth-century Britain were part of a larger argument about the responsibility of the state for poverty (Himmelfarb, 1985; Lis and Soly, 1979). For example, in the 1840s Henry Mayhew contributed a series of very influential articles to the *Morning Chronicle* newspaper which sensationalized and brought to the attention of the London public, almost for the first time, the extent of poverty and style of living of the poor. The *Economist* magazine then commented on Mayhew's work thus (Thompson and Yeow, 1971: 26):

> The people can only help themselves . . . Their fate is given into their own hands; they are responsible for their condition; the rich are no more responsible for their condition than they are responsible for the condition of the rich . . .

If the poor failed to be responsible, for example in matters such as choice of food, then the causes of poverty lay with them, and not with the social structure or 'the rich'. The concentration by social commentators on the

9

wrong choice of food or other irresponsible actions by the poor can be seen as a strategy which located the causes of poverty with the poor themselves. Solutions to poverty were therefore to be found in educating the ignorant poor as to how to manage their households. Alternative views of the poor and the causes of poverty, based on the works of Adam Smith, Tom Paine, William Cobbett and others were also prevalent in the nineteenth century, but the view of the poor as irresponsible remained dominant, and was a major influence on the formation of poverty measurement.

Original 'measures' of poverty, or estimates of poor people's characters, were therefore concerned with deciding who was responsible for poverty. As the nineteenth century progressed this led to more sophisticated divisions among the poor, into separate but not clearly distinct groups. As was common for the time, Mayhew in his articles divided the poor into those who would and would not work – or the moral and immoral poor.[4] This supported the notion that a section of the poor were irresponsible and unwilling to improve themselves, and therefore 'responsible' for their poverty. But it also suggested that some of the poor were 'moral' and willing to work (Thompson and Yeow, 1971). The responsible, moral poor were artisans, the stalwarts of the nineteenth-century industrial system, and more likely to adopt the values of the middle classes, as opposed to the 'dangerous and ragged masses' who needed to be controlled (Hobsbawm, 1975). As Himmelfarb (1985) has shown, the division between pauper and labouring poor established with the Poor Law Amendment Act of 1834 moved away from the eighteenth-century definition of poverty which saw no such divisions.

Measurement and morality – Charles Booth and Joseph Rowntree

It is clear that by the time poverty came to be measured statistically at the end of the nineteenth century, divisions based on moral categories had already been made amongst the poor. Charles Booth continued and expanded this moral categorization in his *Life and Labour of the People in London*, which examined poverty in the 1880s. This study covered 909,000 people in the East End of London, and was based on personal visits, School Board visitors' records, and figures from the Poor Law statistics and the Charities Organization Society. A poverty line based on income was set, the first use of such a measure in modern Britain, and the sample subsequently divided into eight classes based on income – A to H – the first four of which were below the poverty line.

---

[4] See Thompson (1986: 439); Schaffer (1985: 42–3); Lis and Soly (1979: 195); Hobsbawm (1975: 224–29); and for a detailed discussion Himmelfarb (1985). For similar divisions outside of Britain see Hunter on early twentieth-century U.S.A. (1912: 2–5), and Hufton on late eighteenth-century France (1974: 22, 114).

Each of the eight classes mentioned had its own characteristics. Class A led (Booth 1969: 11):

> ... the life of savages, with vicissitudes of extreme hardship and occasional excess ... they render no useful service, they create no wealth; more often they destroy it. They degrade whatever they touch, and as individuals are perhaps incapable of improvement.

It is from Booth's description of class A that I have taken the title for this chapter. According to Booth class A were literally 'beyond enumeration' (that is Booth's researchers could not count them) because there was no record of them on the School Board visitors' records.

One moral rung up this moral ladder of poverty were class B, which included many who (ibid.: 13):

> from shiftlessness, helplessness or drink, are inevitably poor. The ideal of such persons is to work when they like ... They cannot stand the regularity and dulness of civilized existence ...

And so on, through the more respectable and self-sufficient poor, classes C and D, to the upright and 'honourable' class F (ibid.: 19). Booth's classes thus essentially followed nineteenth-century tradition in dividing the moral from the immoral poor, even though he also used a poverty line based on income.

Booth's method of dividing the poor into economic and moral categories was followed by Rowntree in his well-known survey of every working-class household in York in 1899, and in his less well-known book on country labouring families (Rowntree, respectively 1922 and 1913). Rowntree extended the precision of measurement by calculating a poverty line based upon the expense from contemporary scientific views of what constituted a minimum diet,[5] to which were added the cost of rent, clothing, fuel and household sundries. For the first time in Britain poverty measurement was based on contemporary 'scientific' findings.

As noted above, Rowntree's 1899 study is claimed as a forerunner to absolute measures of poverty. However, measurement of subsistence was only one part of Rowntree's work (see Veit-Wilson, 1986). Following nineteenth-century tradition, Rowntree divided the poor into two categories – the 'primary' and 'secondary' poor. The number in primary poverty was decided on a head-count basis (Rowntree, 1922). These were the 're-spectable' or moral poor of nineteenth-century tradition, poor through no fault of their own.

---

[5] An idea originally used by Rowntree's father in his co-authored book *The Temperance Problem and Social Reform* (Rowntree and Sherwell, 1899), a standard Edwardian manual on temperance; see Williams (1981: 356–60).

The number in secondary poverty was worked out using this method (ibid.: 148):

> The investigator, in the course of his house-to-house visitation, noted down the households where there were evidences of poverty, i.e. obvious want and squalor. Direct information was often obtained from neighbours, or from a member of the household concerned, to the effect that the father or mother was a heavy drinker . . . Judging in this way, partly by appearance, and partly from information given, I have been able to arrive at a fair estimate of the total number living in 'secondary' poverty.

Part of Rowntree's survey was therefore based on 'appearance' and hearsay, or in other words (the second of the meanings of 'measure') – 'to weigh or gauge the abilities of (a person) with a view to what one is to expect from him'. Those in secondary poverty were (ibid.: xix):

> Families whose total earnings would be sufficient for the maintenance of merely physical efficiency were it not that some portion of them is absorbed by other expenditure, either useful or wasteful.

Rowntree was equivocal about the causes of secondary poverty, as the reference to 'useful or wasteful' expenditure suggests, but he came down on the side of wasteful expenditure: 'drink, betting and gambling, the predominant factor being drink. Ignorant housekeeping and other improvident expenditure' meant that many 'respectable families . . . have sunk to the low moral level of their neighbours' (ibid.: 176, 88). Nine point nine per cent of the sample were found to be in primary poverty, and 17.9 per cent in secondary. Again following nineteenth-century tradition, Rowntree also commented on the advantages that would accrue to the 'labouring classes' if 'they possessed greater knowledge of the relative value of food stuffs' (ibid.: 284). Education and moral uplift were therefore required to overcome secondary poverty. While developing a measure based on nutritional information, Rowntree's study also therefore used 'opinion' to determine his categories of poverty, and in his schemata the secondary poor were considered responsible for their own poverty.[6] Caught on the cusp of the two centuries, Rowntree wavered between nineteenth-century prejudice and what has become known in the twentieth century as 'hard' science.

Solutions to poverty and regulation of the poor

Alongside such constructions came suggestions for solutions to poverty, which were rife throughout the nineteenth century in Britain (for ex-

---

[6] In his later studies of poverty in York, Rowntree (1941: vi, 461; 1951) abandoned the use of 'secondary poverty' as definition of 'obvious want and squalor' was no longer possible, or comparable to the situation of 1899 when his first study took place.

amples, see Himmelfarb, 1985). One theme that stretched throughout the century was the idea of labour camps and the regulation of movement of the poor. This was connected to increased mobility of the poor, which was seen at the time as a threat to social stability. The utilitarian Jeremy Bentham, for example, developed a scheme for pauper management which was to involve the establishment of a National Charity Company (under Bentham's directorship), based on the model of the East India Company, that would have 'undivided authority' over the 'whole body of the burdensome poor'. In this scheme the poor would be housed in model prisons, the architecture of which would allow visibility from a central point into all the cells (see Himmelfarb, 1985). More radical ideas were also floated. One proposed solution to the 'problem' of prostitution among poor needle-women revealed by Mayhew was the deportation of half a million women to the colonies, a policy supported by Prime Minister-to-be Gladstone, among others (Thompson and Yeow, 1971).[7]

The idea of model prisons surfaced again in Booth's work when he discussed solutions to poverty. Booth's class A, the poorest class and class beyond enumeration, while 'the ready materials for disorder when occasion serves' (Booth 1969: 11), were considered a disgrace but not a danger. But classes A and B together threatened to unsettle the social structure by dragging down the respectable, self-sufficient poor to their own level (ibid.: xxix). Booth's remedy was thus:

> To bring class B under state regulation would be to control the springs of pauperism . . . the Individualistic system breaks down as things are, and is invaded on every side by Socialistic innovations, but its hardy doctrines would have a far better chance in a society purged of those who cannot stand alone . . . my idea is that these people should be allowed to live in families in industrial groups planted wherever land and building materials were cheap; being well housed, well fed, and well warmed, and employed from morning to night on work indoors or out, for themselves or on government account . . . Class A, no longer confounded with the 'unemployed' would be gradually harried out of existence.

The enforced movement of a considerable portion of the population (class B made up 11 per cent of Booth's sample, ibid.: 13) stemmed directly from the moral divisions Booth made among the poor, and from 'estimation' of their character. Identification of the poor allowed repulsion of 'Socialistic innovations' and also provided a means of exorcizing the threat of 'Socialism and Revolution' – a constant preoccupation of those concerned with

---

[7] For details of schemes of deportation intended for the nineteenth-century agricultural labourer, see Snell (1985: 111–13). For discussion of the Poor Law of 1834 as a disciplinary measure, see Snell (1985: 121).

poverty, as we shall see below. It is also of note that Booth's enterprise in examining poverty was begun as a means of disproving contemporary Socialist claims as to the numbers of the poor in London; ironically, his study showed that the number 'in poverty' was higher than the Socialists claimed. But the wider point here is that Booth's enterprise was an eminently political one, despite its pseudo-scientific orientation.

Brown (1968) has pointed out that after the publication of Booth's *Life and Labour of the People in London*, 'a number of detailed plans were brought forward for the creation in Britain of a system of labour colonies', which were also discussed in the House of Commons Inter-Departmental Committee on Physical Deterioration (1904: 85), suggesting that Booth's thinking was representative of that of his time.

Rowntree also had wider social concerns than simply identifying the poor. As a politician and businessman, he was interested in Britain's trading place in the world. A contemporary fear which Rowntree shared concerned the deterioration of the national physique through the movement of country labourers to the towns where they would become 'anaemic' (Rowntree, 1913; see also the Inter-Departmental Committee, 1904). In particular Rowntree saw Britain losing out because of the greater efficiency of the American worker, an efficiency gained because the American worker was better nourished, returning again to a general obsession with poor people's eating habits (Rowntree, 1922). And as part of his interest in Britain as a trading nation, Rowntree was also concerned about 'harmonious social and industrial co-operation' (Rowntree, 1922: xv), which could only be achieved by the presence of a well-fed workforce. Rowntree maintained a similar concern with social order to that expressed by Booth, as can be seen in the following quotation from Rowntree's work (1913: 14):

> Already the country dwellers have given up their best, and this prospect, from the point of view of the maintenance of the national physique, is not bright . . . Work on the land . . . produces a solid strength of character which our English nation can ill afford to lose. The town dweller, on the other hand, suffers from living too quickly and living in a crowd. His opinions are the opinions of the crowd – and a crowd is easily swayed, for evil as well as for good.

Here are Booth's 'ready materials for disorder', the 'lawless and furious rabble' (Thompson 1986: 66; and see Hobsbawm 1975: 211) who were a threat to industry and the moral and social order, and who needed to be controlled.[8]

---

[8] Aronson (1984: 5–6) notes that the nutritional studies conducted by W.O. Atwater, the first Chief of the US Office of Nutritional Investigation, were funded by, among others, a 'network of economists, statisticians, and philanthropists concerned about labour violence.' Rowntree quoted extensively from Atwater (see 1922: 119–25) to support his estimates of the poverty line.

The idea that the crowd may be 'swayed . . . for evil' led to a concern about the foundations of a democratic system which had one quarter of its population living in poverty (Rowntree, 1922):

> There is surely need for a greater concentration of thought by the nation upon the well-being of its own people, for no civilization can be sound or stable which has as its base this mass of stunted life.

These ideas were a part of the overall makeup of Rowntree's industrial philosophy and are representative of views held throughout the nineteenth century on the need for a compliant workforce (see Thompson, 1986; Lis and Soly, 1979; Hobsbawm, 1975).

Booth and Rowntree, the founding fathers of the poverty line, re-defined the moral preoccupations of their time as to the nature of poverty, building on moral divisions of the poor that were developed throughout the nineteenth century. They paid little attention to possible social or structural causes of poverty, focusing instead on weaknesses and lack of responsibility of the poor, and the possible threats society faced from them. Regulatory policy followed naturally from their moral and economic attempts at measurement, and in this they followed closely the moral code of their time. I would argue therefore that from the origins of poverty measurement the three meanings of 'measure' converged; the poor were measured statistically, their characters were estimated by opinion, and an attempt was made to regulate them based on this. The conclusion that can be drawn from this is the simple one that the view taken of the poor, the way in which the characteristics of the poor were constructed, determined to a large extent the solutions that were proposed to the problem of poverty.

While Booth and Rowntree can be criticized as 'moral statisticians', they both also displayed considerable compassion and concern for the poor. Their books contain long, detailed case studies of poor families, giving sympathetic accounts of their lifestyles and insights into the the lives of the poor. This familiarity with the lifestyles of the poor is largely missing from contemporary analysis of poverty in India, where the British tradition has been developed as a concentration on techniques of quantification, while maintaining, implicitly, the moral and political concerns of Booth and Rowntree. This is addressed in the next section.[9]

---

[9] The concept of a 'culture of poverty' has been influential in more modern formulations of causes of poverty, such as those propagated by Oscar Lewis and his followers (see e.g. Lewis, 1966). Lewis picks up on the tradition of nineteenth-century morality studies of the poor, and attempts to identify the characteristics of a social sub-group called the poor. Discussion of the culture of poverty concept can be found in Schaffer (1985: 54–8); Townsend (1979: 66–71); and Wade (1973).

Poverty measurement in India

In India, much of the debate on poverty has involved using macro-level statistics on income and nutrition to set a poverty line and calculate the numbers below it. This is an important debate, because the rise and fall of the numbers below or above a set poverty line is used by the government and its critics to claim the success or failure of its anti-poverty projects and programmes, and also to formulate government policy. However, the central preoccupation of the majority of the authors on poverty has been the accuracy of the statistics and statistical techniques used. One is reminded by these debates of the character of Stein in Joseph Conrad's novel *Lord Jim*, who spends most of his time preoccupied with his collection of rare butterflies in the study of his immaculate mansion, occasionally stepping out to make prophetic comments on the workings of the world. In a similar way economists working on Indian poverty have built themselves statistical towers and mansions from which they can peer down on the poor. Below we step outside their arcane, erudite statistical debates and consider the philosophical foundations of this form of academic inquiry. The discussion below will challenge the idea that statistical measurement is in some way value neutral. To do this I will outline how Indian academics and planners have worked within the same paradigmatic structure, and with the same preoccupations, as Rowntree and Booth, and have followed British tradition and connected the measurement of poverty to a particular view of the poor, and a particular political world view. I will also discuss the language used in documents on poverty, which will support my more general argument.[10]

The history of poverty measurement in India
Prevailing themes on poverty from the British nineteenth century reappear in state documents from colonial India – particularly the view of the poor as apathetic and irresponsible. This is one result of the social background of British administrators and colonial ideology in India (on which, see Guha, 1986; Stokes, 1959). The similarity can be noted between statements in the *Report of the Royal Commission on Agriculture in India*, published in 1928, and that quoted above from the House of Commons Inter-Departmental Committee on Physical Deterioration, as to the lack of entrepreneurship among the poor:

---

[10] The statistical accuracy of different sides in the poverty debate has been summarized elsewhere (Sagar, 1988; Thakur, 1985; Cutler, 1984), and will not be dealt with here. Using the head-count measure, the percentage of the population 'in poverty' has remained much the same between the mid-1960s and mid-1980s (Lipton and Toye, 1990).

at the heart of the problem (of improved agriculture in I.
development of the desire for a higher standard of living . .
nant feature in rural India in the present day is that the will to .
is not a force to be reckoned with. (Government of India, 1928:

Seventeen years later the Famine Inquiry Commission (Government of India, 1945a, b) produced a wide-ranging report on the 1943 famine in India. One of the Commission's terms of reference was 'the possibility of improving the diet of the people' (1945b: vii). The authors complained of poor people's lack of flexibility in their eating habits, in a passage which echoes that of Eden's comment quoted above about the English poor refusing to eat barley and oatmeal (Government of India, 1945a: 176):

> During the famine large supplies of wheat and millet were sent to Bengal and helped to relieve food shortage. They were supplied to rice eaters through the free kitchens but efforts to persuade people to eat them in their homes in place of rice met with little success.

And in a passage almost identical to the earlier opinions of the Inter-Departmental Committee on Physical Deterioration (1904), another theme – on the ignorance of the poor mother – appears (Government of India, 1945b: 108):

> The general experience of those concerned with infant mortality and infant welfare work supports the view that much sickness and mortality among infants are due to the faulty feeding of mother and child.

The echoing of official statements over decades and continents is surely not a coincidence; the political message is clear – it is the faulty and wayward eating habits of the poor that is the cause of hunger, rather than the authorities or social structure.[11] A contemporary example of 'blaming the victim' can be found in Breman's study of migrants and paupers from Gujarat. Breman notes that employers in his study area justified payment of low wages to labourers in general by harping on the characteristics of the latter, which they saw as including (1985a: 285): 'laziness, drunkenness, lack of regularity, ignorance and apathy'. Employers also played on the theme that labourers 'have less needs than "ordinary" people, and can thus make do with less'. (ibid.: 301). In other words, poor people love to eat fish.

The view of the poor as 'ignorant ryots' (Government of India, 1945b:79) fed (sic) into the first attempts to set a poverty line in India, which was based, as in Britain, on the nutritional intake of urban workers. The

---

[11] For a discussion of the 'ignorant mother' as a target of contemporary nutritional education policies, see Wheeler (1985). For other colonial views of the poor as ignorant, lazy and passive, see Dasgupta (1985: 102); Arnold (1984: 63); and Siddiqui (1982: 48).

verty line was first introduced by the Bombay Labour Enquiry Committee in 1937–40 (Thakur, 1985). Following this, the *Report of the Central Wage Board for the Cotton Textile Industry*, published in 1960, fixed a minimum wage based on Rowntree's method of combining nutritional data and expenditure on clothing, housing, fuel, lighting and other miscellaneous items (Franklin, 1967).

However, the first generally-followed use of a poverty line based on income in India was formulated in 1961 by the Perspective Planning Division of the Planning Commission, under the guidance of Pitambar Pant. This report was highly influential and laid the groundwork for future attempts at poverty measurement. It set the minimum necessary expenditure for a family of five to be above the poverty line at 20 rupees a month.[12] According to this measure, the authors found that 'half the population lives in abject poverty' (Pant, 1974:12). The consequences of this were discussed in the first paragraphs of the report, in a passage that would be in place in Rowntree's writings (Pant, 1974: 13):

> Such widespread poverty is a challenge which no society in modern times can afford to ignore for long. It must be eradicated both on humanitarian grounds and as an essential condition for orderly progress. No programme or policy which fails to alleviate the conditions of the poor appreciably can hope for the necessary measure of public co-operation and political support in a mature democracy.

That this influential document should concern itself with the relation between quantification, 'orderly progress' and democracy is consistent with the ideological history of poverty measurement, and the connections I have made between poverty measurement and social progress.[13]

The Planning Commission's report on poverty was followed by two widely-discussed articles, by Dandekar and Rath (1971a,b), on the dimensions and trends of poverty in India, and the number of those below the poverty line. In the same way as Rowntree and Pant, Dandekar and Rath's quantification was indivisible from a fear of the inevitable undermining of the 'democratic foundations of the economy' if the gains of development were not distributed equally (1971a: 47). They repeat these fears in the conclusion to the second article (1971b: 146), where they discuss the possibility of revolution if the 'minimum legitimate needs' of the increasingly 'desperate poor' are not 'attended to'. And in a passage dealing with migration from urban to rural areas in India in the 1960s (1971a: 40), they revoice Rowntree's fears of the crowd being 'swayed, for evil as well as for good':

---

[12] For the arbitrary origins of this 'magic' figure, since used by many authors, see Rudra (1974: 281).

[13] For a similar theme from the same volume, see Vaidyanathan (1974: 215). None of the studies quoted in this section acknowledge their British heritage.

All the latent dissatisfaction about the slow progress of the economy and the silent frustration about its failure to give the poor a fair deal ... appear to be gathering in this form (in slum life in the cities). Its shape today is probably no more than hideous, allowed to grow unheeded and unrelieved it will inevitably turn ugly.[14]

Dandekar and Rath also followed nineteenth-century British tradition by suggesting a policy of the formation of workcamps for the poor (1971b: 14–02):

A rural works programme aimed at offering continuous and regular employment for a section of the agricultural proletariat ... must ... move the people who are willing to work to wherever work exists. It is unlikely to be near everybody's home. It may be within the block, within the district or even outside the district. Wherever it may be, the workers must be moved to where the work exists and when the work in one place is finished, they must be moved to another place. An organization must perform this essential function ...

The poor, or in this case the 'agricultural proletariat', having been measured, can be shipped around by a state organization, in a scheme involving large-scale movement of the population in a fashion similar to that suggested by several nineteenth-century British authors.

Contemporary poverty measurement and 'poverty-line language'

Is it a coincidence that the first major writings on poverty measurement in India should return to the preoccupations of the British Victorians? I would argue that it is not. What is common to both sets of authors is a particular frame of mind that views the poor as passive objects of state planning who are also, paradoxically, possibly dangerous. Most writers measuring poverty in India after Dandekar and Rath have focused exclusively on quantifying the poor at the macro-level by use of the headcount poverty measure, using a single indicator of poverty, and this is now the dominant theme in the literature on poverty in India. A sampling of this literature supports Chambers' view that the preoccupation of academics writing on poverty measurement in India has been with 'flows and measurement', to the exclusion of any examination of the conceptual issues underlying such analyses of poverty (Chambers, 1988: 2).[15]

---

[14] Compare the Draft Fifth Five Year Plan (Government of India 1973: 6) which considers the existence of poverty 'a potential threat to the unity, integrity and independence of the country'. And see also the next section below for similar views.

[15] Poverty measurement studies include Dayal (1989); Singh (1989); Ranade (1988); Ahluwalia (1986); Kurien (1982); B.S. Rao (1982); V.K.R.V. Rao (1982); Bhanoji Rao (1981); Dandekar (1981); Rao and Vivekananda (1981); Sukhatme (1981); Sastry (1980); Chaudhuri (1978); Minhas (1974); Vaidyanathan (1974);[cont. over]

19

Some of these conceptual issues I have already addressed in this chapter, in particular who bears responsibility for poverty and the connection of this to the way in which poverty is constructed. How does the contemporary literature on poverty in India address these issues? Implicit in debates about setting a poverty line are attitudes toward the poor. Contemporary literature on Indian poverty measurement, with its concentration on statistics, has essentially 'demoralized' the debate on poverty, in that there are no explicit references to the poor as 'passive' or 'ignorant'. Instead, the poor have been shunted aside as the main centre of interest, and measurement has taken central place.

This subjugation of moral to statistical priorities does not mean, however, that no view is taken of the poor. What is termed here 'poverty-line language' makes implicit assumptions about those being measured. The assumptions are the same as those made by earlier writers on poverty – that the poor are passive instruments available for measurement and as 'targets' of policy. In planning documents and the literature on poverty measurement the poverty line is visualized as a physical line which separates poor from non-poor. The aim of policy then becomes to push poor people over this line, or help them rise above it. The physical nature of this language is determined by the methodology involved in setting the poverty line.

Reference in this language is made to those 'weaker sections of society' who are 'socially and economically backward', whose 'social and economic status' must be raised (Government of India 1985: 328); to those who could be 'pushed above the poverty line by (the) resource flows' (Sundaram and Tendulkar 1983: 1932); those 'vulnerable sections' who 'through special or specific beneficiary–oriented assistance . . . could be brought above the poverty line' (Government of India, 1981: 170); who 'suffer special disadvantages due to lack of access to both education and health

---

Bardhan (1973, 1970). There have been several criticisms of the use of the head-count poverty line from within the paradigm of poverty measurement. For example, Sen has pointed out that the head-count method ignores both distribution and transfer of income below the poverty line. It also has political implications, in that a concentration of government resources on those just below a head-count poverty line will bring in 'rich dividends', as their income needs to be raised only slightly for them to cross the line, while 'the credit for pushing up even poorer people is likely to be zero in this measure unless they are pushed up quite a bit.' (Sen, 1976: 214, 219; 1974: 78). For attempts to use more sophisticated poverty measures, see Gaiha (1988; 1987; Gaiha and Kazmi, 1981). For a gendered analysis of poverty measures, see Sen, 1990; Agarwal, 1986; Harriss, 1986; and for a review of recent economic literature, Folbre (1986: 11-26). It should be noted that none of these criticisms of the poverty line question its ideological basis, nor do they consider why measurement is being made.

services'; and whose 'isolation severely limits appropriate delivery services for human development'. (Bussink, 1980: 106).[16]

This is a language of bureaucratic planning, with 'targets', 'aims', and recipients ready to be 'pushed', 'raised', accept delivery and be 'attended to'. It is the language of control.[17] The poor have become statistics with which statisticians can play and experiment. It is a short step from this movement of millions above and below lines to the type of policy suggested by Dandekar and Rath, a system to physically move 'willing' workers around the country to wherever work is available. The preoccupation with measurement fits well into a system where policy is created by a centralized state and then imposed on the poor 'from above' in order to shunt the poor above the poverty line. One might and should ask what part the poor themselves have in this process, and why their own experience should be ignored in debates on poverty. The answer is probably that it is far easier to debate with other economists over enumeration or concepts of poverty than it is to speak with the poor. And it is also easier to devise policy from the estimation of numbers than it is to do so from an understanding of the realities of rural life in India.

A further conceptual issue that remains unclarified in contemporary studies of poverty measurement in India is that of the causes of and responsibility for poverty. Booth and Rowntree were clear in their minds that the cause of poverty for at least some of the poor was the inability of the poor to rise above poverty. Are the poor still to blame for poverty, or is poverty the fault of an unequal social structure and exploitation? Or is it a mixture of the two? The current literature on poverty measurement in India gives us no clue. The reader is left with no idea why poverty should have persisted in India, only with an idea of how many people are poor.

This 'science' of poverty measurement may appear both 'objective' and apolitical, in that it deals with statistics. But what remains unstated in debates on poverty is as important as what is included. As far as poverty in India is concerned, the choice of technique to examine poverty is as important as the debates within the particular paradigm chosen. That economists choose to focus on numbers rather than people is as important as the conclusions they come to with regard to how many are below the poverty line. It is difficult to move outside a powerful tradition. The philosophical orientation of economists measuring poverty today remains similar to that

---

[16] See also Saith (1990: 174); Bhanoji Rao (1981: 347); and Mellor (1976: 89). Torry (1986: 14) has also referred (without apparent irony, but perhaps with the Indian mystic tradition in mind) to labourers 'levitated . . . above the official cutoff poverty line of Rs. 346/capita/year.' For use of the terms 'uplift, reform, rehabilitation, guidance and enlightenment' with reference to social welfare organizations in contemporary Tamil Nadu, see Caplan (1985: 202).

[17] For a similar point, see Wood (1985, b, c) on what he calls 'labelling' of the poor as 'targets'.

21

of the founders of the poverty line. As in nineteenth-century British tradition, measurement and the character of the poor are indivisibly connected. In this sense, one may write of a particular dominant paradigm into which most of the literature on poverty measurement fits. Even where the poor are invisible, as in contemporary studies on India, some view of their character is being taken, because by their being made invisible it is assumed that they are characterless, have no voice, and cannot be seen.

The construction of the poor in contemporary political science

There is a telling similarity between the representations of the poor I have already discussed and the construction of the poor in mainstream contemporary north American political science writing on India. I want to look now at the overlapping features from some of the most important authors writing on India over the last twenty years – Francine Frankel, Barrington Moore, and the Rudolphs.

These authors make copious use of moral economy theory, as popularized by Scott (1976, and see the next chapter for a discussion of the origins of this theory). They do this by adapting one strand of this theory for their own purposes – this is, that the penetration of capital into subsistence agrarian systems erodes 'traditional' patron–client relationships that may have been unequal, but provided minimum security for all. The disruption of this security, and increasing differentiation caused by capitalist development, is then seen to be followed by rural instability and peasant protest.

In Frankel's work the erosion of traditional patron–client ties during economic modernization is a key concept. Although what constitutes the traditional is never clearly defined, her most common usage of the term comes in describing a breakdown in past agrarian relations, as is apparent from the following discussion of the effects of the green revolution (1971: 45–6):

> Occurring as these changes are in a local context characterized by an erosion in traditional ties, and an incipient polarization on the basis of class, it would not be surprising if efforts by political parties to mobilize social discontent for power purposes would lead to increasing instances of class confrontation in rural areas.[18]

Rudolph and Rudolph (1987: 384–5) also comment on the nature of traditional agrarian ties in India:

> Under forms of traditional domination, the legitimizing ideologies and power asymmetries of local hierarchies sustained interdependence with

---

[18] For similar comments, see Frankel (1978: 8, 21, 26, 582; 1971: 38, 40, 208). For a critique of the ahistorical nature of Frankel's work, see Harriss (1977: 34–6).

relatively stable local social equilibriums. Legitimizing ideologies sanctioned rights and obligations as well as duties and dependencies by linking putatively nonantagonistic strata in harmonious social order.

Moore (1987) also uses the same idea of the pre-modern harmony existing in 'traditional' Indian rural society.

The formulation of the existence of a pre-modern 'harmonious social order' is dependent on the view that the lower castes and classes passively accepted the ideology of the prevailing order. Frankel notes a contemporary attack on: 'the traditional village system under which harmony was preserved by the mutual acceptance of ascriptive inequalities sanctified by the religious myths of caste'. (1971: 116). In Frankel's work the poor are variously described as 'resigned', 'deferrent', and 'deeply conservative and inert, strongly committed to the traditional social hierarchy of caste, and largely reconciled to their impoverishment' (1971: 10; 107; 177). Almost 20 years later, Frankel returns to a similar refrain (1989: 1):

> Village studies show that . . . asymmetrical obligations among unequals were oriented toward ensuring subsistence for all members according to their ceremonial and productive functions. Religious symbolism became attached to the notion of a 'hierachical collectivity' in which the use of concentrated politico-economic power was circumscribed by moral obligation . . . As a result, it is arguable that commands by the dominant castes were perceived as legitimate and evoked a high level of predictable compliance from the lower castes toward whom they were directed.

A coincident view is also taken by Moore, who writes of the 'passive acceptance' of their situation by the lower castes (1987).[19]

The Rudolphs write in similar terms of the modern agricultural labourer (1987: 387): 'We infer that isolation accompanied by normlessness and apathy has replaced decaying mutual ties in many other local contexts . . .'. The term 'normlessness' here again implies that labourers simply echo élite norms. Breman, whose work is quoted by the Rudolphs as supporting their arguments, has responded (1988: 30):

> To label the behaviour of Halpatis in terms of passivity, amoral individualism and fatalism, as Rudolph and Rudolph are apt to do . . . would negate the forceful opposition shown by these landless workers against their physical and mental oppression.

Breman makes the wider point that calling the poor 'paupers with all the negative characteristics that are linked to that term' (ibid.), is one way of

---

[19] Seavoy (1986: 260) also suggests that the main characteristic of the precapitalist peasant is laziness, and Bauer (1976: 191) comments on: 'The widely prevalent and readily observable torpor and inertia of the population of the Indian subcontinent . . .'.

justifying the exclusion of local workers from the production process in the area he studied, and explaining poverty in terms of poor people's characteristics.

A newer generation of political scientist, Atul Kohli (1990: 385) also wheels out the same patient for operation and follows closely to what has now become the 'traditional' construction of Indian social and political relations:

> Economic development has generated new patterns of division of labor that have undermined traditional caste authority. The spread of commerce has similarly replaced seemingly reciprocal patterns of exchange with the impersonal medium of money, again undermining the traditional bonds of 'solidarity' between social 'superiors' and 'inferiors'. Unequal economic gains have also generated new types of tensions that increasingly resemble class conflict.

And so on. What is not considered in detail in this construction is how far poor people themselves have supported such 'traditional' arrangements. The evidence there is from phenomenological studies of poverty (see the next chapter, and my fieldwork in chapter eight), shows that the poor display considerable scepticism as to the value of such 'traditional' arrangements from which they have supposedly benefited, and that such notions are nearer to the view of society as held by academics than the view of those actually experiencing the social relations they describe.

In conceptualizing the poor as 'passive followers', these authors also view the state or élites as the main actors in poor people's lives (see Kothari, 1988 and Byres, 1988 for further discussion of this point). In Frankel and Moore's work, actions of the poor are seen as reactions to the policies of the state. As well as being open to state manipulation and passive receivers of élite ideology, the poor are also viewed as increasingly susceptible to organization by forces other than the 'traditional'. I have shown above how poverty measurers saw the volatile nature of the poor as a threat to social structure, national stability and democracy. The authors discussed here voice similar fears. As Frankel puts it (1971: 8): '. . . high rates of economic development may actually exacerbate social tensions, and ultimately undermine the foundation of rural political stability'. This leaves room for communist agitation and the possibility that the poor will become convinced by (ibid.: 185): '. . . the Marxist political propaganda that fundamental social change can only be accomplished by the complete overthrow of the existing property system'.[20] The Rudolphs also warn that the 'dissolution of traditional interdependence and absence of a reconstituted moral order' may lead to 'undeclared civil wars', the leading char-

---

[20] For similar comments see Frankel (1978: xii, 3, 21, 580).

24

acteristic of these being 'spontaneous, leaderless violence against property and persons' (1987: 389–90).

Moore is circumspect as to the possibility of violent action by the poor, mainly because, oppressed by the caste system, they have embraced 'hierarchical submission' (Moore, 1987). But, writing a few years before Dandekar and Rath, and like Booth and Rowntree, Moore also saw the spectre of violence in the breakdown of the 'traditional' and the trend of urban migration (ibid.: 406):

> It seems likely that the direction of future changes will be toward further disintegration of traditional ties . . . There is already a huge migration to urban slums where communist agitation does find considerable response. If no place in society is found for this mass of floating labor . . . the political consequences might well be explosive.[21]

I would argue that the construction of poverty is central to the interpretation of Indian society here. It is the received view of the poor as passive, but subject to irrational violence, which is central to the interpretative enterprise of the authors discussed, a remarkably similar view to that found in studies of poverty measurement. Once again, it is the representation of the characteristics of the poor that are a determining factor in establishing how poverty is conceptualized and solutions to poverty determined. It may be that the paradigm of the poor analysed here is found in other writings; for my purpose the examples in this chapter will suffice. It is such psychological and political imposition of unquestioned and untested overgeneralized theories onto the Indian poor that this book aims to challenge.

The story so far

A simple conclusion from this chapter is that the way in which the characteristics of the poor are represented determines external reaction to poverty. Because historically in studies of poverty measurement the poor have been represented as irresponsible or dangerous to the social order, the solutions to poverty have tended to be regulatory. This is not to suggest that there is always a connection between statistics and social control, only that in this one particular case this connection has been a persistent one and has important social consequences. Choice of technique is never politically neutral, even if the workings of that technique can be seen to be

---

[21] This fear of spontaneous violence against 'property and persons' is in addition connected to a fear for Indian democracy and democratic institutions. Although there is no scope to discuss this at length, the political economists also share a similar concern to poverty measurers as to how to 'prevent another breakdown in the democratic process of government' (Frankel, 1978: 582; and see also Kohli, 1990; Moore, 1987: 385–410).

internally logical, as is the case with statistical analysis. Working with numbers is as political as any other area of academic inquiry. I am not (of course) suggesting that statistical or economic analysis has no purpose or role, only that its limitations should be clearly seen.

I have examined in this chapter representations of the poor and the methods by which poverty and solutions to poverty are constructed in academic and planners' discourse. Such examination is, of course, nothing new; rather, it is an established approach developed among others by Said (1978) in his work on Orientalism. But the extended questioning here of the poverty measurement paradigm is new. Poverty measurement is the main prism in our society through which we are permitted to view the poor – the dominant paradigm. Analysis of the historical and contemporary use of this technique can help towards an understanding of its political nature and of how it restricts our vision. In particular, I have argued in this chapter that the dominant paradigm describes a world where the non-poor – statisticians, planners, political scientists – make regulatory decisions for the poor from 'above'. I have looked as well at literature that to a large extent ignores and denies the experience of the poor in favour of the preoccupations of the theorists and academics who have interpreted poor people's world-view for us. In this world, the traditionally subservient, immoral, apathetic, irresponsible, normless but occasionally irrationally violent poor (to use a few epithets and ascriptions from this chapter) are unable to shape their own lives or their society. From my analysis, I would argue that basing policy on received ideas of the poor is unhelpful and potentially damaging, and also that, to stress one of the central themes of this book, those affected by policy should participate in its making. I turn now to alternative ways in which poverty has been constructed that take a different political perspective from the one analysed in this chapter.

26

3   The dimension of human agency

Introduction

This chapter is in the form of a critical review of literature that I have found useful when trying to understand how to approach the study of poverty. I look at several perspectives. The first, Sen's entitlement and capability theories, seeks to extend but ultimately remains within the poverty measurement paradigm. The rest of the literature reviewed – the History Workshop school, the varied and influential writings of E.P. Thompson, and contemporary authors on development – all take a quite different, and in some cases an oppositional perspective on poverty to that of authors discussed in chapter two. In other words, this chapter moves beyond enumeration and numbers, to people and experience.

There are some common themes in this chapter, in particular how authors, mainly from the left, have dealt with the difficult concepts of agency and experience, and whether or not they have been successful in contextualizing agency and experience within what one author has called an 'objective framework', or what I call the structural constraints that limit the action of the poor. As Giddens (quoted below) has pointed out, the question of how best to balance agency and structure is a persistent one in the social sciences, and it is not a question that the following review will attempt to answer definitively. But this chapter does try and illuminate why 'experience' has been chosen as a central organizing feature of this work, and the problems which arise from that choice.

I have been necessarily selective in my choice of literature to review. Other literature, such as the major debate on 'relative' poverty, I have not covered here for reasons of brevity (the debate is summarized in Beck, 1991) and because it did not fit in a discussion of what are basically studies of agency and experience.

Entitlement and capability theory as an alternative to poverty measurement

Firstly, an approach to experience that has attempted to move beyond the constraints of poverty measurement but which I find, in the final analysis, unsatisfactory. The writings of Amartya Sen have had an enormous influence on the discussion of poverty and famine throughout the 1980s, an influence that is likely to continue for some time. Sen has much to say as well about the experience of the poor, and this is the reason his work will be discussed in some detail here. Sen's work came to prominence in development circles with the publication of *Poverty and Famines*, although he

27

had made major contributions to widening the debates on poverty measurement and development before this. *Poverty and Famines* develops 'exchange entitlement' theory, where Sen argues that starvation can be caused by the lack of bargaining power or entitlement of certain groups or individuals, which means that they do not get access to food or other essential items during periods of famine. As an explanation of famine, entitlement theory is a welcome challenge to the simplistic and apolitical theory that food availability decline is the cause of famine, for, as Sen shows, famines can occur when overall availability of food in a given country remains stable (or even increases).

The value and originality of entitlement theory has been much debated and the intention here is not to go over that debate.[1] Instead, I am concerned with Sen's representation of the poor and his attempts to step outside of the narrow measurement paradigm discussed in the last chapter.

Seeming dissatisfaction with an over-emphasis on economics in entitlement theory has led Sen to develop from it another theory of well-being, which he has called capability theory (see Sen, 1990; 1985; 1983; Kynch and Sen, 1983). As Dreze and Sen put it (1989:13): 'The focus on entitlements, which is concerned with the command over *commodities*, has to be seen as only instrumentally important, and the concentration has to be, ultimately, on basic human capabilities.' The capability approach involves examining how far an individual can achieve certain basic aims. Indicators of capability proposed are the ability to survive, be well nourished, free from disease, literate, to receive medical attention, and latterly, the ability of women to work (Sen, 1983; 1985; 1990).

Both entitlement and capability theories were developed as part of Sen's long-term project of moving the analysis of poverty and hunger away from a focus on commodities and food availability, and towards the idea of the individual as an economic actor. Sen argues that the capability approach is an alternative to both 'commodity fetishism' on the one hand, and 'utilitarian mental-metricism' on the other. 'Commodity fetishism', according to Sen, attempts to define well-being in terms of commodities owned or needed rather than what can be achieved with commodities. 'Mental-metricism' focuses on well-being in terms of the 'subjective' perceptions of individuals, unbounded by any 'objective' reality (1983: 366). Hence, steering a middle course between these poles, in capability theory the focus is on what active human beings are capable of achieving, rather than what they possess, or think and believe. As Sen has made clear (1983: 163): 'The capability approach . . . continues to concentrate on human beings – their

---

[1] For some criticisms, see Clay (1991); Arnold (1988). Entitlement theory is discussed in detail, mainly favourably, in the three volumes of *The Political Economy of Hunger*, edited by Dreze and Sen (1990–91).

capabilities in this case – rather than moving with Rawls to incomes, goods and characteristics.'[2]

The view taken of the poor, hungry individual in entitlement and capability theories is ambiguous. In the original hypothesis Sen states (1982: 45):

> The entitlement approach to starvation and famines concentrates on the ability of people to command food through the legal means available in the society, including the use of production possibilities, trade opportunities, entitlements *vis-a-vis* the state, and other methods of acquiring food. A person starves *either* because he does not have the ability to command enough food, *or* because he does not use this ability to avoid starvation. The entitlement approach concentrates on the former, ignoring the latter possibility.

The causes of starvation in the entitlement approach are related directly here to the inability of the individual to command enough food. There is little doubt from the phrasing of the above quotation that the focus of the approach is on the weakness of the poor and hungry, and on their inability. I would argue that a more accurate hypothesis in famine situations or in situations of hunger would concentrate as well on questions of political economy – not only on the ability of the individual, but also on the way in which individuals or groups are denied access to food, by the state, by the local élite, or by other powerful local people. But only one of the four case studies in *Poverty and Famines*, on the Great Bengal famine, considers the role of the state in any detail, and the role of local élites are more or less ignored even in this case study.

A more holistic conceptualization of a poor person would focus on other abilities as well as the ability to command food, and this Sen has attempted in the concept of capabilities. But it is ironic that Sen has chosen to focus almost exclusively on mortality, morbidity and literacy, or the 'capabilities' of being able to stay alive, being free from illness or being able to read and write. These are unfortunately narrow indicators of what human beings are capable of, based on a narrow perception of the abilities of the poor, and follow in a tradition of denying agency to the poor. Sen's more recent work on capabilities has stressed that the poor are 'agents' (e.g. Sen, 1990; Dreze and Sen, 1989), as well as the importance of 'public action' in changing social policy. The type of 'public action' Dreze and Sen invoke, however, is action by the state rather than by the public in the more general sense of

---

[2] The capability approach would appear to be an extension of concepts such as basic needs and the physical quality of life index (PQLI), which consider poverty in terms of access of individuals to basic services. On basic needs in India see Lakdawala, 1988; Rudra, 1981b. The PQLI, for example, uses infant mortality, life expectancy and literacy as indicators of well being (Morris and Mcalpin, 1979), which are similar to Sen's indicators.

the term. Action by the poor, the disadvantaged or the exploited to improve their own quality of life is largely ignored in Sen's work.[3] The later chapters of this book will examine poor people's experience of poverty to include both what poor people feel and think about poverty and power structures, and also what poor people are capable of doing to eliminate their own poverty. For the latter I will be analysing poor people's 'capabilities', but in a much wider sense than that meant by Amartya Sen. I will be examining what poor people are capable of achieving in their everyday lives, how they keep their households going, and how they contribute to the making of their societies. As I indicated in the introduction, this is one method of opposing received ideas about the way in which the poor are represented and poverty is constructed in the mainstream literature.

Let me return to the concept of 'mental-metricism', an important concept to discuss here because its use involves a denial of the worth of poor people's experience. In developing capability theory, Sen argues that individuals are too close to their personal construction of reality to have a clear picture of their state of well being. One can note here the similarity between this thesis and the idea of 'false consciousness', propounded for example by Marxists such as Gramsci and Sartre, where individuals are also considered to be unaware of their true (usually class) situation. Sen gives an interesting example of mental-metricism which appears to represent his general viewpoint when he refers to questions put to survivors of the 1943 famine in Bengal about their health. Of those replying, 48 per cent of widowers thought that they were ill, as opposed to two per cent of widows – obviously disproportionate figures. According to Sen, these widows' perceptions did not accord with reality (Sen, 1985). Using this reasoning and example Sen develops arguments about capability and the need to use macro-level indicators of well-being, therefore avoiding the idiosyncrasy of the individual's perception.

What happens if this example is 'deconstructed'? It may be true that everyone is tied in different ways by their individual perceptions. Looking more closely at Sen's example, one wonders why a male academician should have chosen poor female famine sufferers as an example of 'mental-metricism'. Does this choice of example reveal 'mental-metricism' on the part of Sen himself? Or is the example a scientific and 'objective' one because it was taken from a survey, which was no doubt carried out by trained surveyors using questionnaires? Could a comparative survey of the health of female and male academics who had just failed to get tenure, lost their house and car, and hadn't eaten for three days, be taken as an accurate reflection of their well-being, or would we expect some 'mental-metricism' to creep in? The point here is that any measure, standard, example,

---

[3] For a more detailed discussion, see my review of *Hunger and Public Action* (Beck, 1991a).

or comment can be questioned as biased or too directly related to the personal experience of an individual.

This raises two issues. The first concerns the origins of the information that needs to be interpreted. If we are considering social science surveys involving people's perceptions, it becomes essential to concentrate on the nature of the questions asked, the method of questioning and the way in which it is analysed, because these can be as revealing about the mind set of the analyst as the reply is about the mind set of the respondents. To illustrate this I return to the argument of the last chapter; standards of poverty based on mathematical analysis might appear to be 'objective' because of the inherent logic of calculation and mathematics. But this appearance of objectivity ignores the paradigmatic basis of such analysis. Examining the paradigm on which it is built, the whole exercise of poverty measurement is open to the criticism that it too is 'mental-metric', because it has developed from a specific, scientific mindset, rather than any objective position to which its proponents might lay claim through their use of esoteric statistical techniques. The same point can be made concerning Sen's capability theory – its representation of the agency of the poor means that it is not 'objective' at all.

The second issue is whether the argument that every view, comment, statement, perception or theory is open to the claim that it is 'subjective' invalidates the individual's experience, whether that individual be an academic or poor sufferer of famine. If we followed that argument to its logical conclusion, all communication would be impossible (sometimes the case with academics, of course), because everyone would be trapped within their own language, their own discourse, and their own subjectivity. To step outside of this post-modern maze, each person's experience needs to be contextualized within their socio-economic environment. Taking the example of widows discussing their health after the 1943 famine, it is now well understood that rural women in Bengal have internalized certain patriarchal norms, one of which relates to their conceptualization of their health. This one example of subjectivity, or even several such examples, should not be used to invalidate everything that a poor widow has to say. A sensitive researcher would understand from a knowledge of the social background and context that Bengali women may give particular answers to questions in an interview situation. Poor rural Bengali women may not be able to give their age, or may not admit to illness. This does not mean that they are unaware of who exploits them in the village, how village politics works, or how much food their family needs to eat, as we shall see in chapter eight. Poor rural women may even know much more about certain areas and issues than academics. In effect, they both have different, and perhaps complementary knowledge, about what poverty is and means.[4]

---

[4] See over.

In my travels around West Bengal and Bangladesh villages with government officials I have noted that there is often (not always, of course) a tendency for urban, educated officials to devalue the comments or answers of villagers, both rich and poor. The attitude of these officials is based very much on the mental-metric reasoning – because of their situation, mired as they are in the swamp of petty village life, rural people are ignorant, so what is the point of spending time talking to them? I hope (rather than being caught within my own mental-metricism!) that I am making a wider argument here – that every form of analysis or criticism brings with it bias, political baggage and subjectivity, and needs to be examined for this. So in the case of Sen's work, there is a lack of attention to the abilities of the poor that stems from an economistic perception as to what poverty means.[5]

People's history and agency

To develop my own theoretical preferences, I will return the argument now to the nineteenth century in Britain. In a way perhaps not sufficiently recognized, nineteenth-century rural British society resembles in many features contemporary village Bengal. The patterns of social and economic change, resource distribution, the power structure, even the agricultural labour systems are similar (see Thompson, 1986 for agricultural labour systems; and the discussion of common property resource use below). It is to the reinterpretation and reconstruction of nineteenth-century British history, to the work of the History Workshop school and of Edward Thompson that I turn to now for lessons as to how contemporary Indian rural society and contemporary poverty in West Bengal may be reinterpreted as well.

One strand of people's history stems from the History Workshop, a radical movement which concerns itself with class struggle 'at the point of production', and the cultural dimensions of politics (Samuel, 1980). Samuel (1981) traces people's history theory to Vico's *Scienza Nova* of 1725, and John Baxter's *New and Imperial History of England* of 1796. Samuel also traces the influence of 'bourgeois-democratic' and populist ideas on Marxist thought, in particular their joint concern for the experience of the 'common' people. As Samuel puts it (1981: xxix):

---

[4] The whole idea of questioning the origins of knowledge is central to the postmodern enterprise, for example Said's (1978) book on Orientalism. There is nothing particularly modern about this debate – some eighteenth-century antecedents are discussed in Frye's (1947) work on William Blake.

[5] 'Relative' poverty is a further important alternative method of conceptualizing poverty that will not be discussed in detail here. For an analysis of the work of Peter Townsend, who has written extensively on relative poverty, and Townsend's debate with Sen over the meaning of poverty, see Beck, 1991.

Marx himself certainly practised a species of people's history, and the debt to his predecessors in this respect – Vico, the Scottish historical school of the eighteenth century, the French liberal historians of the Restoration, the German folklorists and peasant historians – has hardly been explored. His whole account of 'Capital' might be described, under one optic, as a history from below – the history of development seen through the eyes of its victims.

People's history theory has opposed 'economic history which insisted on the primacy of the statistical, irrespective of the significance of what was being measured . . .' (Samuel 1980). The central issue for the History Workshop school in recent years has been the 'recovery of subjective *experience*' (my emphasis) of the poor and the peasantry, and experience that was to be contextualized in the relevant political setting (ibid.: xviii). Samuel has also described it as a history from below or 'from the bottom up' (ibid.: xxxi).[6] In addition, people's history attempts to recover the political viewpoint of the poor as they themselves express it, one of the subjects least understood in the study of poverty, and to which I return in chapter eight. Here, then, is a radically different way of looking at poor people's experience from the approach of planners, statisticians and academics discussed in chapter two, and one on which I have drawn in my own analysis.

Apart from its theoretical orientation, the History Workshop approach is also relevant here because of its focus on the rural poor. An example is the volume *Village Life and Labour*, edited by Samuel, which attempts to recapture by use of case studies the life of that 'curiously anonymous figure', the nineteenth-century village labourer (Samuel 1982a: 3). The volume concentrates on an informal economy ignored by poverty measurement studies – poaching, gleaning, common rights, use of common property resources, livestock and migration – which were integral to poor people's lives and experience of class. These 'survival strategies' of the nineteenth-century labourer are areas still crucial for poor people in contemporary rural West Bengal, as I will show in chapters seven and eight. This focus on areas of importance to the poor has led to an examination of extra-economic subjects that might at first glance appear esoteric, because they are little studied. Gleaning is one example of such an extra-economic subject.

Morgan's essay on the place of harvesters in nineteenth-century village life in *Village Life and Labour* illustrates the importance of gleaning in nineteenth-century Britain, and there are close parallels between gleaning as practised in nineteenth-century Britain and contemporary West Bengal. Morgan writes that (1982: 54);

It is difficult to appreciate that the effort of so many days of back-breaking work was thought worth while but to the gleaners the gathered

---

[6] The latter is now a familiar phrase in development studies.

grain represented one of the mainstays of the home – a safeguard against the threatened privations of winter. In the case of wheat, gleanings provided flour for the cottager's loaf. Barley gleanings were fed to the chicken or the pig. For the family who were able to supply themselves with a winter's stock of flour, gleaning might be the most lasting of the harvest 'extras'.

Morgan also makes the point that, because labourers had access to farmers' fields, the practice of gleaning was (ibid.: 61): 'the clearest expression of the psychological advantage which the village labourer and his family enjoyed [over the farmer] in the few brief weeks of harvest'. Because of this, class conflict manifested itself in disputes over gleaning, and Morgan elucidates the nature of this conflict (ibid.: 56):

Gleaning was a universal practice in the corn-growing counties of nineteenth-century England, despite the fact that farmers and landowners, at different times, had attempted to put it down, or to bring it under tighter control. It was an ancient common right, embodied in the Mosaic Law, that harvest gleanings should be left 'unto the poor and the strangers'. It continued to be practised at a time when many other common rights were under attack. In 1787 the right to glean 'indefinitely' by 'poor, necessitous, and indigent persons' had been denied on the grounds that it was 'inconsistent with the nature of property', 'destructive of the peace and good order of society', and 'amounting to a general vagrancy'. This judgement was reinforced and re-stated in more comprehensive terms a year later by Lord Loughborough, the Lord Chief Justice, and two of his fellow judges . . . But rights so deeply rooted in the needs and practices of the local communities could not be extinguished on the mere say-so of a High Court judge . . .'

Here was a classic dispute between 'property' on the one hand, supported by the state in the form of its courts, and common rights on the other. This dispute involved 'infringements' or 'encroachments' from both sides, infringements by the poor on to private property, and attempts at infringements of common rights by the rich; an example of the latter is that while farmers could not prohibit gleaning, they attempted to restrict it, by limiting the privilege to those who had worked for them in the harvest (ibid: 57–8), something I also found occurring in contemporary West Bengal (see chapter seven).

What is the wider relevance of the above discussion to contemporary West Bengal? As was discussed above, and has been noted by Humphries (1990), resource use in industrializing Britain and many parts of the contemporary developing world is similar. Both societies are founded upon unequal property rights, a situation supported by the state. In both societies CPRs (common property rights) make up an important and at times crucial part of poor households' income, and access to certain CPRs is a source of conflict over 'traditional' rights that can be seen to fit into a wider social conflict between poor and rich. In addition, in both societies, gathering of CPRs is mainly the responsibility of women and children, whereas land is owned by men. One might therefore expect patterns of class and gender conflict over common resources in nineteenth-century Britain to be repeated in contemporary West Bengal.

There has been criticism as to how far people's history presents a coherent theory that accounts for both poor people's agency and the socioeconomic structure that restricts their action. The History Workshop ideal is to link the 'particular to general, the part to the whole, the individual moment to the longue duree' (Samuel 1981: xxxii). However, as Selbourne has argued (1980: 15–56), it often errs on the side of the 'narrative and the descriptive rather than the analytical', and can be 'facts without science.' Because of the necessity of concentrating on the particular experience of individuals and small groups, the wider frame is often lost, and this experience remains uncontextualized. For example, he essays in *Village Life and Labour* give detailed accounts of nineteenth-century labourers' lives, but often do not contextualize these experiences within a wider political framework. Similarly, people's history is often weakened because the analysis of the interaction between the agency of the poor and the socio-economic structure that constrains them remains secondary to the recovery of 'subjective experience'. The ability to contextualize satisfactorily the experience and agency of the poor within socio-economic structure remains one of the fundamental problems of authors taking a 'bottom up' approach, and which I consider in more detail in the following sections.[7]

E.P. Thompson, agency and experience

E.P. Thompson has been one of the most influential historians writing history 'from the bottom up', and, as will be seen from the following discussion, has influenced my analysis of poverty measurement in the last chapter. The impetus for much of Thompson's work can be found in the preface to the *The Making of the English Working Class*, a history of working-class experience in the late eighteenth and early nineteenth

---

[7] The literature on people's history is now voluminous, and there is not scope here to discuss it in detail. However, reference can be made to Reeves' (1979) account of working-class lives in London between 1909 and 1913; and the Hammonds' (1948) sympathetic account of the eighteenth and nineteenth-century British village labourer. Literary examples of people's history from urban and rural early twentieth-century Britain can be found in Tressell (1965) and Thompson (1983) respectively. A 'participant observation' account of the London poor can be found in Orwell (1981), and a less sympathetic account in London (1903).

centuries. Thompson's states here that his aim is to oppose prevailing orthodoxies (ibid.: 11–12):

> There is the Fabian orthodoxy, in which the great majority of working people are seen as passive victims of laissez faire . . . There is the orthodoxy of the empirical economic historians, in which working people are seen as a labour force, as migrants, or as the data for statistical series . . . My quarrel (with these) is that they tend to obscure the agency of working people, the degree to which they contributed by conscious efforts, to the making of history.

The organizing feature of much of Thompson's work is an attempt to recover 'the dimension of human agency', and counterpoise this with socio-economic structure (ibid.; Thompson 1971). So for Thompson (1986: 213), the 'working class made itself as much as it was made'. This emphasis on members of the working class as active participants in the making of their societies is closely tied as well to Thompson's opposition to other 'orthodoxies', what he views as Marxist economic determinism where, in Marxist terminology, the economic 'base' or social being determines the cultural 'superstructure' or social consciousness. That all human activity is determined by economic forces is obviously alien to historical analysis that places human beings centre stage as makers of history. Thompson instead views the economic and cultural as involved in a complex dialectic relation (Kaye 1984; Thompson 1978; 1977).

This theoretical stance moves Thompson to focus on the perspective of the subaltern. In *The Making of the English Working Class*, he argues that the 'crucial experience of the Industrial Revolution was felt in terms of changes in the nature and intensity of exploitation' (1986: 218). Exploitation is seen in: 'the reduction of man to the status of an "instrument" . . . (and) turned on issues which are not encompassed by cost-of-living series. The issues which provoked the most intensity of feeling were very often ones in which such values as traditional customs, "justice", "independence", security, or family economy were at stake . . .' (ibid.: 222). Thompson goes on to argue that (ibid.: 239):

> Those petty rights of the villager, such as gleaning, access to fuel, and the tethering of stock in the lanes or on the stubble, which are irrelevant to the historian of economic growth, might be of crucial importance to the subsistence of the poor . . . If one looks at the scene again from the standpoint of the villager, one finds a dense cluster of claims and usages, which stretch from the common to the market-place and which, taken together, make up the economic and cultural universe of the rural poor.

There is a clear opposition here between the 'historian of economic change' who relies on cost-of-living data, and Thompson's attempt to recover the experience of impoverishment felt by the poor.

Also of importance in Thompson's work is his discussion of the differing and opposing values and ideologies held by rich and poor, an idea that informs much of his empirical enquiry (see Thompson 1990, 1978a, 1977). The values, customs and beliefs of the poor are not only different from those of the rich, they are also part of an ideological value system which either challenges the dominant ideological constructions of the rich or reinforces those aspects of the dominant ideology which the poor see as benefiting them.This is in sharp contrast, again, to the view of some of the academics quoted in the last chapter. I return to this subject when discussing below Thompson's idea of the moral economy.

Is Thompson's theoretical approach coherent, and how far does it inform his own writing? There has been voluminous discussion of Thompson's work, and much of this literature can be found referenced in a *Festschrift* to Thompson (Kaye and McClelland 1990). There is scope here only to discuss the main issues. Much of the critical attention has focused on Thompson's concepts of 'agency' and 'experience', and the balance of human agency and socio-economic structure in particular in *The Making of the English Working Class*. The meaning of agency and experience, and the attempts that have been made to deny their relevance, are important to this book, so I will dwell on their definition for a little longer here.

The concept of agency

I have noted above that part of Thompson's endeavour is to recover the 'dimension of human agency'. The term 'agency' is a key but also problematic one in Thompson's work. As Anderson (1980) has noted, Thompson's definition of agency in his critique of Marxist determinism, *The Poverty of Theory*, is imprecise, and his uses of the word are irregular, and this has consequences for Thompson's attempt to build a theoretical framework.

The perceived failure on the part of Thompson to define clearly agency leads Anderson to claim that the main concentration of *The Making of the English Working Class* is on agency rather than structure: '. . . (there is) a disconcerting lack of objective coordinates as the narrative of class formation unfolds'. (Anderson 1980: 33). One can note here the similarity to Selbourne's criticism of the History Workshop school. Missing for Anderson are analysis of structural elements such as capital accumulation and details of the workings of the cotton, iron and coal industries. He concludes (ibid.: 34–5):

> In the absence of any objective framework for laying down the overall pattern of capital accumulation in these years, there is little way of assessing the relative importance of one area of subjective experience within the English working class against another.

As Anderson comments (ibid.: 33), at the end of the book the reader is not aware of 'the approximate size of the English working class', and it is true that the reader does not receive a solid sense of how widespread the movements Thompson describes were.[8]

Yet as Giddens notes, while Thompson lays too little stress on structure, Anderson pays too little attention to agency, emphasizing as he does a more standard Marxist economic approach. As Giddens puts it (1987: 215):

> The debate between Thompson and Anderson carried echoes of long-standing controversies in the social sciences and history as a whole. Schools of social thought tend to divide around the question of agency. Those who, like Thompson, are prone to assert the primacy of agency typically have had considerable difficulty in coming to grips both conceptually and substantively with what might be termed the 'structural constraints' over human action. On the other hand, those traditions of thought that have tended to stress the significance of pre-given social institutions have for the most part generated seriously deficient accounts of action . . .[9]

I will return to Giddens' proposed solution to this problem below, but first I will dwell for a moment on Anderson's attempt to define agency.

In his critique of Thompson's work, Anderson defines agency as (1980: 19) 'conscious, goal-directed activity', and argues that Thompson conflates three meanings of the term, which he differentiates as private, public and collective forms of agency. Anderson defines private agency as the everyday carrying out of individual goals, such as collecting water, 'which have consumed the greater part of human energy and persistence throughout recorded time'. Alternatively, public agency occurs where 'will and action . . . acquire an independent historical significance as causal sequences in their own right'. These public actions, such as political struggles or commercial explorations, have fitted into a known structural framework rather than attempting to change it. Lastly, collective agency is found in isolated 'collective projects which have sought to render their initiators authors of their collective mode of existence as a whole, in a conscious programme aimed at creating or remodelling whole social structures'. (Anderson 1980: 19). Anderson notes that Thompson's use of the term permits a 'sliding' between its different meanings (ibid.), and therefore Thompson has been unable to outline clearly what Anderson in the quote above refers to as the importance of different 'subjective experiences' of the working class. Anderson's typology itself is perhaps too general, and ignores the interlocking

---

[8] The same point can be made of Christopher Hill's (1975) book on radical movements during the English revolution; there is little intimation in the book as to how widespread such movements were.

[9] The tension between agency and structure is also one area of enquiry that has been central to recent geographical theoretical analysis. See Johnston, 1989; Kobayashi and Mackenzie, 1989; Sayer, 1989; Jackson and Smith, 1984.

nature of the types of agency he distinguishes, and the way in which the political and the personal mesh; in particular, it would appear to fail to give sufficient stress to the way in which 'private' agency can shape society. But his definitions provide a useful reminder that there may be different types of agency which will have different political implications.

In turn, Giddens, in a review of the debate between Thompson and his critics, has criticized Anderson's definition of agency, noting (1987: 21–56): 'Anderson confidently equates agency with 'conscious, goal-directed activity', finding only in the notion of 'goals' anything which merits serious analytical reflection. Such is surely not the case . . .'. For Giddens, agency 'presumes the capability of "acting otherwise" '. He goes on (ibid.: 216):

> Human beings have an understanding of themselves as agents, thus allowing for a reflexive appropriation of knowledge denied to non-human animals. They are also able conceptually to 'bracket' time and space, connecting future and past in a manner not open to the remainder of the animal kingdom. There is no reason to doubt that the behaviour of animal agents is purposive. But in the case of human agents purposiveness is integrated with a continuous monitoring of what the actor does, intrinsic to what 'doing' is.[10]

Giddens' definition is certainly more comprehensive than that of Anderson, and from the above argument, Giddens has developed the theory of 'structuration', his proposed solution to the long-standing controversy over agency. Briefly outlined, this involves a redefinition of the inter-relations of structure and agency; in structuration theory, neither agency and structure is dominant, but rather they constantly reconstitute each other. So, according to Giddens there is a 'duality of structure' where (1987: 61):

> . . . structure is not as such external to human action, and is not identified solely with constraint. Structure is both the medium and the outcome of the human activities which it recursively organizes. Institutions, or large-scale societies, have structural properties in virtue of the continuity of the actions of their component members. But those members of society are only able to carry out their day-to-day activities in virtue of their capability of instantiating those structural properties.

While this proposed symmetrical relation between agency and structure is aesthetically satisfying, provides a theoretical framework for the consideration of the interaction of agency and structure, and has been recently lauded (for example, see Sewell, 1990), to operationalize this model in a study of human society would be a daunting task. Giddens' theory is useful in that it provides a *map* of processes within everyday life. Once any

---

[10] Thompson makes a similar point in *The Poverty of Theory* (1978: 8).

particular event is selected for study, however, the problem remains as to what weight to give to individual circumstances, agents and structures. A further problem remains in terms of the scale or scope of a study. For example, Thompson's *Whigs and Hunters* is in many ways more satisfying than *The Making of the English Working Class* as far as the balance of agency and structure is concerned, in that careful attention is given to the formation of legal constraints on 'traditional' rights of the rural population. But *Whigs and Hunters* is a local study which lacks the scope and wide range of *The Making of the English Working Class*. And being a local study, *Whigs and Hunters* leaves itself open to the criticism that it neglects the international economy that was important to the maintenance of hegemony of the English landed classes (see Anderson, 1980). Given the difficulties of satisfactorily operationalizing Giddens' structuration model, and the major unresolved debates in the social sciences concerning the nature of agency, it may be necessary to accept that the problems outlined above concerning agency and structure are unlikely to be easily resolved, and will certainly not be resolved in this book.

The concept of experience

One can find a similar concern in academic discourse to that about agency over Thompson's use of the word 'experience', another key word in his writing. The meaning of experience is more than just a question of semantics. If we wish to validate the experience of the common person or the poor, to claim that experience is more important than data on wages or statistics, then a clear meaning of experience is necessary. This is particularly so as the term is closely related to other words that have been denigrated in social studies, for example 'subjective' (note Anderson's reference above to 'subjective experience'; presumably all experience is 'subjective' and the adjective is irrelevant).

One of the interesting features of Thompson's work is that he has been inspired by the writings of the early Romantic poets, in particular Blake and Wordsworth, and their validation of the experience of the 'common people'. It is not surprising to find Thompson quoting William Blake on the importance of experience:

What is the price of Experience? Do men buy it for a song?
Or wisdom for a dance in the street? No, it is bought with the price
Of all that a man hath, his house, his wife, his children . . .

In Thompson's work, the stress on the experience of common people is clearly connected to his opposition to economic determinism and structural Marxism, and the importance of experience can also be seen in its crucial contribution to the forming of class consciousness (Thompson 1986: 8–9):

40

. . . class happens when some men, as a result of common experiences (inherited or shared), feel and articulate the identity of their interests as between themselves, and as against other men whose interests are different from (and usually opposed to) theirs. The class experience is largely determined by the productive relations into which men are born – or enter involuntarily. Class consciousness is the way in which these experiences are handled in cultural terms: embodied in traditions, value-systems, ideas, and institutional forms. If the experience appears as determined, class-consciousness does not. We can see a *logic* in the responses of similar occupational groups undergoing similar experiences, but we cannot predicate any *law*. Consciousness of class arises in the same way in different times and places, but never in just the same way.

An attempt to deny the importance of this common experience will also therefore be an attempt to deny the importance of the contribution of the working class to history. However, it is the 'productive relations into which men are born', what Anderson calls 'objective co-ordinates' or an 'objective framework', which are not always clearly defined in Thompson's work, and the importance of experience is therefore clouded as it is not seen in relevant context.

Thompson has also used 'experience' in a more complicated and possibly confusing sense, as a mediating force between social being and social consciousness. For example, in *The Poverty of Theory*, Thompson wrote of himself and fellow Marxist historiographers (1978: 170):

We explored, both in theory and in practice, those junction-concepts (such as 'need', 'class', and 'determine') by which, through the missing term, 'experience', structure is transmuted into process, and the subject re-enters history.

Here experience would appear to be a mediating force between structure and process, and at other times Thompson uses the term to mean a mediating force between social being and social consciousness (Sewell, 1990). Various critics have pointed out (the debate is summarized in Sewell, 1990) that Thompson uses the word imprecisely, and tends to conflate its different meanings in a confusing fashion. This is partly to do with the complex nature of the word. Williams (1989: 126) gives its two main contemporary meanings, focusing on different states or levels of consciousness at different times, as: '(i) knowledge gathered from past events, whether by conscious observation or by consideration and reflection; (ii) a particular kind of consciousness that can in some contexts be distinguished from "reason" or "knowledge".' Experience here means both going through a process of learning, and coming to a particular state of mind. It is these two meanings of the word that Thompson tends to conflate; it is not always

41

clear in his writings whether he refers to the learning experience or to the state of mind and consciousness that the working class has achieved.[11]

While Thompson is not always consistent in his use of key terms, this should not detract from his contribution to the study of agency and experience, and his ability to link theory and practice in his analysis; nor should it detract from the importance of exploring such concepts empirically. I have used the title 'The Experience of Poverty' with an awareness of the complexity of the word experience (as well as an awareness of the complexity of the word poverty!). Let me clarify now what I mean by experience. I use it to encompass both what the poor feel about poverty, as well as how they respond to poverty at an individual and collective level. I will show in chapters seven and eight that this experience of poverty is inextricably tied to relations of power, and I argue throughout this book that the poor face great structural constraints or structures within which they have to function, and with which they interact. The particular structural constraints I focus on are control over political, social and economic resources by the rich, and I discuss these where relevant. I return here to my conclusions about mental-metricism. It is only by presenting both the constraints the poor face and their responses and interaction with these constraints that the experience of poverty can be comprehended, and the real 'capabilities' of the poor can be understood. This is for the most part a book about poverty and power; it does not attempt to set up a theoretical model to explain structure and agency, something Giddens has termed a persistent difficulty in social thought (1987: 215). Instead, it proceeds with an awareness of the complexity of this issue.[12]

Thompson and moral economy theory

We need to examine one other approach of Thompson's, because it gives a theoretical lead as to the nature of relations between poor and rich which

---

[11] Giddens, on the other hand, in a discussion of Thompson's work, notes (1987: 211): '. . . experience may refer to the subjective outlook of an individual participating in a given range of activities; or it may refer to what that individual actively learns from such participation', a subtly different definition to that of Williams.

[12] There is no scope here to discuss the work of other British Marxist historians such as Christopher Hill and Eric Hobsbawm. For an assessment, see Kaye (1984). The output of these historians has been crucial in determining the approach of the school of Indian historiographers who form the Subaltern Studies group. For this literature see the six volumes of *Subaltern Studies* edited by Ranajit Guha, as well as Guha's text *Elementary Aspects of Peasant Insurgency in Colonial India*. It is of interest that critics of the Subaltern school have also focused on the inability of its members to adequately locate the subaltern experience within the wider social structure (see Bayly, 1988; Mukherjee, 1988: 2110–12; O'Hanlon, 1988: 200–92, 212).

will be discussed later in the book, and because of its influence on contemporary development studies. Moral economy theory has been used by both political scientists and Marxist historians as a means of describing historical process and peasant action. Thompson (1991) reviews twenty years of use and mis-use of the term in a recent essay, including many of the studies from developing countries that have taken up the term.This section will concentrate on Thompson's concept of the moral economy, and make only a few brief comments about later uses of the term.

As Thompson makes clear, his use of the term is tied to a particular time and example, in both the *Making of the English Working Class* and in his essay 'The Moral Economy of the English Crowd in the Eighteenth Century'. As he puts it (1991: 337–8):

> But while the term is available for every development which can be justified, my own usage has in general been confined to confrontations in the market-place over access (and entitlement) to 'necessities' – essential food. It is not only that there is an identifiable bundle of beliefs, usages and forms associated with the marketing of food in time of dearth, which it is convenient to bind together in a common term, but the deep emotions stirred by dearth, the claims which the crowd made upon the authorities in such crises, and the outrage provoked by profiteering in life-threatening emergencies, imparted a 'moral' charge to protest. All of this, taken together, is what I understand by moral economy.

In his original account, Thompson shows that peasants' protests and riots over state attempts to change their eating habits in the late eighteenth century, or set higher prices for grain, were both ordered and had a clear intention – that of maintaining historic rights to subsistence. Diametrically opposed to the accounts of the political scientists discussed in the last chapter, Thompson views the poor as neither deferrent or passive until provoked. Thompson instead sees the peasant protests he describes as part of a 'passionately held . . . notion of the common-weal, and a struggle for maintenance of rights for the poor that could be dated back at least to the mid-seventeenth century'. (1971: 79, 98–100). Riot was often accompanied by threats to landowners and millers, and by political warnings. For Thompson, the interaction of patron and client was one of class struggle where the paternalist tradition was re-echoed loudly by the people so that 'the authorities were, in some measure, the prisoners of the people' (ibid.: 79). Thompson's notion of the moral economy therefore centres on contestation over resources and ideology, and it was through the experience of this struggle, as was seen above, that Thompson saw the working class in Britain making itself.

This concern with contestation over resources and ideology is further elucidated in an essay by Thompson, 'Eighteenth-century English society: class struggle without class?', where he considers the nature of patronage and class struggle. As noted above, struggle between poor and rich is seen by Thompson to involve struggle over ideology as well as over physical resources. Discussing cultural hegemony, Thompson comments (1978a: 163):

> But it is necessary to say what this hegemony does *not* entail. It does not entail any acceptance by the poor of the gentry's paternalism upon the gentry's own terms or in their approved self-image. The poor might be willing to award their deference to the gentry, but only for a price. The price was substantial. And the deference was often without the least illusion: it could be seen from below as being one part necessary self-preservation, one part the calculated extraction of whatever could be extracted. Seen in this way the poor imposed upon the rich some of the duties and functions of paternalism just as much as paternalism was in turn imposed upon them. Both parties to the equation were constrained within a common field-of-force.

This concept of a common field-of-force is a useful one for the consideration of power relations in contemporary West Bengal, where, as shall be seen in chapter eight, a similar pattern operates, and there is 'class struggle' prior to the formation of formal classes of a nature similar to that analysed by Thompson.

As should be evident from my discussion of contemporary political science writing on India, there are various strands of moral economy thought presently in use, both politically conservative as well as radical. Thompson has commented in his review of these studies (1991: 344):

> Much of the very interesting discussion which is now extending under the rubric of 'moral economy' from African to Asian to Latin American or to Irish studies has little to do with my (1971) usage but is concerned with the social dialectic of unequal mutuality (need and obligation) which lies at the centre of most societies.

Some of the most interesting uses of the theory, for example Scott's (1985) book on class relations and 'weapons of the weak' in Malaysia, which present important examples of the relations of poor and rich in village societies, are used in my later discussion for comparative reasons. But for the purposes of theory there has been, in my opinion, little progress made since Thompson's original propositions.

Understanding poor people's priorities and knowledge

There is now a strong movement within development studies, influenced directly or indirectly by people's history theory, that focuses on the perspective and abilities of the poor. Given that this approach is central to my own endeavour, this chapter would be incomplete if it failed to review relevant literature on rural development, and from South Asia, that presents such a focus.

Of note in the recent literature on rural development that has focused on the abilities of the peasant and the poor is the work of Paul Richards and Robert Chambers. Richards' discussion of 'people's science' (1979) draws its theoretical framework from populist ideology, a coherent approach as populism has been concerned historically with the experience of the common person who has not benefitted from bureaucracies and governments (Midgley, 1986).[13] Richards' main concern is not with the political or social aspects of agrarian populism, but with the ecological aspects of the populist case. He has developed populist arguments of the following kind (1985: 16–17):

> Whereas much of Africa's rural population is scattered and poor it is also inventively self-reliant. . . . inventive self-reliance is one of Africa's most precious resources. Development initiatives should aim to maximize the utilization of this resource.

Richards gives in *Indigenous Agricultural Revolution* a number of examples of inventive farmer techniques in West Africa, and in his second book, *Coping with Hunger*, describes how Sierra Leone farmers adapt their farming practices to exploit the local environment and cope with seasonal risk. His work gives ample evidence of the coping abilities of farmers. The emphasis in Richards' work is on the state supporting farmers' own strategies.[14] This emphasis is part of a wider approach, into which this book fits, that aims to develop indigenous technical knowledge with external support (Chambers, Thrupp and Pacey, 1989; Biggs and Clay, 1981; IDS, 1979).

While Richards considers farmer knowledge and farmer agency as central issues, does he adequately detail the socio-economic context of that knowledge? In the Sierra Leone village he describes in *Coping with Hunger*, a moral economy framework is postulated with patron–client relationships as its most important factor (1986). One reason given for the support of this system within the village is the high degree of household mobility, which means that a patron may be a client in the not too far off future (ibid.). In the pre-harvest lean season: 'Households short of rice expect to be able to borrow from households with a surplus', but: 'Rice loans to ward off pre-harvest hunger are not necessarily seen by those who take them as

---

[13] Populism has been used as a perjorative term particularly by Marxists who view populists as being insufficiently concerned with analysis of class (see for example Byres, 1979). For a discussion of 'supply side' and 'demand side' populism, see Richards (1987).

[14] Rather than, in much literature on participation, the poor participating in state development programmes. The literature on participation is reviewed in Beck (1991). Oakley (1991) provides a useful overview of themes in participation studies.

unduly "exploitative".' (ibid.: 115, 116). There is an echo of E.P. Thompson in Richards' comment that (ibid.: 49): 'Poorer villagers . . . expect (*even demand*) that those with a little wealth or good fortune should begin to act as patrons'. (my emphasis). However, Richards gives little data to support his claims concerning loans and patronage. One wonders how far the local government officers, traders and literate men he describes as powerful patrons (ibid.) control village life, and whether their positions are, as might be expected, permanent ones. There is in the book no break-down of village socio-economic structure or patterns of mobility, no details, for example, of the amount of land operated or yields per household, which would have allowed for a detailed discussion of these matters. In common with many authors who have focused on agency, structure is not well covered in Richards' work.

In a number of publications Robert Chambers has written of the need for rural development practitioners concerned with poverty to change their attitudes and consider poor people's experience of poverty and priorities, and his writing has been one source for my approach in the last chapter (for example, Chambers, 1983). Chambers (ibid.: 103) notes that learning from the poor and empirical research may change attitudes to-wards the poor:

> Outsiders' comfortable views of the poor as improvident, lazy, fatalistic, stupid and responsible for their poverty, are reassuring but wrong. Case studies show that poor rural people are usually tough, hard-working, ingenious and resilient.

The fieldwork chapters of this book attempt to provide just such a case study.

A concentration on poor people's priorities requires a widening of the definition of poverty to include those priorities. Chambers has therefore attempted to differentiate poverty from vulnerability, the former concern-ing income, and the latter being closer to poor people's ideas of depriva-tion, and which Chambers defines as (1989: 1): '. . . not lack or want, but defencelessness, insecurity, and exposure to risk, shocks and stress . . . vulnerability, and its opposite, security, stand out as recurrent concerns of poor people which professional definitions of poverty overlook'. With this definition Chambers has widened the meaning of poverty to include what he feels are poor people's concerns, although his definition includes mainly negative features (on which, more below).

Again taking the perspective of the poor, Chambers has outlined a useful typology to describe what he calls 'integrated rural poverty', a deprivation trap that includes poverty, isolation, powerlessness, vulnerability and physical weakness, although again all of these features are negative ones (1983: chapter five). Powerlessness remains the most pressing of problems (1983: 60):

The gravest neglect in analysis for practical rural development has been political feasibility . . . the ignoring of power and interests of local elites, more perhaps than any other factor, has been responsible for failures to benefit the poor.

Chambers acknowledges that intervention to disrupt such interests of local elites are likely to be difficult. Related to this, he raises the question of who will take the consequences of development action. If professional 'outsiders' intervene in an unequal social structure, this may lead to a backlash against the poor by indigenous elites once the professionals have departed. Chambers suggests instead looking for programmes that will either benefit both rural elites and the poor, or not harm the elites (ibid.); and for 'soft spots' or 'weak links in a chain' in village power structures (ibid.), a concentration on which will allow benefits to reach the poor without instigating a backlash against them (ibid.). The type of agency that Chambers is interested in therefore tends to be 'private' (as defined by Anderson) – everyday and individual, or peacefully collective. This practical approach excludes traditional methods of poor people's organization that have focused on their political priorities, such as bargaining for wages before the harvest or strikes by agricultural labourer unions. However, following Chambers, one of the main foci of the fieldwork of this book has been just such an analysis of the means by which poor people negotiate for themselves a better quality of life, although the fieldwork findings extend Chambers' discussion by also concentrating on relations of power and poor people's passive and active resistance to exploitation.

By focusing on negative aspects of poor people's lives, Chambers' work presents at times a view of the agency of the poor as severely constrained. For example, Chambers has written (ibid.: 2–3):

But who should act? The poorer rural people, it is said, must help themselves; but this, trapped as they are, they often cannot do. The initiative, in enabling them better to help themselves, lies with outsiders who have more power and resources and most of whom are neither rural nor poor.

Similarly, Chambers (1981: 5) has noted that for the poor: 'The knowledge that there will be future seasonal crisis constrains them [the poor] to keep on good terms with their patrons. They are thus screwed down seasonally into subordinate and dependent relationships in which they are open to exploitation'. This is perhaps a simplification of the way in which poor and rich interact, and the different forms of agency open to poor people. While poor people are certainly exploited or 'screwed down', this does not necessarily make them deferrent, as the discussion of Thompson's work has shown. Chambers' concentration on the relationship between the poor and the rural development practitioner tends to ignore historical examples of

47

poor people's passive and active resistance to exploitation. But these critical points should not detract from the positive influence Chambers' work has had in refocusing studies of poverty towards the priorities and experience of the poor.

The perspective of the poor from contemporary South Asia

There has been a handful of studies which have carried out detailed fieldwork in contemporary South Asia that specifically set out to consider the perspective and experience of the poor. These are briefly reviewed, and then an attempt will be made to find common themes that contextualize my own findings at field level. I draw on many of these studies again for purposes of comparison in the later fieldwork chapters.[15]

On the sociological side, of note is Breman's study of changing labour relations and migration in Gujarat (1985a; 1979). Breman's work is the only major longitudinal study from India I have come across that specifically sets out to examine the condition of the poor, contextualized within local power structures. Breman's work looks specifically at changes in the material condition of the poor and the development of different forms of exploitation, and also reports on how the poor experience these changes.

Another excellent sociological case study is Jodha's work on poor people's perceptions of poverty in village Rajasthan. Jodha notes (1989: 175): 'The concepts and categories used to identify and classify rural realities are often too restrictive . . . .'. Jodha compares changes between 1964–6 and 1982–4 in two villages in Rajasthan, western India, using two 'measures'. The first is the standard measure of poverty, i.e. income, and the second is what Jodha calls 'qualitative' indicators (ibid.), which were based on farmers' own perceptions of change. These qualitative indicators included reduced dependence on low paid jobs, improved mobility, and shifts in consumption. Jodha found that, using the standard income measure, there had been an increase in the number of households below the poverty line, but by the qualitative indicators used, the overall situation of 35 households whose per capita annual income had declined by more than 5 per cent during the period under review had actually *improved*. Jodha concludes by stressing the importance of combining both 'quantitative' and 'qualitative' indicators of well being, and calls for 'a fresh look at the conceptualization underlying the measurement of the level and change in rural poverty'. (ibid.: 194). B. Harriss (1987: 14) has sounded a cautionary note with reference to Jodha's findings, commenting: 'That peoples' own criteria do not include longer life, less disease, more freedom for women makes one sceptical about gender bias in this phenomenological approach'.

---

[15] For a general review of literature on poverty in India, including phenomenological studies, see B. Harriss (1987).

Such a criticism does not invalidate the phenomenological approach, however, but it should make advocates of such an approach more sensitive to possible bias that comes from using it.

Mencher's research in Tamil Nadu on untouchables' rejection of Brahminic ideology is also of note, as it is a rare account of the view of the power structure as seen by the exploited (Mencher 1980; 1975). The account by the Jefferies and Lyon (1989) of gender roles, child bearing and patriarchal ideology in Uttar Pradesh is a vital record of the complex nature of female oppression, much of it in the villagers' own words. Details of grassroots organization among untouchables and women can also be found in Joshi (1986), Kishwar and Vanita (1984), and I. Sen (1990).

Important research can also be found from Bangladesh, in particular BRAC's account of peasant perceptions of famine (BRAC, 1984); in Chen and Yunus's description of the formation of credit and employment groups among poor women, with, again, much of the account being in the women's words (Chen, 1983; Yunus, 1982). In addition, Hartmann and Boyce's (1983) investigation of village life in Bangladesh remains one of the most vivid, sympathetic and powerful of village studies (in particular, the account of the death of a landless labourer, chapter twelve). White's (1988) analysis of gender and class from one Bangladeshi village is valuable for insights it presents into the role of women within and outside the village.

Oral history remains another important method for representing the viewpoint of the poor, but apart from the work of Freeman (1979), and studies concerning poor people's uprisings (Stree Shakti Sanghatana, 1989; Cooper, 1984) no significant work appears to have been carried out in this area.[16]

What can one learn from this scattered evidence concerning poor people's priorities and how they experience poverty? Firstly, with the exception of Breman's work, which uses a moral economy approach, the literature cited above is for the most part descriptive, and lacks either a theoretical framework or clear theoretical direction. It is, in Selbourne's words 'facts without science'. Secondly, and in stark contrast to the theoretical propositions of the political scientists discussed at the end of the last chapter, it is clear from this literature that poor people do not always subscribe to the dominant ideology, Brahminic or otherwise. Rather, they assert their own identities, identities which are usually closely tied to the material circumstances of deprivation and exploitation in which they find themselves. Thirdly, poor people feel sympathy for and identify with their

---

[16] Fiction can also be a powerful method of portraying the lives and views of the poor. Bengali literature is rich in short stories and novels concerning poverty where villagers are the main protagonists (see for example Bardhan, 1990). Representation of the experience of the poor can also be found in Marathi literature and songs (Omvedt, 1977; Miller and Kale, 1972).

fellow poor, and help other poor people where this is possible.[17] There is a common note here with the nineteenth-century authors on poverty in Britain, many of whom commented (often with astonishment) on how poor people manage to support each other despite their own brutal poverty (see Booth, 1969; Rowntree, 1922; Thompson and Yeow, 1971). Of course there are converse findings which show how Untouchables or others have internalized dominant ideologies or do not support each other (Bandyopadhyay and von Eschen, 1988; Moffat, 1979), but these go against the trend of the literature. Lastly, the authors discussed all express, covertly or overtly, a political sympathy with the 'struggles' of the poor, and attempt to use their work as a means of forwarding these struggles. In this endeavour they have much in common with the British Marxist historians such as Thompson and Samuel, who express a similar political sympathy with the historical poor. Again, this is in sharp contrast to the poverty measurers discussed in the last chapter.

The literature discussed in this section shows that concentrating on the viewpoint of the poor can be an important theoretical and practical corrective to unsubstantiated opinions of the poor such as those discussed in the last chapter, and the assertion of identity and mutual support by the poor will be seen to figure prominently in the discussions in chapter eight.

The saga continues . . .

It should be clear from this chapter (if not, a re-reading or re-writing of it may be in order!) that there has been significant discussion of the experience and agency of the poor. Much of this literature has been a reaction and challenge to the representation of the poor person as 'economic man', a narrow and passive recipient of external interference from the environment, state or local elite. As such, it takes up an oppositional stance to the literature discussed in chapter two. It draws on different, more explicit and more coherent theories of the operation of society, whether Marxist or populist, than studies of poverty measurement. Much of the literature is also politically motivated by a general sympathy for the poor, and follows in a quite different political tradition from economic studies of poverty which, as I showed in the last chapter, tend to be connected to policies of 'blaming the victim' and social control. The literature discussed in this and the last chapter thus form part of a wider theoretical debate about the nature and capabilities of poor people and their place in society, and how the problem of poverty is to be resolved. A question that arises from the review is: If historians can reconstruct with the limited evidence

---

[17] This does not mean that there are no divisions among the poor (fostered by indigenous elites or otherwise), or that they do not compete with each other, as Breman's studies makes clear.

available the strengths of the poor in nineteenth-century Britain, why have so few modern-day social scientists over the last twenty years working on rural societies in developing countries chosen to ignore similar strengths that might exist among the poor of today, and why do poverty measurement studies outnumber studies of agency by 50 to 1?

Where the literature reviewed in this chapter has explained the causes of poverty, these are seen to be located for the most part in exploitation or other structural socio-economic constraints, rather than being located in the characteristics of the poor themselves. However, the literature reviewed (with the exception of Sen's contributions) has tended to examine agency and experience more closely than structural constraints, and leaves itself open to the criticisms made by Giddens concerning the inability of studies which focus on agency to come to grips with structure. However, to address the interaction of various forms of agency and structure remains a major challenge, as the review has shown.

From the discussion in this chapter and the last chapter it is possible to suggest a theoretical framework with which to proceed. Essential to an analysis of poverty and survival strategies is a consideration of agency and structure. The poor should be seen neither as 'free agents' with unbounded ability or whose moral or physical failings make them responsible for their own poverty, nor as 'economic men' whose actions are determined by market forces or the state. Rather the interaction of agency and structure, and the corresponding mutual ties and bonds of poor and rich, should be investigated empirically in specific circumstances. It is to this endeavour that the book now turns.

4   West Bengal – the case study area

Introduction

This chapter will give a contextualizing background to the case study area, examining the structural factors that constrain activity by the poor and have ensured the production of poverty in West Bengal historically and in the present day. It discusses geographical, agricultural and demographic features of Bengal and West Bengal,[1] and then considers historical and political features, concentrating on the formation of social structure and protest by rural groups in Bengal in the nineteenth and twentieth centuries. Finally I examine the contemporary agrarian structure, and agrarian reform and politics in West Bengal. I seek to answer the following questions: What are the state-wide features of the agrarian economy, and how have these developed; how successful has the present West Bengal government been in alleviating poverty; and who is in control of rural resources?

Geography, agriculture and population in Bengal and West Bengal

West Bengal (see Map 4.1) is about half the size of England and Wales, and has a present-day population of about 60 million people. It is one of the poorest states in India, with the second largest scheduled caste and scheduled tribe population, groups generally accounted to be the poorest, in the country (Sengupta, 1991). Some relevant, self-explanatory figures concerning West Bengal are given in Table 4.1.

Table 4.1   Statistical profile of West Bengal – 1981

Per capita annual income (US $)	139
Life expectancy (all India)	51
Female literacy (%)	30.3
Male literacy (%)	50.5
Overall literacy (%)	41
Pop. scheduled tribes (millions)	3.07
Pop. scheduled castes (millions)	12

Sources: Boyce, 1987: 2; Government of West Bengal, 1986

Modern West Bengal can be divided into two main geographical areas, the Gangetic delta to the south, and Himalayan West Bengal to the north, and it is in the former that the case study area lies. The changing course of the river systems of the region since the seventeenth century, towards present-day Bangladesh to the east, combined with human intervention with

---

[1] 'Bengal' should be taken to mean present day West Bengal and Bangladesh.

drainage in the nineteenth century, has meant that most of the West Bengal portion of the Gangetic delta now makes up a moribund area of old alluvium (Bose, 1986), which will be termed here the 'moribund delta' or simply 'delta'. To the west of the moribund delta soils are more laterite, but are exchanged for alluvium as one moves eastwards (Mitra, 1953).

Rainfall in the delta region is very high, averaging around 1500 millimetres a year, as compared to about 250–500 millimetres for semi-arid areas to the west of India (Jose, 1984: 138). There are three principal cropping seasons in West Bengal. The most important agriculturally is the monsoon season, when mainly rainfed *aman* rice is grown, and which lasts from May/July to November/December. After this comes the winter *rabi* season, from December to about April, during which a variety of irrigated crops are grown, including *boro* rice, wheat, vegetables, oilseeds and pulses. Completing the agricultural year is the *bhadoi* or spring season, when the main crops are *aus* rice and jute. The state *aman* paddy yield in 1988 was some six million tonnes, and the *boro* paddy yield some two and a half million tonnes. By contrast, production of wheat was some 655,000 tonnes (Palmer-Jones, 1989: 24). It is on the *boro* season that this book concentrates, when the varieties of paddy used are almost exclusively 'high yielding' or 'modern'. During the *bhadoi* and late monsoon seasons traditional varieties of rice are generally grown, dependent on region. Despite high rainfall and some of the world's most fertile soil (Boyce, 1987), yields in West Bengal are low by south Indian and also by international standards. Average yield of rice is currently some 1.4 metric tonnes per hectare, only 17 per cent higher than in 1928–32 in Bengal (ibid.: 1,10).

Bengal and West Bengal have for several decades supported high population densities. From 1901 to 1931 population growth was generally low, with a decline in 1911 to 1921 caused by malaria and influenza epidemics. The high mortality after the 1943 famine slowed the increase of the 1930s, and growth was again high in the 1950s and 1960s (Boyce 1987: 139). Population growth at 2.46 per cent per annum in West Bengal during this period can be compared to the figure of 2.15 per cent per annum for all-India (Jose, 1984: 140). The contemporary population density figure of 614 persons per sq km is one of the highest in the world. Bandyopadhyay (1983: 17) noted that West Bengal has a net sown area of roughly 13.6 million acres and a rural population of about 40 million, or an average of one-third of an acre a person, some three times lower than the all-India average. Such high and steadily increasing population density has meant a decrease in land-related resources per person,[2] and this is one constraining

---

[2] One should be careful about making a simple connection between *agricultural* growth and population growth, as some economists have done (e.g. Jose, 1984: 138). Boyce (1987: 153), opposing Malthusian theory, has argued that population growth is positively correlated to agricultural growth in Bengal.

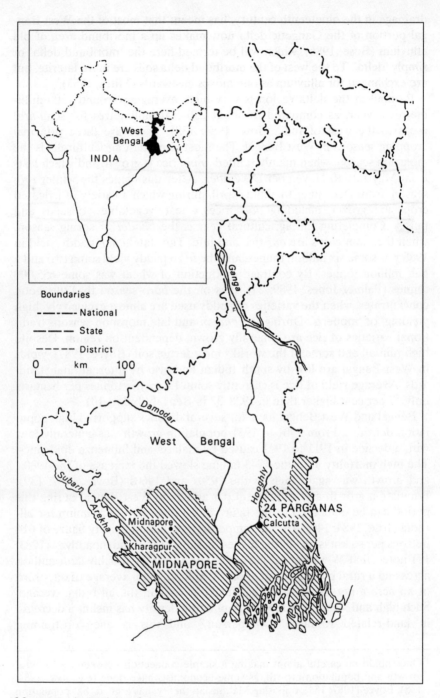

Map 4.1 Location of the study area

factor on the poor, and a cause of immiseration. Increase in population should not, however, be isolated from other socio-economic and structural causes of poverty, discussed below.

Historical and political background to Bengal and West Bengal

Bengal has therefore been a region with a relatively large population and high agricultural potential, but which has developed into one of the poorer regions of India (Rogers, *et al.*, 1989). This section considers factors other than population increase that have contributed to the serious decline in living standards between the turn of the century and the present day, as well as the history of peasant protest in the region.

The contemporary agrarian structure in the moribund delta, which features a high proportion of agricultural labourers and multiple small holdings, was already set by the beginning of the twentieth century, and can possibly be traced back to the eighteenth century (Ray, 1979). Bose has charted the decline in living standards in West Bengal from the beginning of the twentieth century to independence. Causes for this decline at the national and international levels concerned adverse terms of trade and geography. Bengal's increasing integration into the world market meant that external and internal terms of trade worked against the agrarian sector concerning the price of jute, the main export crop, as well as of rice (Bose, 1986). Bose (ibid.: 44) has also described the deteriorating physical environment in the western moribund delta in the nineteenth century: 'In West Bengal, as the river system atrophied . . . disease and decline set in, and the population languished.' This natural atrophying of the river system, along with the construction of rail and road embankments from the middle of the nineteenth century: 'played havoc with the fast deteriorating drainage system of the region.' (ibid.: 44–45).[3] This led to decreasing soil fertility and stagnating yields, and along with the increase in population and pressure on land, was a prologue to the famine of 1943 in Bengal, when up to three million people died. While the famine did have specific local causes, including maladministration and siphoning off of food from the rural economy (Greenough, 1982; Sen, 1982), the general economic decline from the beginning of the century also contributed to its occurence.

Declining living standards and exploitation were met with protest by Bengali labourers, peasants and sharecroppers. In the two study areas discussed in this book, for example, protests took place throughout the nineteenth century. Guha (1986) describes protest in 24 Parganas District in 1830 to 1832, of particular interest as it centred on Barasat, a large town about 12 kilometres from the main study village of this book. It was led by

---

[3] For a more detailed analysis of nineteenth-century ecological developments, see Biswas (1981).

Titu Mir, a convert to the Islamic Wahabi sect, a professional fighter and *lathial* turned rebel. Titu Mir began to preach Wahabi doctrines secretly in Barasat from 1827, and violence against Hindus began in 1830 to 1831. O'Malley (1914: 49) noted that the Wahabis set up headquarters in 24 Parganas in 1831 'within a few hours' ride from Calcutta', and 'the whole of the country north and east of Calcutta, including the 24 Parganas, Nadia and Faridpur, lay at the mercy of insurgent bands, between three and four thousand strong'. O'Malley treats the uprising as communal disturbance. Guha on the other hand sees the insurgency as a 'sustained class struggle' of Muslim tenants against Hindu *zamindars* (1986: 107–8). Evidence of widespread Wahabi protest against the Government of Bengal in the 1860s, including in 24 Parganas, can be found in Khan (1961). Elements of the agrarian structure which led to this Muslim–Hindu/tenant–landlord conflict were still present in the contemporary case study area, and this is discussed in chapter six.

For Midnapore, the other case study district of this book, Dasgupta (1985) has outlined the exploitation of tribals in terms of expropriation of land and restrictions on forest 'rights' from 1760 to 1924. The incursion of outsiders, mainly Hindu and British landowners, was seen by the tribals as an affront to their way of living and particularly their honour. As Dasgupta puts it (ibid.: 117): 'the notion of honour figured very prominently in *adivasi* (tribal) consciousness'. As to the relative importance to tribals of food and self respect, another area of enquiry in this book, Dasgupta notes (ibid.: 120):

> During the 1886 famine in Chota Nagpur, British officials found to their astonishment that starving Santals refused to eat the food distributed by the relief committee because it had been cooked by the hated Brahmins.

This is an interesting perspective, and might explain why the poor in Britain in the 1790s may have refused to eat food that, in Frederick Eden's words, 'was served at a gentleman's table'.

The most widespread of rural protests was the *Tebhaga* movement, which took place throughout Bengal in 1946 and 1947, although concentrated in the east and frontier regions. *Tebhaga* was a movement carried out mainly by sharecroppers, in an attempt to gain two-thirds rather than the traditional half share of the crop from the land they farmed. Rather than being a purely economic protest, it was also a protest against the exploitive relationship between sharecroppers and landlords (Cooper, 1984). The movement also had wider goals, and 'land to the tiller' was a frequent demand. Sharecroppers were ringed in by a set of petty prohibitions which symbolized their low status. These included being forced to sit on the ground or on a lower seat than a landlord; violence by the landlord's hired personal armies; and sexual and economic exploitation of women in the sharecropping households (ibid.: 89–92; see also Dasgupta, 1984a). The system of advances of pre-harvest credit in cash or kind to sharecroppers, to be repaid with extortionate interest or by labour after the harvest, which operated in the 1940s in Bengal (Cooper, 1984), was found to be still in operation in 1989 in the field study villages.

By November 1946 *Tebhaga* protests had extended to most districts in Bengal, and were taken up all over 24 Parganas in December 1946. Protests included attacks on landlords' granaries, and violence against landlords and the police. Agricultural labourers were actively involved, and it was women who took the lead in many incidents (Cooper, 1984; Dasgupta, 1984a; Ghatak, 1983). Although the *Tebhaga* demands were not met at this time, this and other protests undoubtedly helped shape government policy in the post-Independence period.

There has been, therefore, a long history of protest against exploitation and the decline of living standards in Bengal, by tribals, sharecroppers and 'middle' peasants, which should counter any idea of the rural population in Bengal as passive.[4] These protests have continued after Independence, particularly, as in the past, in frontier regions such as north Bengal (see Bandyopadhyay, 1977), and during the recent Naxalite movement (Bannerjee, 1984), which was mainly a tribal agitation. There have no doubt also been many local protests by agricultural labourers over wages or exploitation of the kind described by Davis (1983) and Westergaard (1986), which have gone unrecorded, as agricultural labourer protest in general has not been well documented in Bengal (Van Schendel and Faraizi, 1984).

Rural protests have been one important factor, as Dasgupta has suggested (1984a), in shaping subsequent government legislation in favour of poorer peasants; for example, the *Tebhaga* movement led directly to the West Bengal Bargadars Act of 1950, and the post-1977 Communist government has made rights of share-croppers a central issue for its legislation (Ghosh 1986: 6; and see below). This collective form of poor rural people's agency and protest against exploitation and decline in living standards should be borne in mind when present day forms of exploitation and agency are considered in chapter eight. They are also examples of the way in which poor people's 'public' and 'collective' agency (in Anderson's typology) is meshed and interacts with the structures imposed by the state and local elites.

The agrarian structure in West Bengal

At Indian Independence in 1947 Bengal was partitioned into West Bengal and present day Bangladesh, a division impractical in terms of communica-

---

[4] For an all-Bengal perspective on peasant protest between 1928 and 1934, see Sarkar (1987). Sarkar also documents the active role played by women in peasant protests.

tions and the functioning of the important jute industry (Boyce, 1987). After Independence West Bengal's economy declined. Meso-level data suggests that consumption of food in West Bengal stagnated and private consumption of non-food items showed a mild improvement between 1972–3 and 1985–6, while public services such as education and transport have remained poor, and rural housing conditions have deteriorated (Bhattacharya *et al.*, 1987a, b, c). Boyce (1987: 81) estimated that: 'the overall rate of agricultural output growth in West Bengal from 1949 to 1980 has been below the rates of rural and total population increase.' Only 40 per cent of net sown area was irrigated in West Bengal in 1978–9, as opposed to 78 per cent in the Punjab. Post-1980 agricultural growth will be discussed below.

Lack of agricultural growth is one constraining feature on activity by the poor, because low yields mean low profits for small and marginal farmers and less work for labourers. The agrarian structure is a further possible constraining feature. Evidence from macro-level state figures reveal an unequal pattern of resource distribution within West Bengal. The available evidence shows that about 70 per cent of rural households operated 30 per cent of land in West Bengal, in holdings of less than 1 hectare. In contrast, a further 30 per cent of land was held by 20 per cent of households operating 1–2 hectares, and about 4 per cent of households operated more than 10 hectares, covering only 0.02 per cent of the area of the State (Lieten, 1990: 2268). Sengupta has commented on this land-operating pattern as follows (1981: A71):

. . . in pre-reform [i.e. pre-1977] West Bengal we already observe, compared to the whole of the country, a much higher preponderance of small and marginal farmers and farms, a higher incidence of sharecroppers and agricultural labourers . . . and a relatively weak existence of big landowners at the other pole of the economy.

The agrarian structure is therefore 'minifundist'. However, while few 'big landowners' exist in West Bengal, it is the group that I will refer to as 'middle' farmers, and who own or operate approximately 1–2 hectares, who have been seen by various authors as dominant in the villages of West Bengal.[5]

The large percentage of smallholdings found below one hectare is complemented by a high degree of fragmentation of holdings. Boyce (1987:

---

[5] Webster, 1989: 45; Bandyopadhyay and Von Eschen, 1988: 127; Kohli, 1987: 100–101; Bandyopadhyay, 1983: 61, 63, 73. For a survey of 11 village studies, see Beck, 1991. Nossiter (1988: 120–1) has written that, as opposed to north India, in West Bengal there has not been a tendency for one middle or lower caste to dominate, and that, unlike most other parts of India, caste has not been a major axis of conflict.

210) has calculated that in 1970/71, for all size classes of rural households, there were 7 fragments of land per holding and 5.6 fragments per acre, a figure that will have increased over the last twenty years. As only 0.07 per cent of holdings in West Bengal were operated on a joint basis in the same years (Ghose 1983: 131, fn. 43), it can be seen that the spatial pattern of land operation involves a major disarticulation of many small plots with very little co-operative farming taking place.

These figures on land operation are complemented by data on the increase in the number of agricultural labourers. Historically, agricultural labourers have been amongst the poorest occupational groups in Bengal, and the group most affected by the general decline in living standards (Van Schendel and Faraizi, 1984). Agricultural labourer households were also found to be the main group among the poorest households selected for intensive interviews in all three case study villages in this book. They are generally landless or landpoor, and receive their main income through manual labour in agricultural operations. According to all sources, the percentage of agricultural labourers has increased steadily since Independence. One study estimates that agricultural labourers in 1981 made up 33 per cent of all rural workers, up from 19 per cent in 1951 (Dasgupta, 1984c: A141; for further details, see Beck, 1991). However, rural employment possibilities have not increased alongside the number of agricultural labourers, which has led to large scale un- and under-employment in rural areas, a further cause of the immiseration of the Bengal poor.

There are three further features of agrarian relations that make the agrarian structure 'move' and are central to power relations at village level. These are tenancy, absentee landlordism, and credit relations, which will be seen in operation at micro-level in the chapters following this one.

The rural economy in West Bengal is marked by tenancy relations, the main form of which is sharecropping. About 23 per cent of land was sharecropped in Bengal in 1931, and about 31 per cent in 1951 (Cooper 1984: 342–345), declining to about 19 per cent in 1971/2 (Boyce 1987: 214). As we have seen above, distribution of the crop from sharecropped land has been an axis of class conflict in West Bengal. Sharecropping remains an exploitive practice in the state, with the profits often divided in favour of the owner of the land; given the unequal landholdings in rural areas, it is often absentee landlords or middle farmers who sharecrop out land. The risk of farming remains with the sharecropper, who often makes only a very small profit.[6]

The second complicating feature of the agrarian structure is that evidence suggests that a 'substantial' proportion of land in West Bengal is controlled by absentee landlords (Dasgupta, 1984b). 'Absentee' is defined

---

[6] Sharecropping in West Bengal has generated a large academic literature, which I have summarized elsewhere (Beck, 1991).

here to mean landowners who live outside the village, and who earn their primary source of income in some way other than agriculture (i.e. they are not agriculturalists nor do they supervise agricultural operations). Nossiter (1988: 116) has noted that many Bengali *bhadraloks* were urban rent receivers who retained a rural connection through land ownership. Ghose (1983: 103–4) also mentions the historical acquisition of land by non-agriculturalists, for example during the 1943 Bengal famine. Empirical evidence of a significant degree of absentee landlordism can be found in several rural surveys.[7] Kohli (1987: 100) has noted that the Government of West Bengal has declared absentee landlords 'enemies' of the rural people, because they do not participate in agricultural activities; however, no detailed study appears to have been carried out as to their number or power in the State.

The third factor which fuels the agrarian economy is credit and market relations. As B. Harriss (1982: 195) has noted in a study of the system of circulation of rice in Birbhum District:

> Rice mills stand dominant over the rural economy. Though their land ownership is sizeable, . . . profits are extracted through usury, through rent on property and land, through buying and selling, usually accompanied by processing.

This 'extraction of surplus' from and control of the rural economy goes hand in hand with a similar extraction at village level involving control of credit by employers and petty traders. J. Harriss, in a complementary study to the one just quoted, has written (1984: 26–7):

> . . . while the system of advances [of credit to landless people and small-holding peasants from rich peasants/landlords] does not necessarily constitute a powerful siphon of extraction of product, it certainly *secures* the appropriate surplus for speculative trading by the dominant class.

This 'dominant class' in Birbhum District which controls village credit relations is also described by Harriss as 'middle farmers' (ibid.), that same group that I suggest control village relations in West Bengal in the moribund delta.

This section has outlined structural features of the agrarian economy that one can expect to find replicated to a lesser or greater extent throughout villages in the moribund delta. The complex interplay of people and their environment has meant that village power structures have also become imprinted on the local environment, and ensure that the poor are constantly 'squeezed' by the dominant in their villages who control the most important village resources of land and credit.

---

[7] Webster, 1989; Kohli, 1987; Westergaard, 1986; ; Bandyopadhyay, 1983; B. Harriss, 1982; Khasnabis and Chakravarty, 1982; Frankel, 1971; and my fieldwork below.

Politics and agrarian reform in West Bengal

State reform may have significant impact on the lives of the poor either by its presence or absence. The effect of agrarian reforms and the benefits the poor have gained is charted below, after a discussion of macro- and micro-level politics in the state.

Apart from two brief interrupted periods of Left Front (Communist) rule between 1967 and 1970, the post-Independence government in West Bengal was before 1977 exclusively Congress. Since 1977 West Bengal has been ruled by a Left Front coalition, of which the Communist Party of India (Marxist) or CPM has been the main partner. The long history of peasant protest in the state has been seen as one reason for the success of left wing parties (Bandyopahdyay, 1983: 111). The Left Front is now dominant politically in West Bengal, having gained 85 per cent of seats in the state parliament in 1987 (with 53 per cent of the vote, an increase of 7 per cent over 1977). As well, the Left Front have a stronghold in the rural *panchayats*, which the Left Front reconstituted in 1978, and which have successfully consolidated rural power for the party.

The Left Front have benefited from party discipline and strong leadership at state level (Kohli, 1987). Despite rhetoric to the contrary (see Government of West Bengal, 1986; Rudra, 1985), the party has been more in the liberal democratic than in the socialist mode, and has taken a more moderate path in its agrarian reform than, for example, governments in Kerala (Webster, 1989; Kohli, 1987; Bandyopadhyay, 1983). This has partly to do with the federal situation in India where opposition states have been consistently 'toppled' by the Central government. As important, given the Kerala comparison, has been the internal agrarian structure in West Bengal, and the need for the Left Front to retain its power base among the middle farmers.

Since 1978 *panchayats* have been in control of land reform and rural development programmes, and at present 50 per cent of rural development resources are being channelled through the *panchayats*. In order to describe which groups hold political power in West Bengal at village level, it is necessary to look at membership of the *panchayat* organizations. Evidence on *panchayat* membership is conflicting. Several studies, including my own fieldwork, suggests that the *panchayats* at village level are controlled mainly by middle farmers who already have significant resources under their control, with a large percentage being teachers or other professionals.[8] These farmers are supporters of the CPM, and hence the 'concessions' made to this group in terms of subsidies on irrigation water rates, exemption from land revenue payments, and subsidized supplies of fertil-

---

[8] See Nesmith, 1990; Mallick, 1988; Nossiter,1988; Kohli, 1987; Westergaard, 1986: Ghose, 1983.

izer (Dasgupta, 1984b; Sengupta, 1981). As Kohli (1987: 142) has concisely put it:

> . . . the CPM leadership finds it difficult to balance the needs of the middle peasantry, who often employ landless labourers, against the task of organizing the struggles of landless labourers for wage increments.

On the other hand, some recent evidence has suggested that representation of the rural poor on village *panchayats* has been fair, and that there has been increasing representation of scheduled tribe and caste members as opposed to women, whose representation is more or less non-existent (Sengupta, 1991; Lieten, 1988).

The main agrarian reform attempted by the Left Front has been as follows (Government of West Bengal, 1986: 2):

> The first object of land reforms programme (sic) is to reduce, as far as possible the disparity and irregularities in the rural economic structure by bringing about a change in the ownership of land and land tenancy system. With this end in view a comprehensive multi-purpose pro-gramme has been undertaken to distribute surplus lands among the landless and to safeguard the rights of the sharecroppers.

There is extreme divergence of views as to the effectiveness of the Left Front Government in accomplishing these aims, so much so that one wonders if critics and supporters are always addressing the same phenomenon. Much academic attention has focused on the attempt to 'safeguard the rights of sharecroppers', one of the state's poorer occupational groups. Since 1978 the government has attempted to register the names of sharecroppers to prevent their eviction and ensure their continued right to cultivate land they have farmed for three consecutive years; and to provide these sharecroppers with credit, other institutional support, and a lawful (75 per cent) share of the crop. This programme has been called 'Operation Barga', and can be seen to have stemmed directly from peasant agitation over sharecroppers' rights. According to the West Bengal Government (1986: 3), before 1977 only 300,000 sharecroppers had registered their names with the land revenue office, while by the beginning of 1986 about 1.4 million had done so, out of a total of about two million sharecroppers in the state.

While there is some consensus as to the success of registration (Kohli, 1987; Westergaard, 1986), registration may mean nothing more that having one's name recorded. It would be difficult to say how many sharecroppers have resisted eviction after registration, or even if eviction has decreased since the 1970s. There is also some consensus that the Left Front has been unable to provide credit for registered sharecroppers (Westergaard, 1986; Bandyopadhyay, 1983; Rudra, 1981a). In addition, the programme has been criticized because the share of the crop is still divided illegally in the landowners' favour (Bandyopadhyay, 1983).

While 'Operation Barga' has been successful in some areas, it awaits detailed contemporary state-wise assessment. Of more relevance here, given the constitution of the group of the poorest, and that there are twice as many agricultural labourers as sharecroppers in rural West Bengal (Bandyopadyay, 1983), is the effect of government policy on agricultural labourers. Labourers could have benefited from at least three areas of policy – land reform, increases in wages, and state-sponsored development programs – which I will discuss now.

West Bengal's achievements in land reform have been claimed as considerable, in comparison to other Indian states. For example, Sengupta (1991: 28), in support of the Left Front Government, notes that: 'West Bengal's coverage in land distribution programmes either in terms of area or in terms of intended beneficiaries was qualitatively on a different plane compared to the country's. While only 1.23 per cent of the net sown area in India was distributed under the redistribution programme, in West Bengal this was more than 6 per cent [up to 1991]. What seems more remarkable is that nearly 48 per cent of the land distribution beneficiaries in the country belonged to West Bengal alone . . .'. In addition, the government has stated that much of the land in West Bengal, about 55 per cent, had been given to scheduled tribes and scheduled castes, an impressive performance (Government of West Bengal, 1986: 3). On the other hand, Mallick (1992) has claimed that the Left Front Government has included in its redistribution figures land redistributed by governments prior to its own. It does appear, for example, that during 1972–77, when the Congress were in power, 250,000 acres were distributed, or a quarter of all land distributed to date in West Bengal (Lieten 1990: 2267). Looking at the quality of land distributed, micro-level studies suggest that this may have been poor (Sengupta, 1991; Westergaard, 1986). It is not possible to come to any conclusion to this complex debate here. However, as we shall see in chapter six when I analyse the government land reform programme at village level, from the poor person's perspective even receipt of a small piece of poor quality land can be psychologically important.

The Left Front Government does not appear to have prioritized the enforcement of a minimum wage for agricultural labourers (Kohli, 1987; Westergaard, 1986). Nor is it likely to do so in the future, given the nature of its support among 'middle' farmers who are wage payers. Wage rates in Bengal have remained steady but at a low level in the last hundred years (Van Schendel and Faraizi, 1984); and Mallick (1988: 180) has calculated that: '. . . there does not appear to be any significant differences in ratios of change between Congress and Communist regimes in terms of money or real wages.' There is some evidence, however, that agitation by labourers is becoming effective in increasing the wage rate (see Ghosh, 1988; Bardhan and Rudra 1980b).

Programmes for rural development with a pro-poor focus undertaken by the Left Front Government have had mixed success, but have been as good or better than those in other parts of India. Westergaard's study suggests that the National Rural Employment Programme has had considerable, if regional, success in providing employment for the rural poor (1986). Chaudhuri's (1980) and Kohli's (1987) studies of food for work in Birbhum, Burdwan and Midnapore districts accord the programme some success, and Dreze (1988b: 71–2) also found that, for one village in Birbhum, and despite party bias, the Integrated Rural Development Programme (IRDP) in West Bengal 'overwhelmingly benefited landless labourers', a finding echoed by Swaminathan (1990), comparing the state's performance in implementing IRDP in West Bengal and the southern state of Tamil Nadu. Ghatak, on the other hand, found that in Purulia and Bankura Districts, for the Rural Labour Employment Guarantee Programme (1985: 78):

> There is more concern at all levels, beginning from the State, down to the Gram Panchayat, in getting more resources, somehow or the other, than in their proper utilization . . .

And for the Development of Women and Children in Rural Areas for the same districts Ghatak found that there had been a 'failure of the administration and Panchayat leadership' which meant that the performance of West Bengal had been 'miserably poor' (Ghatak, n.d.: 40). These findings undermine Kohli's statement that (1987: 139):

> For the first time in modern India, political institutions capable of facilitating rural development with redistribution are being developed at the behest of the CPM leadership.

In addition, health and education do not seem to be much improved under Left Front rule, although nutritional levels do appear to have improved (Mallick, 1992; Sengupta, 1991).

One last point should be made concerning the Left Front's agrarian policy. This is that, as a number of academics have pointed out (Bannerjee, 1992; Lieten, 1988; Bose and Bhadoria, 1987; Kohli, 1987; Ghosh, 1986), Left Front policies have had a significant effect concerning the conscientization of poorer groups. For example, as Ghosh suggests (1986: 78), for the first time, under the Operation Barga programme, government officials have been going to villages to meet sharecroppers at the sharecroppers' convenience, to discuss their rights with them. The Left Front programme cannot be judged, therefore, only in quantitative terms; that poor village people can now live, as one of Lieten's respondents put it (1988: 2070), with 'human dignity', as opposed to the situation ten years ago, is a significant achievement, one of relevance to the approach of this book, and also one of its field findings.

Conclusions

The following conclusions can be drawn about the agrarian structure in West Bengal. Firstly, present-day features of the rural economy, such as a high degree of landlessness and sharecropping, a high percentage of (mainly landless) agricultural labourers, and an exploitive rural credit system, have been in operation since at least the beginning of this century. Secondly, a combination of high population growth, low agricultural growth and stagnating yields have, since the beginning of this century, led to increasing poverty in Bengal and West Bengal, and to a comparative scarcity of resources. This increase in population has taken place in the context of an unequal agrarian structure where a majority of resources, and control of local government, in the moribund delta at least, are now in the hands of a group of middle farmers. Thirdly, present-day West Bengal has an agrarian structure that is complex, and which defies easy categorization. Complicating features are: overlapping groups of agricultural labourers, landless labourers, sharecroppers and small land operators, all of whom may have conflicting interests; ownership of small fragmented plots by a large number of smallholders; complex tenancy arrangements; absentee landlordism; and credit relations. It is within this unequal and complex structure, with increasing immiseration and poverty, and decreasing access to resources, that poor people must continue their livelihoods. A further constraint on the poorest has been that the Left Front Government has forgone 'radical' attempts at reform because of fear of alienating 'middle' land operators, which has meant relative loss for agricultural labourers. However, while poorer groups may not have received significant material gains from land reform and rural development programmes, these gains have been of disproportionate psychological and qualitative importance. Many of the structural features outlined in this chapter will reappear when socio-economic structure in the case study villages is investigated in the next two chapters.

5   The villages and the study

How the study came to be done and how it was carried out

This chapter continues at village level the contextualization begun in chapter four. This section on methodology describes how and why I came to carry out a field study, and the relation between theory and method in this book. I give some background information on the case study villages, and make comparisons between them and West Bengal as a whole. I then discuss land operation and employment in the three villages, and finally set out the method of categorization and differentiation of village households used in this book to analyse the socio-economic constraints faced by poorest households.

I can still remember vividly arriving at Calcutta airport for the first time in 1981. I had wanted to 'get out into the world'. What surprised me on the road from the airport into the city was not the shacks of slum dwellers or the cows wandering over the road, but the palm trees fringing the road and the lushness of the vegetation. I got a job for several months soon after arriving with a Bengali NGO working for rural development, who invited me back at the beginning of 1984 to act as their administrator. I did so for a year and a half, and the Bengali I know was learnt during this time. The NGO compound was in a rural area and when I first arrived I shared the rigours of village life – no electricity or running water, little variety and poor quality food, the heat of the summer and the humidity of the monsoon, snakes, red ants, mosquitoes and sickness. Gradually I came to be accepted by the local community. As part of the work we established a health and education programme for poor village women from ten local villages, but the women who came were not the poorest as I had hoped. The classes were held outside, and I was struck one day when watching one of the classes to see some of the very poor women from one of the local villages, babies on hips, standing and watching the class from a distance, trying to figure out what was going on. Like most development programmes, ours had failed to get through to the poorest.

After returning from India, I decided to return to academic life for a few years, and write the thesis on which this book is based. My contact with the poor in rural West Bengal, and my admiration for their ability not only to survive but to do so with dignity, led to my choice of subject. This choice was further determined by the relative neglect in research on rural India of work on poverty or poor people's, and particularly poor women's, abilities. As Breman has suggested (1985b: 9): 'a systematic illumination from the bottom up has remained very rare'. He goes on (ibid.: 34):

66

The distortion which results from analysing situations of poverty from outside often arises from incomprehension and appalling inability to empathise among researchers who allow themselves to be guided by the judgements of the higher social classes to which they belong . . . It has become standard practice to point to defects in the lives of poor people as explanation for the situation in which they live. Only study at closer range can contribute to the combating of the notion that poverty is perpetuated primarily by a subculture rather than by a larger social structure . . .

From this quote it is possible to extract the methodological approach taken here – that both the world-view and abilities of the poor, and the social structure with which they interact, need to be studied if poverty is to be understood.

I decided to take the village next to the compound of the NGO for which I had been working as a study village, as I already had some contact with the villagers there through my work. This village I call Fonogram.[1] I also decided to select two other villages in a different agro-ecological setting for comparative purposes, and to ensure that my discussions with poorest households would allow me to describe their activities in general terms. These villages were situated in Midnapore District and were chosen because of their large Scheduled Tribe and Scheduled Caste populations, two groups reportedly among the poorest in India.

In all I made three field trips. The first was a preliminary visit to Fonogram from December 1986 to March 1987. An informal census survey of the village households was initially made, collecting basic socio-economic data with the assistance of Hamedchha, a Fonogram villager, agricultural labourer aged about fifty, who was a local guide, and an invaluable source of local information. After this survey I formulated a general questionnaire, the aim of which was to get basic socio-economic data on each household. Fonogram was badly flooded in the 1986 monsoon season; this offered the opportunity of discussing with poorest households how they had coped in a period of difficulty, and for some, crisis. All communication with the villagers and those who assisted me in the research was in Bengali.

From the initial census survey, my knowledge of the village and the views of villagers, a 15 per cent sample of 22 poorest households was selected for more detailed informal interview. Subsequently, three more households were added in 1988/9, bringing the sample nearer to 20 per cent. A staff member of the NGO for which I had worked assisted in these detailed interviews with poorest families. These interviews concentrated on how respondents had coped after the floods during the 1986 monsoon, a period still fresh in their minds. Their answers were grouped under common headings,

---

[1] All local names are pseudonyms.

and with these answers in mind a second check list of questions was produced. This check list listed questions under headings that reflected the
priorities of the poor – 'Hunger, collection and survival', 'Economic experience', 'Social experience' and 'Political experience'. Census survey interviews with all village households will be referred to below as first-round
interviews. The more detailed discussions with the poorest will be referred to
as second-round interviews. The formation of questionnaires after initial
discussions with villagers allowed for greater flexibility in including questions
concerning areas which respondents considered important.

During this field trip I also mapped land use, ownership and operation in
Fonogram through a plot to plot survey of about 600 plots, a process
repeated in 1987/8 and 1988/9. The aim of this was the evaluation of an
irrigation project, which involved the introduction of 14 shallow tubewells
(STWs) into the Fonogram area in 1985, and which is discussed in the next
chapter. My own data was carefully cross-checked with official information,
so that data given here on land operation in Fonogram can be considered
as accurate.

I made a second field trip from October 1987 to January 1988. During
this trip I visited five villages in Birbhum District and four villages in
Midnapore District where I had previous contacts, in order to choose two
other study villages. I returned to Fonogram and conducted more detailed
second-round interviews with 22 poorest households, most of whom were
interviewed informally in the previous year. A third field trip followed
from October 1988 to February 1989 to complete the fieldwork. This visit
enabled the completion of a three-year land use survey in Fonogram, so as
to ensure the representativeness of data. For the secondary study villages I
chose Midnapore over Birbhum. With its laterite soil, central Midnapore
provided a quite different agro-ecological setting to 24 Parganas or the
more fertile areas of Birbhum that I had visited. It also gave access in close
proximity to Scheduled Tribes and Scheduled Castes, and, importantly, the
possibility of an introduction to local villages through the West Bengal
Forestry Department.[2]

We set up house in Kharagpur town (see Map 4.1), and I cycled daily to
these two villages, subsequently named Bithigram and Keshipur. First-
round interviews were carried out in both of the villages with the aid of an
'assistant', a local student. Nineteen poorest households in Bithigram and
sixteen in Keshipur were then selected for re-interview on the basis of
these first-round interviews, that is approximately a 20 per cent sample
from each village.[3] During this trip first-round interviews were also

---

[2] Mallick (1988: 229) estimates that Scheduled Tribes and Castes make up 33 per
cent of the West Bengal population.

[3] In Bithigram for half of the second-round interviews one of the poorest household
members who acted as a guide was also present.

repeated for each household in Fonogram, to cross-check the socio-economic information gathered in 1986.

The approach taken in the second-round interviews was to sit informally with poor people, privately and in their homes, at a convenient time for them. As much scope as possible was given to respondents for replying and speaking their mind. This was a time-consuming and often draining practice, as there was much unhappiness and anger in many of the respondents' lives, and discussion with them could last for two hours or more; several respondents broke down in tears during the interviews when discussing personal tragedies. Mutual respect between respondent and interviewer was essential during interviews. This respect made it possible for me to ask very personal questions about respondents' lives, and about emotional subjects such as death of family members.

Key informants in each village, some of whom were among the poorest, were another useful source of information, and being accompanied by a poor person (Hamedchha) in Fonogram, and later in Bithigram, made me less of an outsider. Informal chats along the roadside, in the local teashops, in my or others' houses in the evening with tea as a lubricant, often provided revealing information. Many of the most enjoyable and animated discussions took place in the evening, and it is difficult to describe the experience of discussing village matters with several villagers on the verandah of one of their houses, our shawls wrapped tightly around us to keep out the cold, sipping tea, the sky a mass of stars. The daughter of one of the respondents in Fonogram, who lived in a dilapidated shack on the side of the approach road to the village, would often be cooking as I passed by. She was happy to chat and talk about her responsibility for cooking, and proved a source of inspiration about how, what and where poor people eat. I also held about twenty group interviews with both better-off and poorer people; again the evenings were a good time for these. Interviews in the Lodha (tribal) *para* of Bithigram often turned into group discussions, which I welcomed, and which often became animated. I interviewed as well, often in substantial depth, richer farmers, village leaders and local government officials, to find out their views on the village and farming, and their attitude towards the poor.

There was little 'random sampling', therefore, in the choice of study villages, although an attempt was made to ensure the representativeness of the villages by surveying them and checking census details before selecting them. As will be seen below, I have no reason to believe that the study villages are unrepresentative of moribund delta West Bengal. A criteria for choice of villages as important as representativeness was ease of access to the poorest, as lack of such access has been one reason for past failure of rural surveys to address the experience and problems of the poor.

Apart from the problem of 'mental-metricism' discussed in chapter two, a further methodological problem arises from the kind of 'bottom up', qualitative approach taken and advocated here. This is that even if poor people's views are considered as valid, and are understood in social context, can they be taken as representative of anything other than their immediate locality, and if not, are they of greater value than simply being the thoughts and opinions of a few poor people? A solution to this problem is to use comparative analysis. For example, if a particular coping strategy or opinion of the poor is found to be widespread in rural studies, this strategy can then be taken as representative. This comparative method is used when presenting the fieldwork material in later chapters.

Method in this book is closely related to theory. Chapter two has shown that method and choice of subject are not 'value-neutral', and that, historically, a quantitative approach to studying poverty has been likely to have a built-in bias against poor people, to be elitist, and to involve both moral judgements about the poor, and regulatory policy. Equally, chapter three analysed studies which have taken a qualitative approach in pointing out the importance of the poor person's perspective, but have not always addressed structural socio-economic issues. My own work has attempted to keep close to the agenda of the authors discussed in chapter three, and in my choice of subject and methodological approach, I recognize that there is an explicit political sympathizing with the poor. But I also recognize the problems associated with such an approach, and have also attempted to locate the experience of poverty within the socio-economic framework with which the poorest interact.

Background to the case study villages

This section gives background information on the three study villages in terms of location, population, caste, politics, occupation and land operation. More detailed analysis of market linkages, farming practices, soil and topography for Fonogram can be found in the next chapter. All figures in this section are for 1989, unless otherwise stated.

Dasgupta (1975) has outlined differences in the Indian context between 'A' (or agriculturally advanced) and 'B' (or less agriculturally advanced) villages. 'A' villages, of which Fonogram is one type, are larger, more accessible, more irrigated, with less equal landholding, more landless households and higher-yielding land than 'B' villages, into which category the Midnapore villages fit. This suggests that the agrarian structures described below are representative of a wider pattern.

Fonogram
Fonogram lay about 40 km north east of Calcutta, or three hours from that city by public transport. A metalled road, on which plied an irregular and always over-crowded bus service, was located 2 km from the village. One then walked to Fonogram along a brick and earth road, which ended

70

abruptly at the first house in the village. The village roads were all *kaccha* (for a village and *mouza* map, see the next chapter).

Fonogram lay within an area that was mainly agricultural. Local villages, which were both Muslim and Hindu, bore a similar appearance to Fonogram, being mainly groups of mud walled and red tiled houses surrounded by an irregular chess-board of fields in different states of cultivation throughout the year. No evidence was available as to when Fonogram was founded, although older residents suggested that the area had been settled several generations back. The village was exclusively Muslim. Households were grouped into family settlements, with the better-off households having inner courtyards, in traditional Muslim fashion. Pressure on village land was great. In 1989 there were 141 households in the village, and total village population was about 840. In 1951, the Government Census gave Fonogram's population at 405, so the population more than doubled over the last 30 years. Fonogram households operated just under 50 hectares of land, giving a person–land ratio of 14 decimals per person. Several villagers saw the increase in population as one historical cause of increasing poverty in the village, and most villagers agreed that poverty was increasing.

Local health services included a hospital in Barasat (a town about 12 km from Fonogram, and the centre of Wahabi protest mentioned in chapter four), and two allopathic doctors in Dabu, a very small town about 3 km distant. Water supply in the village was from tubewells and ponds. None of the houses had electricity, although since the introduction of the STWs there had been one street light in operation on the road into the village. When there was no moon, the village was black except for the hurricane and oil lanterns that villagers kept on their verandahs, and the torches of the few villagers who owned them. A market was held twice weekly at Dabu, and most Fonogram villagers shopped there or in local shops which lined the approach road to the village and whose proprietors, as will be seen, were among the main sources of village credit.

The majority of Fonogram villagers were supporters of the CPM, through choice or otherwise. As one wealthier farmer put it: 'I used to be a supporter of Congress, but I thought that I would be beaten up if I continued to support them, so I changed to the CPM.' The village had an unelected 'committee' (to use the local term) made up of four men from the most powerful households in the village.[4] This committee called occasional meetings to discuss matters that affected the whole village, for example rates of payment for land leased during the *boro* season. The

---

[4] Half of Fonogram was covered by a *gram* (village) *panchayat*, and the other half, despite its rural setting, came under the jurisdiction of the local municipality. The reason for this, as informants told me with some amusement, was that a water pipe ran around its outskirts, and this pipe was the responsibility of the municipality. The local authorities appeared to have little influence on events in Fonogram.

committee members had considerable influence concerning village affairs, and, for example, evicted two households that had supposedly been involved in immoral activities (the story of one of the households will be told in chapter nine), as well as helping to settle a virtually homeless third household on a piece of land of an absentee landlord outside the village. Although there were some differences of interest between these four households, as became apparent when discussing village matters with them, it would not be going too far to say that village power was largely in their, and their close relatives', hands. They were the middle farmers indicated earlier as the most powerful group in the moribund delta villages of West Bengal, each household operating about 1–2 hectares of land.

Fonogram farmers followed traditional cropping patterns. *Aman*, the most important crop, was poor to indifferent in the 1986, 1987 and 1988 seasons, because of flooding or insufficient rainfall. This increased economic pressure on all villagers, but particularly the poor as they lost employment at the harvesting period, the peak period of employment in the agricultural year.

Bithigram and Keshipur
These two villages lay about 14 km south west of Kharagpur, a railhead and small town 225 km west of Calcutta. A metalled road but no bus service ran near the villages, so they were approachable from Kharagpur town by car, bicycle or foot, with some circumnavigation needed for the first method. Roads within the local villages were all *kaccha*. The area was mainly agricultural, although there was local employment connected to the railways.

The two villages lay in a transitional agro-ecological zone between the alluvial soils of eastern Midnapore and the laterite soils of the west. The area surrounding the villages had a desolate feeling, especially compared to the cramped and fertile surroundings in Fonogram. There was much more space here, but less in it. Approaching the villages one traversed a barren red soil and apart from the vegetation around the occasional village there was little of green colour in sight. In both villages, households operated about half each of *sali* (or paddy land), used for growing *aman* paddy, and *danga* (or high, poorer quality land with lateritic soil) used for an *aus* crop, and for grazing of livestock. This division of land confirmed the position of the villages in an agro-ecological transitional zone. In the late 1980s a handful of farmers in Bithigram had begun farming *boro* paddy and vegetables using low-lift pumps to pump water out of a nearby canal branch. Some *danga* land had also been used for growing eucalyptus under a government-sponsored rural development programme.

Table 5.1 gives details of population and land operated, and shows that the person–land ratio was considerably higher in Fonogram than the two Midnapore villages.

Table 5.1 Population and land operation in the three study villages

	No. of households	No. of people	People/ household	Area operated (hectares)	Decimals/ person[1]
Fonogram	141	843	6	49.7	14
Bithigram	97	502	5	92	45
Keshipur	57	299	5	48	39

[1] 1981 Census figures give a West Bengal average as 33 net sown decimals per rural person (Bandyopadhyay, 1983: 17)

The Midnapore villages were much closer to the West Bengal average than Fonogram. Part of the reason for the lower person–land ratio in Bithigram and Keshipur was the poorer quality of land operated there. Average yields in Fonogram for *aman* paddy were 60 *maunds* a hectare, the equivalent in the Midnapore villages being 45 to 50 *maunds*. This fits with the typology formulated by Dasgupta for higher yields in 'A' villages. As well as this, about 90 per cent of land owned by Fonogram households was double cropped, as opposed to 11 per cent and 13 per cent of land owned by Bithigram and Keshipur villagers respectively. The difference in soil quality must have been built into land measures by the colonial government for taxation purposes, as the Midnapore *bigha* at 0.25 hectares is almost twice the 24 Parganas *bigha* at 0.13 hectares.

Both of the Midnapore villages were made up of Hindu households. The most influential and numerous caste in Bithigram, with 58 of the 97 households, were Mahatos, a farming caste which was probably originally an aboriginal tribe who became caste Hindus (Bose, 1986; Ray, 1979). It was several Mahato households, including the village leader (who came from the wealthiest household), who were the main centre of village power. Most of the rest of the village was made up of Lodhas – that is, 36 households – an aboriginal tribe that had the misfortune to be labelled a 'criminal tribe' by the British colonial government, under which title they remained until 1952. The pall of criminality still hung over the Lodhas at the end of the 1980s. According to Davis (1983), the Lodhas came from western Midnapore and were displaced from 'forest living' by Hindus clearing land for farming, a common experience of tribals in India. These Lodhas were mainly agricultural labourers, and considered themselves Hindus, although they retained a separate cultural identity.[5] The Mahatos and Lodhas lived in spatially distinct *paras* (or living areas). It was the Mahatos from Bithigram and surrounding villages who were the main employers of the Lodhas; a good example of the latter's subordination was that during agricultural operations richer Mahatos would sit in their fields, usually under an umbrella, and ensure that the Lodha labourers worked hard enough.

[5] For the history and culture of the Lodhas in Midnapore, see Bhowmick (1963).

73

Lodha houses tended to be very small, with no windows, as compared to some of the large houses of the better-off Mahatos. The remaining three households in Bithigram came from the *narpit* or barber caste, a service caste who earned their main sources of income from agricultural labour, although still acting as barbers within the village and receiving yearly payment in paddy for this.

In Keshipur the dominant and most numerous caste were also Mahatos, with 36 households, while the remaining 21 households were Challuks, a scheduled caste group. The *panchayat* member from Keshipur related the village's history. He said that the original Keshigram villagers used to be inhabitants of Bithigram, but three families, including his own and two other powerful families in the present village, left Bithigram, which lay 2 km away, forty years previously. Keshipur consisted of a scheduled caste *para* and a Mahato *para*. Male Mahatos and Challuks mixed (and ate) together more freely in the village than women, who were more restricted by caste. There was no inter-caste marriage in either of the Midnapore villages.

Access to services in the two villages was similar to Fonogram. Neither of the two villages had electricity, the main source of water coming from tubewells and artesian wells. The nearest allopathic doctor and market were about 5 km distant. The main sources of credit were the local shops and employers of labour, although there was in a nearby village a co-operative society which made loans to farmers. A *gram sevak*, or government village extension officer, made sporadic appearances in Bithigram, but was not seen in Keshipur.

Both Bithigram and Keshipur returned CPM candidates at the 1988 *panchayat* elections. The Bithigram village leader thought that 75 per cent of his village supported the CPM, and the rest supported the Jharkhand party. The percentages were about the same in Keshipur.

Villagers did benefit from government development programmes and land reform (the latter to be discussed in the next chapter). Nine wealthier households in Bithigram had built biogas plants, taking loans of 5,500 rupees and receiving subsidies of 3,300 rupees under the IRDP scheme to do so. The village leader was the first villager to build such a plant. Six other villagers had taken loans under IRDP to buy livestock. In Keshipur five richer households had built biogas plants, and six households had taken other IRDP loans.

Land operation and employment in the three villages

Land ownership and operation patterns in all three villages were roughly correspondent with macro-level West Bengal data, which shows that the villages were not unrepresentative of the wider situation in the state (for details, see Beck, 1991). Land was more equally operated in the Midnapore villages than Fonogram. This can be seen in terms of holdings over 2.5 acres, with 10 per cent of households with more than 2.5 acres operating 48.5 per cent of land in Fonogram, as opposed to 29 per cent of households operating 66.5 per cent in Bithigram and 27 per cent of households operating 60.4 per cent in Keshipur. The minifundist nature of farming in Fonogram was apparent from the finding that 72 per cent of households were landless or operated less than one acre, which is barely enough land to provide for an average-sized household given good harvests. Given the poorer quality of land, the Midnapore villages followed a similar pattern to Fonogram, with a large number of 'landless' (or households with a small amount of poor quality land) and small operators existing alongside a much smaller group of middle farmers.

Seventy per cent of households in Fonogram and 68 per cent of households in Bithigram depended on agriculture for their primary source of income, a figure similar to all West Bengal, as opposed to 46 per cent in Keshipur. For 36 per cent of Keshipur households and 15 per cent of Bithigram households the primary source of income was railway work, in Kharagpur or along the railway tracks. Access to this source of employment was almost exclusively in the hands of the richer farming caste, the Mahatos. This employment was secure and paid relatively well, at 700–800 rupees a month, five to six times as much as an agricultural labourer might expect to earn in an average month. That this resource was captured by the higher castes shows that caste in the Midnapore villages related closely to household income. This was also symbolically represented by the head of one of the richest households in Keshipur also being the temple priest. Equally, in Fonogram it was wealthier villagers who carried out religious functions, and the *imam* came from one of the wealthiest households.

As opposed to this regular and well-paid employment available to some Midnapore villagers, employment external to the village and agriculture in Fonogram, by which 30 per cent of villagers gained their primary source of income, was mainly in the form of daily labour loading and unloading lorries, petty trading in local markets, in local factories, or by plying cycle vans. Despite Fonogram's proximity to Barasat and Calcutta, only two of its households (one of the poorest and one of the richest) worked in urban areas, the former as a petty trader and the latter in business.

Different forms of agricultural labour contracts existed in the two study areas, following on from their degree of agricultural development. Wages for agricultural labourers at 14–15 rupees a day in Fonogram were higher than the 10–12 rupees paid in the Midnapore villages. An agricultural labourer would be expected to be employed for no more than 180–210 days in any of the villages, and probably less in the Midnapore ones. In Fonogram most employment for agricultural labourers was on a daily basis, and payment was by cash. In contrast in the agriculturally 'backward' Midnapore villages, labourers were often 'tied' to employers under *dadan*. This

75

was a system whereby agricultural labourers took loans from employers in the pre-harvest lean period, and the loans were repaid by harvest work, usually at exploitive rates of pay at about half the market rate. This credit system was more exploitive than the one found in Fonogram, where most loans to the poor were from shopkeepers who charged 10 per cent more per item bought on credit, although labourers in Bithigram and Keshipur also took loans from shopkeepers under similar arrangements. The Fonogram shopkeeper with the highest proportion of loans had the sizeable figure of about 50,000 rupees on loan in 1988–9. In addition in Bithigram and Keshipur payment of some wages, especially for women, was in kind, usually paddy. Credit did fuel the rural economy, and these exploitative systems are similar to those found elsewhere in West Bengal and India (see B. Harriss, 1987; Breman, 1985a; and for *dadan* Bose, 1985; and J. Harriss, 1984).

As to gender relations in the three villages, women were certainly subordinated by a well-documented patriarchal system that ensured male control over resources within the village as a whole, and probably within most households (see White, 1988; Mayoux, 1982). For example, land and other productive assets were almost always passed down the patrilineal line. Strict *purdah* did not operate in any of the villages. In Fonogram the restrictions were more severe, and it was only widows and women in a few of the poorest households in Fonogram who were permitted to work outside their homestead; as this work was only allowed to take place outside of the village, *purdah* 'norms' were maintained within the village. Work for these women was low paid and in an exploitive and sometimes dangerous environment. There were no such *purdah* restrictions in the Midnapore villages, although pay for female labour was about 20 per cent less than for male labour. Female-headed households were found to be over-represented among the poorest in all three villages, and one cause of this was the male control of village resources.

Economic categorization

There has been considerable attempt over the last twenty years to develop a system for classifying rural households in developing countries. Despite some excellent work in this field, there appears to be no definitive model built which could be used for the type of analysis required in this book. As Howes (1985: 45) has remarked for the country neighbouring West Bengal: 'Unfortunately there is no commonly-agreed procedure for classifying rural households in Bangladesh'. From a methodological and theoretical point of view, an attempt to build a comprehensive model for such classification deserves a book of its own, and will not be the focus of discussion here.

In the absence of a formal model, I decided to analyse village socio-economic structures by firstly ranking households by income, and secondly differentiating households into four 'income groups', based mainly on income, employment and land operation. These methods appeared the most suitable for the purpose of understanding the distribution of all important village resources, including resources external to the village, and finding a method of analysis that left the data open to comparative analysis. Following Scott (1985), I have calculated total yearly household income, based on the questions asked in the first-round survey on income, and then ranked households by income per household consumption unit, with children below six counting as one-third of an adult and children from six to twelve as two-thirds. This method takes into account not only land operation but also land quality (as it deals with yields, as well as amount of land operated), ownership of cattle, income earned from labour and all other sources, and debt. Because of its comprehensiveness, this method was also suggested by Lipton (1989) as a suitable method for categorizing households in order to study the effects of the 'green revolution' on village economy, which is the focus of the next chapter. To use such a method is considerably more time consuming than categorization by land ownership or operation alone, but also more accurate in terms of ranking households. This method does ignore, however, the important 'informal economy', such as gathering of common property resources, which is of greater relative importance to the poor, and which is discussed in chapter seven.

After ranking by income, village households were divided into four groups, an arbitrary number, but one which was convenient for analysis and equated to that used in past studies. Households were differentiated in the following manner. When households in the three villages were ranked by income, the level of income started at a low level and increased gradually until the first natural break occurred in the data at about 2,000 rupees. This is consistent with the existence of a large number of landless and small operators, in conjunction with a smaller number of dominant 'middle' farmers. I decided that the wealthiest income group should be above the figure of 2,000 rupees. Given no other breaks in the data, the other divisions in the ranked households were made on the basis of occupation and land operation. The majority of households in income group 2 were agricultural labourers, while those in group 3 were either 'small' farmers or worked on the railways, so a division was made between these two groups on this basis. The fact that income group 1 households were effectively landless, while group 2 households operated a small amount of land, was the basis for the division between the two groups. The number of months respondents said home production of crops lasted for was consistent with these divisions, particularly in Fonogram and Bithigram. The four categories fitted the following levels of income – 900 rupees or below per consumption unit per year (income group 1), between 901 and 1,400 rupees (income group 2), between 1,401 and 2,000 rupees (income group 3), and above 2,000 rupees (income group 4).[6] These income groups should be understood only as categories that enable a discussion of the distribution of resources in the village in an economic sense, and that allow for a general discussion of village socio-economic structures.

Tables 5.2 to 5.4 give further details of income groups in the three villages. Figures for income, land operated and the months that home production lasts for (in the columns denoted as 'Months rice lasts') are average figures for the whole income group. Footnotes to the three tables are given after Table 5.4.

Table 5.2 Fonogram village income groups

Income group	No. of households (a)	Income (b)	Land (c)	Months rice lasts (d)	Occ. (e)	Dep. ratio (f)
1	51 (36)	668 (18)	17 (7)	0.5	AI (60)	2.7
2	40 (28)	1132 (25)	45 (15)	0.9	AI (65)	2.1
3	31 (22)	1659 (28)	132 (33)	3.5	F (45)	2
4	19 (14)	2838 (29)	291 (45)	9.1	F (74)	2

Table 5.3 Bithigram village income groups

Income group	No. of households (a)	Income (b)	Land operated (c)	Months rice lasts (d)	Occ. (e)	Dep. ratio (f)
1	18 (19)	799 (9)	102 (8)	2.2	AI (72)	1.3
2	42 (43)	1117 (32)	140 (26)	3.9	AI (63)	1.1
3	16 (16)	1787 (19)	283 (22)	6.6	F (38)	1.8
4	21 (22)	2789 (40)	460 (44)	8.1	R (52)	1.3

Table 5.4 Keshipur village income groups

Income group	No. of households (a)	Income (b)	Land operated (c)	Months rice lasts (d)	Occ. (e)	Dep. ratio (f)
1	13 (23)	744 (10)	108 (11)	2.2	AI (63)	0.7
2	14 (25)	1133 (16)	208 (25)	3.7	AI (43)	1.3
3	10 (18)	1662 (16)	222 (19)	4.9	R (40)	1.7
4	20 (34)	2939 (58)	268 (45)	5.1	R (85)	1.9

[6] The four categories decided upon also correspond roughly to the five classes delineated by Marxists, with the class of 'rich peasants' and 'landlords' excluded. This can be seen in the following equivalence:

Category in this book	Marxist category
Income group 1	Landless labourer
Income group 2	Marginal peasant
Income group 3	Small peasant
Income group 4	Middle peasant

For further details on the methodology of classification, see Beck (1991).

The tables show that income distribution in all of the villages is both similar and unequal, with most resources in the hands of the higher two income groups. The percentages of households in each group are less similar, with Fonogram having a higher percentage of households in group 1, almost double the number in Bithigram, and suggesting that Fonogram contained a higher percentage of poor households when income was the measure used. In Keshipur there is a higher percentage of households in group 4, because of the access to railway related work by Mahato households. The percentage of income earned by group 4 is absolutely higher in Keshipur than in the other two villages, but not higher when the relative sizes of the groups is taken into consideration.

Income is unevenly distributed in all villages. For example, in Fonogram the 14 per cent of households in income group 4 earned 29 per cent of village income, whereas the 36 per cent in income group 1 earned 18%. In Bithigram and Keshipur income can be seen to be even more firmly in the hands of income group 4. Intra-village group differences in absolute income were higher in Fonogram, where absolute income for group 4 is 4.25 times that of group 1, the figure for Bithigram being 3.5, and for Keshipur 4. Figures for land operated and the number of months respondents said that home production lasts the household support the contention that resources were unevenly distributed and located in the hands of a village elite. A further general feature of Bithigram and Keshipur, not shown in the tables, was that, as would be expected, being a member of a scheduled tribe or caste overlapped with a low household income (for details, see Beck, 1991).[7]

---

[7] See over.

Footnotes to Tables 5.2–4 (opposite).

(a) The figures in brackets are the percentage of households in each group.

(b) The figures are for each consumption unit per year, in rupees. The figures in brackets are percentages of total village income earned by each group.

(c) Land operated is in decimals. The figures in brackets give the percentages of land operated by each income group.

(d) This is an estimate by respondents of the number of months that all production from household land operated would last for in an average year if consumed within the household or sold.

(e) Occ. = occupation, Al = agricultural labourers, F = farmers, R = railway work. The occupation in the column is the occupation of the income group by which the majority of households in that group earned their primary income. Figures in brackets denote the percentage in each income group with that particular occupation.

(f) Dependency ratio here means the number of workers aged over twelve working for more than three months in a year, divided by all other household members. Average dependency ratios for the whole villages were:

Fonogram 2.3
Bithigram1.3
Keshipur1.5

Conclusions

The characteristics of the two types of study villages fitted the typology set up by Dasgupta (1975) for agriculturally 'backward' and 'advanced' Indian villages, in that Fonogram was larger, irrigated, had more landless and a more unequal landholding pattern. Despite this, the socio-economic structure of the moribund delta of West Bengal, with a large number of landless, land-poor and small operators existing in conjunction with a small group of dominant 'middle' farmers, could be seen to hold in all the study villages, and in two quite different agro-ecological settings, and this was supported by the data on income distribution which showed similar patterns.

In the study villages the 'middle' farmers controlled the main village resources, both economic and political, as well as remunerative jobs outside of the villages, and were located mainly in income group 4. They made the major decisions and were the dominant political and social figures in the villages. The landless, agricultural labourers and tribal and scheduled caste groups were mainly located in income groups 1 and 2. 'Small' farmers were the main group in income group 3. Caste relations reinforced dominant control over resources in the Midnapore villages.

The purpose of this chapter was to analyse socio-economic structure in the study villages to contextualize the data to be presented in the following chapters, particularly the information on poor people's experience and agency. Income categories, land operation or occupation describe only the bare bones of village life; it is the flesh on these bones to which the book now moves.

---

[7] In the case of Keshipur, ranking and categorization on the basis of land operation alone would have shown a more equal distribution of resources than when all household income was considered. Categorization in Fonogram on the same basis would have shown a more unequal distribution of resources. This is an example of the greater sophistication involved in using income rather than land operation as a method of categorization.

Fonogram income group 4 respondents estimated that their home production would last for eighteen times as long as income group 1 respondents, very similar to the difference between land operation figures (a difference of seventeen). This is of particular interest as Fonogram figures on land operation can be taken as accurate. Estimates of home production could therefore be used as a check on or supplement to estimates of land operation.

6 'There may have been some benefits from the new farming, but I haven't seen any': Agricultural development and land reform in the study villages

The purpose of this chapter is to examine the effect of two government-sponsored anti-poverty programmes on village economic structure and the poor. The chapter analyses, first, the effects of an irrigation scheme in Fonogram and, second, the government land distribution programme carried out in the Midnapore villages. How successful have such initiatives been in promoting equity and helping the poor overcome the constraints they face in improving the quality of their lives? Who has received the main benefits from these initiatives, and why? It is these and related questions that this chapter will answer.

The 'green revolution' in South Asia

As many words have been written on the 'green revolution' as farmers in India have harvested *maunds* of high-yielding variety (HYV) paddy. The discussion here is necessarily selective; it gives a brief introduction to the green revolution in South Asia, but does not review in detail any of the debates concerning it. Instead, comparative findings are included below when considered relevant to my own research findings.[1]

The HYV package, including HYV cereal seeds, chemical fertilizers and pesticides, and irrigation facilities, was introduced into selected agriculturally 'progressive' areas of India in the mid-1960s, and has been one factor that has led to a doubling in crop production in India between the mid-1960s and the mid-1980s. Did the initial planning behind the green revolution mean it was likely to benefit particular rural groups? The background to experimentation with the HYV package was a series of crop failures in India (Dasgupta, 1980), and there was an association made between the introduction of the HYV package and fears of agrarian unrest. As J. Harriss (1987: 229–30) puts it:

> Research foundations established by the American capitalists Ford and Rockefeller played a very important role in organizing and funding the

---

[1] The 'swings of fashion' in this debate – from the optimism about increases in crop production in the late 1960s, to pessimistic fears of polarization and agrarian unrest in the early 1970s, to a new optimism in the 1980s – have been reviewed elsewhere (see Farmer, 1986; Chambers, 1984). Lipton's (1989) volume gives a good summary of important debates on the green revolution.

research which produced the HYVs. And the strategic, geopolitical interests of the United States in changing rural social and economic conditions in Asia and Latin America, with a view to the containment of communist expansion, were clear.

This point is also dealt with by Oasa (1987), who attempted to show that one of the aims of the International Rice Research Institute, which propagated newer agricultural technology, was to concentrate on small, resource-poor farmers, to halt 'proletarianization' and increasing differentiation between poorer and richer farmers and possible agrarian tension that would result from this. A crucial point to make here therefore is that the effects of the HYVs cannot be separated from wider social processes of which the HYVs are a part.

One of the main debates concerning the green revolution, led by Marxist analysts, has been its effects on social process. For example, Dasgupta (1980: 372) stated that, contrary to the hopes of its propagators, the HYV package had led to:

proletarianization of the peasantry and a consequent increase in the number and proportion of landless households, growing concentration of land and assets in fewer hands and widening disparity between the rich and poor households . . .

These assertions have been modified by others (J. Harriss, 1987; Bhaduri, *et al.*, 1986; Howes, 1985; Byres, 1981), who discuss a process of what Byres calls (ibid: 432) 'partial proletarianization'. In this process, some poor peasant households become landless labourer households through enforced sale of land to richer households, and others maintain a hold on land by mortgaging or renting out land to 'rich' peasant households, while at the same time expanding their off-farm income opportunities. As J. Harriss noted (1987: 241): 'even in circumstances where the introduction of the new varieties has been relatively successful . . . the dissolution of small peasant production with a process of 'depeasantization', does not necessarily occur'. Further, Harriss suggests (ibid.): '. . . any potential antagonism between rich and poor peasants has been dampened because of the participation of poor peasants, too, in the "green revolution" . . .'. If this is true, then the forces behind the green revolution can be seen to have achieved their purpose of reinforcing village socio-economic structures, as outlined by Oasa above.

Despite over twenty years of study on the green revolution, Lipton has written after a comprehensive survey of relevant literature (1989: 300):

Our grasp of how village micro-structures of power (involving tenure and credit as well as land) affects MVs (modern varieties) impact on the poor is at present crude and undifferentiated.

This chapter will attempt to provide a greater understanding of such micro-structures. And it will also discuss extra income benefits from hired labour, another subject that has received little attention in the literature, but has, according to Lipton (ibid.), the most potential for reducing poverty.

The green revolution comes to Fonogram

The introduction of irrigation facilities and subsequent agricultural development needs to be seen in the context of general industrial development in the Fonogram locality. Urban linkages increased through the 1980s. Two large pharmaceutical factories were built about 3 km from Fonogram in the late 1980s, although unionization within the work force meant that no Fonogram villagers could get employment in them. There was an increase of lorries owned locally, discussed below. 'Plotting' – the division of land into plots for housing – was also taking place near to Fonogram, which would increase requirements for building materials and the value of land. The presence of new shallow tubewells (STWs) meant that mechanical hand tractors were used in selected local areas for the first time in 1986. Local shops also grew larger and more numerous in response to new opportunities, selling, for example, chemical fertilizers; and a new market grew up around the maintenance and repair of STWs. The STWs were part of a larger rural industrialization that was affecting the whole of north 24 Parganas in the late 1980s.

The information below concerning the introduction of irrigation facilities into Fonogram comes from two sources. Firstly, from interviews with Fonogram villagers responsible for their introduction, particularly a local entrepreneur whom I shall call Romesh Ali; and with the Director of the Rural Development Consortium (RDC), a body which coordinates and channels support to about 250 voluntary projects in West Bengal, and through which Romesh Ali and others applied for foreign funding. And, secondly, from the files on the Fonogram project at RDC, and through correspondence with the Stuttgart office of Bread for the World (BFTW), an aid agency which funded the Fonogram facilities indirectly through RDC.[2]

There were several actors in the introduction of irrigation facilities into Fonogram and surrounding *mouzas*. The first was Romesh Ali, whose household had the second highest income in the village. Romesh's father had been an agricultural labourer; through hard work and cutting consumption over many years, Romesh's family sent him to school and through college where he took a Commerce degree, becoming the first Fonogram villager to receive a degree. After this he worked as a teacher

---

[2] The project application and subsequent evaluation can be found in Beck (1991).

locally. Romesh's wife had a clerical job, and his elder brother, with whom he lived, ran a small poultry business. Romesh's household had bought about two hectares of land, and operated in 1989 more land than any other household in the village.

In the mid-1970s Romesh was involved in setting up a committee called the *Udayan Samaj Kalyan Samity*, (literally 'the committee for the uplift of society', and henceforth called the *samity*), a voluntary organization registered under the Registration of Societies Act, modelled on similar organizations in nearby villages, and formed by villagers from Fonogram and, in theory, seven other local villages. In practice, the *samity* appeared to be mainly run by Romesh Ali, who was its Secretary, in association with the heads of two other households with the highest incomes in Fonogram, and the eldest son of a further household, the head of which had in the past been acknowledged as village leader. The aim of the *samity* was, to quote from an RDC project application, to 'build up a self-reliant community in which the economically and socially depressed people are capable of taking their place as equal partner of the society'.

The Treasurer of the *samity* lived near to Fonogram, and also worked for the RDC, the second actor in the scenario. RDC's involvement with the *samity* appeared to be limited to funding and evaluation. Some small initial funding from RDC to the *samity* led to a larger scheme, first suggested by RDC to BFTW at the end of 1980. The main object of this was, to quote the pilot project plan sent by RDC to BFTW:

> to assist the landless agricultural and other landless labourer families by increasing employment opportunities and creating avenues for subsidiary income and also to extend irrigation facilities to the weaker section cultivating families to step up agricultural production by adoption of improved cultural practices and introduction of multiple cropping pattern.

The intended objectives of the project, and its evaluation, are of direct relevance here, as 'landless agricultural and other landless labourer families' are among the poorest in rural West Bengal.

Following the funding of the project proposal, 14 STWs were installed in the Fonogram locality throughout 1985 (see Map 6.1). The cost of these STWs was 196,000 rupees. Half of this money, the 'people's contribution', came from a District Rural Development Agency subsidy, through the Department of Rural Development of the Government of West Bengal.[3] The other half came from a bank loan, which had to be repaid over seven years at 10 per cent interest from sale of water to farmers. Funding of

---

[3] BFTW's terms for allocation of funds was that half of any project costs should be met by a 'people's contribution' from those to benefit from the project.

50,000 rupees that had been provided by BFTW was retained under bank rules as guarantee money or, as Romesh put it, 'security money'.

The project proposal of RDC and its subsequent report included an analysis of the socio-economic status of Fonogram and surrounding villages. It stated that most of the cultivated land in the area was: 'owned by the weaker section families of the marginal and small farmers', and banded together 'landless working (sic), marginal and small farmer families' as the 'target group', estimating that the latter two groups owned 70 per cent of cultivable land in the area. However, in the RDC analysis a 'small farmer' family was said to own 2.5–5 acres of land, and is contrasted to affluent families likely to own more than 5 acres. My fieldwork showed that only 11 households in Fonogram owned more than 5 acres, so that 'small' and 'marginal' farmers in the RDC categorization made up almost the entire cultivating population of Fonogram. This group could not therefore be considered as the 'weaker section'. The following discussion will show that using such gross figures as '2.5–5 acres' is counter-productive when creating development programmes in the West Bengal context, given the minifundist nature of farming in the state.

The project proposal also stated that: 'almost (the) entire area can very conveniently be brought within the command of shallow tubewells . . .'. It added that: 'While the irrigation facilities will be concentrated in the lands of the small and marginal farmers, some land of more affluent farmers will also have to be covered in the group irrigation scheme. At the instance of the Project Holder (the *samity*), the affluent have agreed to bear their respective share of loans with informal share croppers.'

In its 1985 analysis of the first season of operation of the irrigation scheme, RDC remarked that: 'It was evident from the performance that the project holder has created a good impact among the target group through different appropriate programmes as detailed above . . . The area was mono-cropped but now the beneficiaries have been able to raise more than one crop in the same piece of land . . .'. And in an appraisal made at the end of 1986 the same RDC staff member stated: 'this project created a good impact among the target group of population . . . thereby extending avenues for landless labour families . . .'.[4] These claims and assertions are considered in detail below. One other point is worth making here; the project ignored gender issues, and shows no recognition of the fact that its attention is directed specifically towards agriculture and men.

The following evaluation has wide implications. The development of STWs and other minor irrigation is now a priority for the Government of West Bengal. A government review states (Government of West Bengal 1986: 31): 'great weightage has been given to (promote) minor irrigation

---

[4] The reference here is to RDC files.

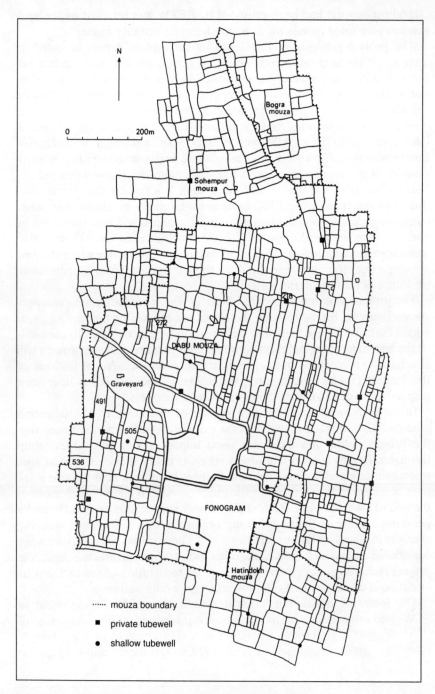

Map 6.1 Fonogram village and its environment

... in areas which cannot be covered by canals and channels in the major irrigation areas, attempts have been made and are also being made to give subsidies to sink DTWs, STWs . . .'. In 1988 there were some 340,000 STWs in West Bengal, as opposed to 78,000 in 1976–7 (Palmer-Jones 1989; Government of West Bengal 1986: 32). Subsequent to this increase in STWs has been increased production of paddy during the *boro* season, estimated by Palmer-Jones (1989: 2) to have grown from some 8 per cent to 25 per cent of total State food grain production between 1977 and 1988. So the following evaluation is of relevance in assessing one of the major state initiatives in West Bengal.

In West Bengal over 95 per cent of STWs are owned privately. The Fonogram scheme, on the other hand, was a public scheme, and in this sense the Fonogram programme is not representative of wider developments in West Bengal. Because of this, the following analysis adds to the bias of academic attention on public as opposed to private irrigation development, a bias only recently recognized (Palmer-Jones, 1989). However, the way in which the water market was managed by the *samity* did resemble private use of STWs in various important ways. Similarities were: that the control of the resource was in the hands of a wealthy few, who restricted the amount of water distributed; water rates of 300 rupees a *bigha* from the STWs were the same as for private tubewells owned by individuals (Palmer-Jones, 1987); and the Fonogram scheme had received a subsidy from the Government of West Bengal, as have many private owners.

In addition, several authors (e.g. Chadha and Bhaumick, 1992; J. Harriss, 1984; N. Bandyopadhyay, 1983) have suggested that the formation of co-operatives should be a next step forward for the Left Front Government. The evaluation of what is essentially a co-operative venture, half funded by the State government, may provide suggestions as to possible future developments in this field.

Land type and land use in the Fonogram area

This section discusses natural and social variables which combine to determine land use in particular, fragmentation and position of holdings, land height, and soil type. Land 'owned' should be taken here as meaning self-operated land belonging to Fonogram households, including land mortgaged in; land 'hired' means land sharecropped; and land 'operated' means a combination of land owned and hired.[5]

Fonogram village and its immediate surroundings, including the land operated by Fonogram households, is shown in Map 6.1, along with *mouza*

---

[5] Mortgaged land was included with self-operated land as it tended to pass to the mortgagee.

boundaries, the position of the thirteen of the *samity*'s STWs, and private STWs.[6] Map 6.1 is made up of parts of four different *mouza* maps where Fonogram villagers operated land, as neither the village nor the land the villagers operated lay within one *mouza*. In addition, as Map 6.1 is based on the settlement survey carried out 1954–8, it does not show contemporary divisions of individual plots, about half of which had been further sub-divided by 1989. These are not shown on the map for purposes of clarity, although such sub-divisions have been included in the following analysis. The minifundist nature of land operation and the extent of fragmentation of holdings is visually apparent in Map 6.1.

In 1988–9 Fonogram villagers operated some 50 hectares of land, owning 490 separate plots on about 39 hectares of land, and hiring a further 130 plots on the remaining 11 hectares. This gives an average figure of about 21 decimals per plot operated, although this average hides the fact that some single operated plots were up to one hectare in size. On average, each Fonogram household operating land cultivated seven and a half plots and 150 decimals of land. These plots were not only very small, but were also scattered throughout the *mouza*, to ensure a mix of land qualities and heights. This increased the possibility of growing a mix of crops, and insured against natural disaster which might affect some parts of a *mouza*. Larger land operators operated a proportionately larger number of plots, which meant that they would be able to take greater advantage of irrigation facilities wherever they were located.

Muslim land inheritance systems in Fonogram also contributed to the scattering of plots in two ways. Firstly, equal amounts of land were inherited by all sons of the household when the head of household died. In theory females inherited half of an equivalent male relative, but in practice usually waived this right to their brothers in return for future expected support from them. Secondly, to ensure equal distribution of the same qualities of land, inheritors generally received one part of each of the

---

[6] One *samity* STW fell outside the map, but was not in any case used by Fonogram households. The maps in this chapter are based on settlement survey operation maps (or *mouza* maps) first produced in 1928. Map 6.1 shows an updated version of the 1928 maps made by the Land Revenue Office between 1954–8.

Details on land holding were gathered through plot to plot surveys. These details were cross-checked in the local Land Revenue Office, which maintained records of land ownership for 1956. The land settlement for the Fonogram area completed in February 1989 was unavailable during the fieldwork period, so I updated the records myself. I noted the size of 600 relevant plots in this office, and a random sample of 50 plots from my survey was checked against the 1956 records. In almost all cases the information corresponded, after accounting for inheritance or land sale. Details of land operation were also checked with the local land surveyor.

household's plots; this meant that a household with three plots and three inheritors would split the plots into three divisions each.

Map 6.2 shows soil types, land heights, and the yearly cropping pattern of land operated by Fonogram households by physiographic zone. Land height in particular determined crop choice by farmers. The area in which Fonogram households operated land sloped quite gradually from south to north (i.e. from the bottom to the top of the map), so that the land near to the graveyard was about one *hat* (or about 45 cm) lower than the land to the south of the village, and the land to the north of the map was one *hat* lower than land around the graveyard.[7] At the same time, land to the east and west of the Map was 15 to 30 cm higher than the land to the centre. The effect was as if a river had cut a bed through the centre of the village land and left banks on each side, before widening to the north. This may have been the case in the past, as the skeleton of a crocodile was found when a grave was being dug in the graveyard, suggesting fresh water there in the past. Soil type was less variable than land height. All of the local land was classed as *etel* of which there were two types, *kaloo* and *lal* (or black and red). Red soil was more clayey and retained more water than black soil. *Boro* paddy farming and the farming of most vegetables was best on red soil. Black soil was friable and fertile and could be used for growing most crops. On Map 6.2 black soil is located mainly in physiographic zones 3, 4, 5 and 6, while in the other zones to the south of the farming land there was a mixture of black and red soils. The annual cropping pattern engendered by this height and soil regime is also found in Map 6.2. Differences in flooding heights partly determined choices of rice and other crop varieties.

To the eye the farming land around Fonogram seemed almost flat and monotonous, but the local farmers were well aware of how to take advantage of the complex mix of land heights and soils. To the south of the graveyard the height of the land was a protection against flooding during the monsoon, when land here generally flooded to the depth of one *hat*. On the farming land to the north of the graveyard flooding was deeper despite the less retentive nature of the soil, up to the *kurmo* (90 cm) and occasionally the *bukh* (120 cm). Villagers said that boats could sail on this lower land during the monsoon. Retention of soil moisture due to greater flooding also meant that *boro* farming was superior here.

The difference in land height could also have dramatic effects on yields. The 1987 *aman* season is a good example of this. There was serious flooding that year to the north of the graveyard, because of monsoon rain. Standing water was in places above chest height and the crop was seriously

---

[7] Local measures were the *hat*, or hand, from the elbow to the top of the fingers, about 45 cm; the *kurmo*, from the ground to the small of the back, or 90 cm; and the *bukh*, from the ground to the chest, or 120 cm.

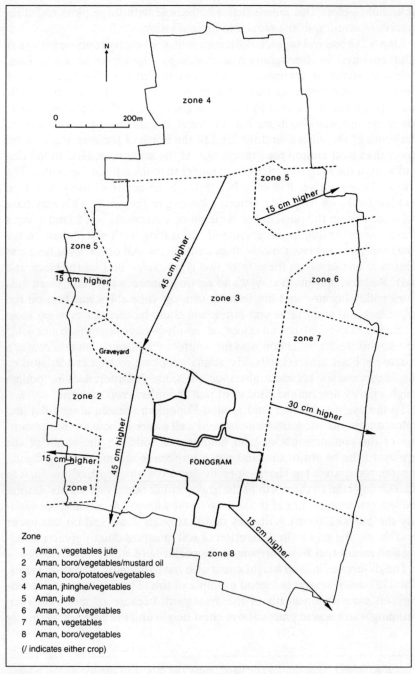

Zone
1 Aman, vegetables jute
2 Aman, boro/vegetables/mustard oil
3 Aman, boro/potatoes/vegetables
4 Aman, jhinghe/vegetables
5 Aman, jute
6 Aman, boro/vegetables
7 Aman, vegetables
8 Aman, boro/vegetables
(/ indicates either crop)

Map 6.2 Land heights and physiographic zones, Fonogram 1988–9 *boro* season

damaged. In early December I talked to farmers as they harvested their crop from these overflooded areas. They estimated that they were harvesting only three or four *maunds* of paddy a *bigha*, or about half of normal average yield. By contrast, farmers in the relatively higher land to the south were harvesting their paddy at the same time and said that their yields were average, at about eight *maunds* of paddy a *bigha*, although there had been a slight *shortage* of water. Within a distance of only 50 metres there was thus a great variation in flooding and yield. This is further evidence as to why households chose to spread their landholdings throughout land operated by the village, and why households with larger holdings had an added advantage in owning a greater number of plots.

Cropping patterns and adoption rates in the *boro* seasons, 1986–7 to 1988–9

As already noted, a three-year survey of cropping patterns was carried out in Fonogram, as findings from any one year might have been unrepresentative. The findings from the 1986–7 and 1987–8 seasons are not considered in detail here because by 1986–7 a general cropping pattern had developed that was similar in the following two years. Nor were there large variations in tenancy arrangements, so that the data for 1988–9 can be taken as representative of a three year period.

Prior to the introduction of the *samity*'s STWs, village land had been irrigated by private pumpsets run on diesel, and from ponds or tanks. These were owned almost exclusively by larger land operators in income groups 3 and 4. A reconstruction made with farmers of cropping patterns for the period prior to the 1985–6 *boro* season showed that the crops grown were vegetables, mustard oil and wheat. Land was not therefore left fallow during this season prior to 1985–6, as the RDC report suggested. However, after the introduction of the STWs, farmers tended to substitute paddy for former crops during *boro*, experimenting with the new HYVs and looking for higher profits.

Loans for *boro* farming were available from the local bank, organized through the *samity*, at 12 per cent per annum interest. Sixteen households took institutional loans for *boro* farming in 1988–9, totalling 42,700 rupees. They were divided in this way: 6 per cent to income group 2, 74 per cent to group 3, and 20 per cent to group 4. Not all households could avail of such loans, as land was usually necessary as collateral. However, loans were also available from relatives, urban money lenders and the local shopkeepers, and lack of credit did not appear to stop poorer households farming *boro* paddy (see below). Income group 4 households also had access to substantial credit from other sources, as they had more urban connections, or richer relatives. For example, Romesh Ali's household had borrowed an estimated 100,000 rupees, half of which had come from government loans

91

that had enabled him to buy two lorries and start a transport business. One of the other members of the *samity* had taken a loan of 35,000 rupees from his father-in-law in order to build a new house. These dwarfed most of the other loans in the village.

Maps 6.3 and 6.4 show the cropping pattern on land operated by Fono-gram households for *boro* 1986–7 and 1987–8, as well as land under paddy farmed by non-Fonogram households. Under the *samity* regulations, the STWs irrigated only paddy. In addition, the *samity* restricted the supply of water of each STW to an area of 17 *bighas*, only 46 per cent of their capacity of about five hectares, to stop disputes between farmers about theft of water.[8] Paddy was being grown on the lower-lying land around the STWs, rather than the peripheral higher land. The exception was the STW just to the south of the Fonogram village boundary. The only rationale for the positioning of this STW seemed to be the existence of land in its immediate vicinity owned by two of the wealthiest Fonogram households who were also members of the *samity*.[9] Elsewhere, households continued the past pattern of growing a mix of vegetables with a scattering of wheat and fallow plots, and a small number of plots were also cultivated under different types of trees or bamboo.

The cropping pattern remained very similar for 1988–9 *boro*. Land under paddy owned by Fonogram income groups is shown in Map 6.5. This map displays the comparative advantage of the wealthier income groups in terms of growing paddy. For purposes of clarity a separate map, 6.6, shows land under paddy hired in by Fonogram households as well as land owned by absentee landlords. Details shown in Map 6.5, as well as information on other crops grown by Fonogram income groups, can be found in numerical form in Table 6.1.

Taking into account both land owned as well as land hired in, percentages under paddy for the 1988–9 season were:

Income group 1 – 55 per cent
Income group 2 – 47 per cent
Income group 3 – 42 per cent
Income group 4 – 40 per cent

Adoption of HYVs was not therefore restricted to richer households. It was the two lower income groups that had planted more of their land under paddy and had taken greater advantage of the possibilities of the green revolution. This is consistent with much other evidence, summarized by

---

[8] Such limitation is common throughout West Bengal. Boyce (1987: 242) quotes Government of West Bengal figures published in 1978 which estimated average STW capacity utilization at about 55 per cent.

[9] The most southerly STW on the maps did irrigate paddy, but not that operated by Fonogram villagers, and is therefore not shown.

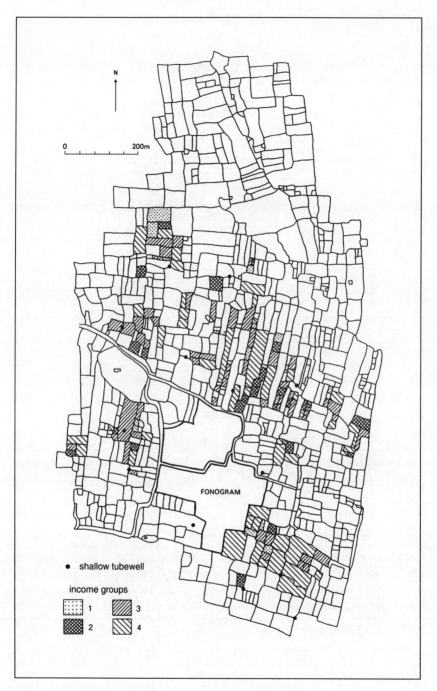

N

0   200m

FONOGRAM

● shallow tubewell

income groups

1   3

2   4

Map 6.3 Cropping pattern, Fonogram 1986–7 *boro* season

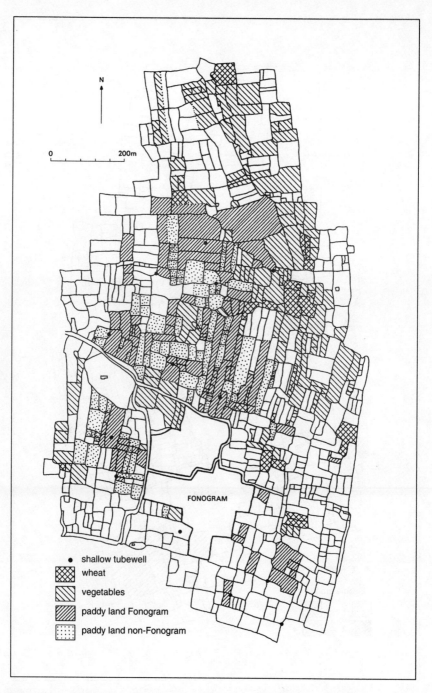

Map 6.4 Cropping pattern, Fonogram 1987–8 *boro* season

94

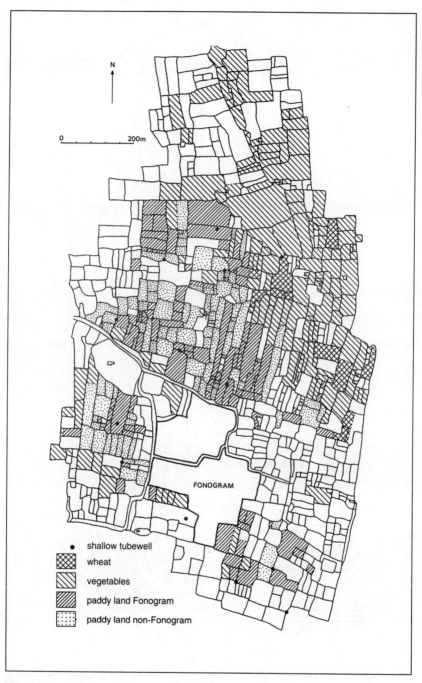

N

0 _____ 200m

FONOGRAM

● shallow tubewell

⊠ wheat

▨ vegetables

▨ paddy land Fonogram

⠿ paddy land non-Fonogram

Map 6.5 Land owned under paddy by income group, Fonogram
1988–9 *boro* season

95

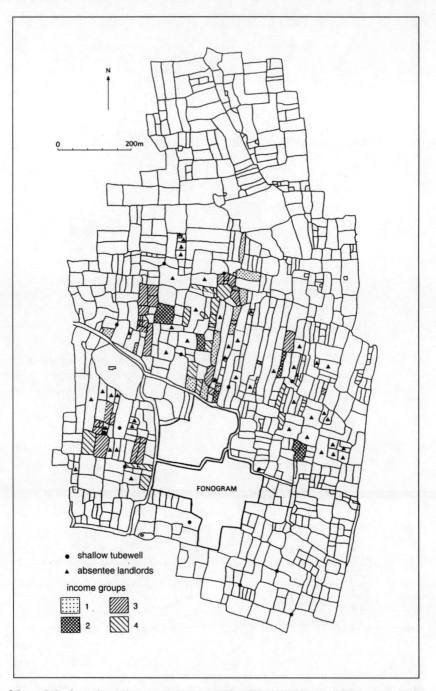

N

0   200m

FONOGRAM

● shallow tubewell
▲ absentee landlords
income groups

| | 1 | | 3 |
| | 2 | | 4 |

Map 6.6 Land under paddy hired by Fonogram households, and operated by absentee landlords, 1988–9 *boro* season

96

Table 6.1 Crops planted on owned land by income group – Fonogram, *boro* season 1988–9[1]

Income group	Land owned by crop in decimals (per cent)					
	paddy	wheat	vegetables	garden	fallow	total
1	151 (37)	–	189 (47)	34 (8)	34 (8)	408
2	449 (47)	–	324 (34)	68 (7)	115 (12)	957
3	1141 (38)	8 (–)	1702 (52)	136 (4)	241 (7)	3228
4	1906 (38)	111 (2)	2384 (48)	139 (3)	433 (9)	4973
Total	3647 (38)	119 (1)	4600 (48)	377 (4)	823 (9)	9566

[1] Rounded figures in brackets in the first four rows are percentages of total land owned under the particular crop.

Lipton (1989: 120): 'the *proportion of land* that adopting smallholders sow to MVs is frequently higher than for adopting large farmers'. In turn this suggests that more rigorous land reform is likely to lead to more planting of HYVs and higher productivity.

Given the scattering of plots noted above, however, the finding that all income groups had similar percentages of land under paddy (as well as other crops) has important implications for irrigation development projects. If wealthier households scatter their landholdings, they will receive a disproportionate benefit from irrigation facilities wherever they are positioned. The findings here therefore support the comment by Chambers *et al.* that (1989: 94):

> Where . . . (irrigation) group members have some land, . . . the location is critical. Much depends on topography and the distribution of landholdings. It can be difficult to serve only SFs and MFs (small farmers and marginal farmers) where their holdings are interspersed with those of larger farmers as is often the case in water-abundant areas . . .

Who gained most from the green revolution?

By 1988–9 some 40 per cent of all land operated by Fonogram households was under paddy. The Fonogram *boro* season farming had been 'green revolutionized'. But because farmers in the lower income groups had been more assiduous in planting HYV paddy did not mean that they gained the most from the agricultural changes. Between them the two richer income groups operated 74 per cent of the 20 hectares of land under paddy, a similar figure to the 78 per cent of total village land operated by the two groups. Shares of income to different income groups, or 'factor shares', from land under paddy are given below in Table 6.2. Figures in this table take into account both profits from cultivation (calculated by taking the profit from the amount of land under paddy operated by each income group, after costs, and dividing this by the total number of households in the group); and extra income from employment (calculated by taking the numbers in each group whose main source of income was agricultural labour divided by the total number of households in the group).[10] The calculations are approximate, but the Table gives sufficiently accurate estimates to allow a general discussion.

Table 6.2   Average returns to Fonogram income group households from the 1988–9 *boro* paddy crop (rupees)

Income group	Land owned[1]	Land operated[2]	Employment[3]	Total (%)
1	73	81	132	286 (6)
2	276	127	125	528 (12)
3	906	219	62	1187 (25)
4	2468	205	10	2683 (57)

[1] Estimating 812 rupees per *bigha* profit.
[2] Estimating 406 rupees per *bigha* profit.
[3] Estimating 192 rupees per hired labourer (16 days extra work at 12 rupees a day), adjusted for numbers of labourers per household. 12 rupees was the sum earned for working from 6 am to noon. If the labourer worked until 3 pm, he earned a further 3 rupees.

This table shows that a disproportionate amount of the income created from the *boro* crop has accrued to the higher income groups. Income groups 3 and 4 have retained the relative advantage that control over 78 per cent of land allowed them; between them they gained 82 per cent of the total income from the *boro* paddy crop. In particular, the 19 households in group 4 gained 57 per cent of this income. The fact that even income group 1 households received more benefit from cultivation than labour shows both the profitability of the HYV crop and the low relative returns to labour. An income group 4 household on average gained over nine times more income from the crop than a group 1 household. This is not to suggest that 286 rupees is a small amount of extra income for a poorest household, only that their richer neighbours were making much larger relative gains.

Absentee landlordism

A further group which gained significantly from the irrigation project were wealthy absentee landlords. Fonogram households hired in about ten hectares of land from absentee landlords, 90 per cent of all land hired in in the

---

[10] Calculations were based on Howes' (1985: 92–110) analysis of a *boro* crop in Bangladesh. For further details, see Beck (1991). Table 6.2 shows total income rather than extra income, a distinction not always made in studies of factor shares (Prahladachar, 1983).

village. Fifty-nine per cent of this land was under paddy. In addition to hiring land out, absentee landlords owned six hectares within the command area of the *samity*'s STWs which was being farmed under paddy in the 1988–9 season (see Map 6.6). This land was farmed by labourers, share-croppers and cultivators from villages other than Fonogram. Absentee landlords therefore benefited significantly from the introduction of the STWs, with a total of 12 hectares under paddy in the 1988–9 season, equivalent to one-quarter of the total Fonogram holding. Who were these absentee landlords? I will describe them briefly, as so little systematic attention has been given to absentee landlordism in West Bengal, despite its importance to the rural economy.

About 60 per cent of the land hired out to Fonogram households be-longed to four families. The largest landholding (three and a half hectares) belonged to four brothers who lived locally and who came from one of the wealthiest and most powerful families in the area. Two of the brothers owned local factories in which Fonogram villagers, and in particular women from the poorest households, were employed at exploitive rates of pay. The oldest brother, G., also ran a business in Calcutta, involving among other things the export of shrimps, and boasted to me on numerous occasions about his wealth. The brother of one of the members of the *samity*, a competent and hard-working farmer from an income group 4 household, with whom I also spent much time discussing farming matters, was, according to one Fonogram villager, 'in and out of G.'s house'. The comparison between G.'s lifestyle and that of the poorest of Fonogram could not have been greater.

The second of these four absentee families, owning two hectares, consis-ted of three brothers, one of whom acted as surveyor for the local Land Revenue Office. The third family, owning three hectares of land, were local traders and businessmen. The fourth were 'cultivators' (to use the term by which they described themselves) who lived adjacent to Fonogram and sharecropped out their two hectares of land. They were not as well off as G.'s family, but were as wealthy as Fonogram income group 4 households (and were also notorious for holding late-night parties and keeping their neighbours awake).

Other absentee landlords included a sweet-shop owner and other local businessmen from Dabu. There was also one landowner who lived in Cal-cutta who sharecropped out half a hectare of land throughout the year to an income group 2 household, an arrangement that had been in place for many years.

Almost all of these landlords were Hindus renting out land to Muslims, continuing an exploitive pattern that dates back at least to the 1830s. *Operation Barga* had had no effect in Fonogram; records at the local Land Revenue Office in 1989 showed that no *bargadars* from Fonogram had been registered under *Operation Barga*. Adjacent Muslim villages had fared no better, although in two nearby Hindu villages of a similar size to Fonogram there were a total of 48 *bargadars* registered. This situation prevailed in Fonogram despite sharecropping arrangements that had continued for at least two generations, and several cases of land operated by *bargadars* for three consecutive years, which under the terms of the post-1977 amendments to the Land Reforms Act qualified them for registration and security of tenure. When I asked *bargadars* why they did not register they had a simple answer – they did not want to go through a procedure that might lead them to future trouble and conflict with landlords, and possibly to the law courts where cases might drag on for several years, as had one local case.

It is clear that any rural development initiative in West Bengal or neighbouring Bangladesh needs to take account of the fact that a relatively large percentage of land in the command areas of irrigation facilities could be owned by town dwellers or local rich absentee landholders, and that the benefits of such programmes might 'trickle up' to the non-poor in this way.[11]

Land sales and land mortgaging

The foregoing discussion has dealt with benefits from the STWs in a static sense; it has not discussed the process of change that ensued as a result of their introduction. This is covered in the present section, although the discussion is limited by the shortness of the period of fieldwork in comparison to the length of time that is usually taken by large-scale social change.

Proponents of the theory that differentiation is likely to increase because of the green revolution have stressed that land sales from poor to rich might be one effect of agrarian change (e.g. Dasgupta, 1980). Is this true for Fonogram? During the plot to plot surveys details were gathered of land sales to and by Fonogram households between 1986–7 and 1988–9. Land exchanges between Fonogram income groups are given in Table 6.3.

Table 6.3 Land exchanges between Fonogram income groups, 1986–7 to 1988–9 (decimals)

Income group	Buyer				Total
	1	2	3	4	
1	–	–	27	–	27
2	4	–	–	63	67
3	–	35	5	85	125
4	–	–	5	33	38
Total	4	35	37	181	257

[11] For evidence of absentee landlordism in West Bengal, see chapter 4.

In total, the 257 decimals of land that changed hands between Fonogram households for the three year period was just under 2 per cent of land operated by the villagers. There was a clear movement of land towards income group 4 households, who bought 70 per cent of all land sold. About 83 per cent of all land sold was sold to a higher income group. About half of the land sold and bought was between relatives, which adds an interesting perspective to the idea of sale of land being an exploitive transaction.[12]

Sales also took place between Fonogram households and villagers from other neigbouring villages nearby, or absentee landlords, details of which are given in Table 6.4.

Table 6.4 Land sales between Fonogram income groups and non-Fonogram households, 1986–7 to 1988–9 (decimals)

Income group	Land bought	Land sold
1	–	6
2	9	106
3	96	–
4	261	33
Total	366	145

Another 511 decimals therefore changed hands between Fonogram households and outsiders. A clear pattern emerges from Table 6.4 with income group 4 households buying in 71 per cent of land and group 2 households selling 73 per cent of land involved in transactions with outsiders.

Group 4 therefore gained 57 per cent of total land bought from within and outside the village; total transfer of land to this group was 371 decimals, or 7 per cent of land owned by this group in 1988–9. Group 2, the income group with a substantial amount of land at risk (group 1 owning only a very small amount of land), made a net loss of 129 decimals. This amounts to some 18 per cent of land held by this income group in 1988–9. This is particularly serious given the importance of land as an asset and the hardships suffered by poor households to retain or acquire land. Each land sale by poorer households probably involved several months of cuts in consumption prior to the sale, the disappearance of an inherited and vital

---

[12] 'Relative' here means a close relative, i.e. a sister, brother, aunt, uncle, niece or nephew or first cousin (many Fonogram households were related in a more distant sense). Details of pre-1986–7 land sales that were collected for occasional plots support the idea that a large percentage of land sales were between close relatives. A reason for this may be that in times of particular hardship, when households would be expected to sell land, a relative may give a better, if still below market, price than a non-relative. Intra-family land sales in Bangladesh are also discussed, as a negative phenomenon, by Jansen (1986: chapter 4), Howes (1985: 70) and Cain (1981: 465).

resource to a wealthier neighbour or relative, and decline towards landlessness.[13]

Of all land bought by group 4 households, 56 per cent was bought by three households. One of these was in the *samity*, and of the other two, one had a nephew in the *samity* and the other had benefited significantly from the introduction of the STWs. Land moved away from households most likely to become landless, although scarcity regulated the land market. Landlessness was likely to increase, but at a slow pace.

Were land sales in Fonogram 'exploitive'? Thirty per cent of land bought by group 4 was from wealthy absentee landlords, who probably sold when the market price was high, and no exploitation was involved. But at the same time the consecutive poor *aman* crops during the period of fieldwork increased pressure on poorer households to sell assets, and some of this pressure, as I heard during discussions, came from wealthier relatives within the village. Data gathered on the price of land sold shows that income group 3 and 4 households were not paying lower than market prices for land, which may have been due to the general scarcity of land in the area as well as the occurrence of intra-family sales. 'Exploitation' as a term to describe land sales in Fonogram has therefore to be defined carefully; wealthier households were taking the opportunity to buy land, but were not paying lower than market prices for it.[14] On the other hand, land prices were increasing markedly in the area, particularly land located near to either a road or an STW. For example, half of PN 491 (Map 6.1), making up two *bighas* of land, had been bought in 1979 for 6,000 rupees a *bigha*. In 1986 it was sold at 9,000 a *bigha*, and was in 1989 estimated to be worth 20,000 a *bigha*.[15] This rise in prices meant that it was unlikely that poorer households would be able to remain in the land market except as sellers, but also that they would receive very high prices for their land.

Land mortgaging
Studies from two villages in Bangladesh with a comparable socio-economic structure to Fonogram identified land mortgaging as an essential feature of the rural economy (Howes, 1985: 64–5; BARD 1976: 140–1). The second of these studies found that 43.5 per cent of households owning land had some land mortgaged out, and that: 'mortgaging . . . represents the principal device by which land is transferred between households in the village.'

---

[13] For similar findings from a Bangladesh village, see Cain (1981).

[14] A qualitatively different system of land sales operated in the Midnapore study villages, where past land sales by tribals to non-tribals were seen as exploitive by the sellers.

[15] A rapid rise in land prices was confirmed by the examination of ten land deeds held by the institution for which the author previously worked, as well as discussion with Fonogram villagers and other local people.

Mortgaging (i.e. land given from one household to another for hire over a negotiated period for a fixed cash sum) was not found to be of such importance in Fonogram (nor in the two Midnapore study villages, where it hardly existed). Only 3 per cent of village land was found to be under mortgage arrangements. In addition, as opposed to land sales, mortgage transactions in Fonogram did not in general involve the movement of land from poorer to richer households. Almost 40 per cent of intra-village transactions involved land mortgaged from group 3 to group 4, and a further 20 per cent involved land mortgaged in by group 1 households.[16]

These results on mortgaging reveal the dangers of attempting to generalize from the findings of a single (or even triple) village survey. As Farmer suggests (1986: 191): 'Conclusions drawn and generalizations made at one point in time for a given area are not valid a few years later.' Features of the West Bengal or Bangladeshi agrarian economy such as mortgaging arrangements or the extent of absentee landlordism appear to have been poorly covered in rural surveys, and until they are investigated more carefully, especially concerning their effect on socio-economic structure and the rural poor, it would be unwise to comment further in this study, except in attempting to consider their effect on the power structure within Fonogram.

'There may have been some benefits from the new farming . . .': Benefits to the landless and perceptions of the poor

As noted above, the literature on the green revolution has not focused on its effect on agricultural labourers, who were the main group targeted in the RDC's project proposal. The effects on the non-agricultural poor, and their perceptions of agricultural change, have been studied even less. This section discusses the benefits that accrued to these two parties, including the perceptions of the 25 poorest households whose lives were the main focus of the fieldwork in Fonogram.

Benefits to agricultural labourer households
Households with agricultural labourers as the main income earner were asked in the first round survey how many *extra* days of hired employment they received from the HYV crop. The reply was standard – 15 to 20 extra days. In this case the return to a household with one labourer would have been between 225 and 300 rupees per *bigha* farmed (at the 15 rupees for a full day's work the labourers estimated). A calculation of total extra labour supplied for the new paddy crop divided by the number of agricultural labourers in the village showed that the labourers' replies were accurate.

---

[16] Further details of land mortgaging can be found in Beck (1991).

The labourers' estimates are also in keeping with other findings which show that HYV farming increases employment (see Beck, 1991, for calculations, a summary of the literature on employment, and a more detailed discussion of real wage rates than will be found below).

Agricultural labourers might also have benefited from higher wage rates. However, using the price of rice in the whole of 24 Parganas District as a deflator (taken from Kynch, 1990), it appeared that there had been little increase in the real wage rates of labourers in the 1980s, despite the intro-duction of the STWs.[17] Wages in the Fonogram area during the *boro* season, at 15 rupees for a full day's work in 1988–9 were high compared to other parts of West Bengal. For example, wage rates for men in the Mid-napore study villages and in Birbhum District were about 25 per cent lower than the Fonogram figure (and even lower for women). The higher level in Fonogram was probably partly caused by the prevalence of cash cropping in north 24 Parganas in the *boro* season for many decades before the introduction of the STWs, which meant a higher demand for labour in this season than in the mainly mono-cropped Midnapore area. On the other hand, there was virtually no agricultural labour organization in Fonogram to press demands for higher wages, as opposed to the informal organization found in both Birbhum and Midnapore villages, and discussed further in chapter eight.

Benefits to the non-agricultural poor
Some non-agricultural employment was created by the rural industrializa-tion taking place in the Fonogram locality, of which the introduction of the STWs was one part. This employment was mainly labouring on lorries, involving five income group 1 and three income group 2 households. In total a team of six to eight labourers worked on these lorries loading and unloading bricks, sand and earth, and it was only the stronger labourers who were employed for these arduous tasks. The wages for this employ-ment were between 20 and 25 rupees a day, onto which was added *par routi* (leavened bread). In Fonogram, Romesh Ali owned two lorries (bought after the introduction of the STWs), and one lorry was owned by another member of the *samity*. Fonogram villagers did not tend to work on these

---

[17] Lipton (1989: 186) has also commented from a survey of relevant literature that: 'MVs seldom raise real wage-rates'.The trend noted in Fonogram may be repres-entative of a wider pattern, although there is conflicting evidence concerning this (see Kynch, 1990, who suggests a slight increase in male wage rates in West Bengal between 1977 and 1987; and Jose, 1988, who notes a decline in such rates). Labourers in Fonogram also gained little from extra employment outside of the village, as they tended not to work outside the village, or from extra employment on non-irrigated land, as the introduction of the STWs did little to raise the cropping index.

lorries, because of the tension this caused between the lorry owners and the labourers. One Fonogram labourer complained bitterly that he was owed wages for several days labour by Romesh, money which he was unlikely to ever receive. He, like the other Fonogram villagers, worked on lorries owned outside the village, and Romesh hired in external villagers, suggesting that new forms of extra-village employment contracts were being established. Romesh and the other lorry owners may have seen this as a way of maintaining an acquiescent labour force and keeping the wage rate down.

There was little other evidence found in Fonogram over the three-year period of fieldwork of 'trickle down' to the non-agricultural poor, a possibility hypothesized by Mellor (1976). Factories had opened up in the area, including bakeries to provide bread for the local factory workers and others, and one member of a group 1 household had got a regular job in one of these bakeries. There were also more grocery and tea shops opening, and a boy from another group 1 household had a job in one of the tea shops. There were, therefore, a few limited gains, which were nevertheless significant for individual households. However, employment in local factories was at an exploitive wage rate and in unpleasant and sometimes dangerous working conditions. It should also be remembered that one wealthy family of absentee landlords owned the local factories in which the Fonogram household members found employment; it was not in the long-term interests of these factory owners that poor households in Fonogram receive substantial benefits from agricultural technology, as this would have meant a possible loss of local sources of cheap labour.

Perceptions of the poorest on the green revolution
When asked what they had gained from the green revolution, poorest respondents (interviewed in the second-round survey) said that they received a little more work, although one respondent thought that farmers were generally using their own labour to farm the *boro* paddy crop. A female respondent thought that: 'People who are farming paddy might be happy with it. Those who are farming it are going to get richer whereas the poor can't farm.' Another replied with sarcasm: 'There may have been some benefits from the new farming, but I haven't seen any.'

Neither was there much evidence of 'trickle down' to this poorest group from their richer neighbours. None of the 25 poorest households reported receipt of *zakat*, or post-harvest donations of grain, which usually takes place from the rich to the poor in Islamic societies (e.g. Scott, 1985). They said that such donations may have taken place in the past, but now no-one ever heard of them.

Nor were poorest households able to glean after the *boro* crop, which might have provided them with an important source of subsistence (see the next chapter); according to them, the HYV paddy husks did not fall as easily

105

as those grown during the *aman* season, leaving little for them to pick up. In addition, post-harvest processing work was not passed on to poorer households, but carried out mainly by the household which grew the crop. As one female respondent put it: 'There is no more work after the harvest in terms of processing. People will sell paddy in the market and buy rice rather than give work to the poor.' Another woman expressed this anti-rich feeling more vividly: 'If we asked for rice-processing work the rich would say "Go off and die!" – they wouldn't give us any paddy to process'.[18]

Apart from watching their neighbours get richer, the green revolution passed the poorest by. As one woman, a factory worker, said: 'I don't know anything about farming – I go out to work at seven in the morning and come back at eight at night.' Poorest people agreed almost unanimously that the rich were getting richer and the poor poorer, and that they were not the people receiving benefits from the new irrigation facilities.

The analysis above shows that RDC's objectives were not met. To recap, according to RDC: 'The main object of the (STW) proposal is to assist the landless agricultural and other landless labourer families . . .' and 'This project created a good impact among the target group of population . . . thereby extending avenues for landless labour families.' Agricultural labourer families certainly did benefit from the STWs. They received an *extra* 225 to 300 rupees in wages for each worker. Given an average agricultural labourer yearly wage of 2,700 rupees, the absolute increase to a single labourer was about 10 per cent every year, no doubt very welcome to the individual households. However, this gain was small compared to that of a household from income group 3 or 4 with six *bighas* under HYV paddy which was making a total profit of about 4,900 rupees and an extra profit (over previous non-HYV crops) of 1,500 rupees in a single season. In percentage terms of their own total incomes, the returns to the different income groups were less extreme. However, poorer villagers did not tend to think in percentage terms of incomes. They were involved in daily relations with other villagers, both economic and extra-economic. They looked at the improvement in the standard of living of the *samity* members and the other richer villagers, and compared it to their own. This comparison was central to their experience of poverty. Bitterness and anger was the outcome.

Social change and the green revolution

What was the overall effect of the introduction of STWs to Fonogram? This must be viewed in historical context. As was seen in chapter four,

---

[18] There may have been some benefits to poorest people in that the paddy crop may have produced a larger amount of stubble than previous vegetable crops, allowing more material for fuel collection and grazing of animals. No data was collected on this matter.

processes such as increasing landlessness and pauperization have been taking place in West Bengal for several decades. It appears likely that recent developments such as the green revolution will intensify changes that were already in process.

Even before the introduction of the STWs, an unequal social structure had become established in Fonogram. It was into this power structure that the irrigation facilities were introduced. And as Lipton has noted (1989: 401): 'MVs are an evolutionary technique . . . not one that requires (or stems from) a transformation in the structure of rural power. An evolutionary technique . . . tends, when introduced into an entrenched power structure, to be used so as to benefit the powerful.' This is precisely what happened in Fonogram.

Poorer households certainly gained more employment subsequent to the introduction of the STWs. They also cultivated a higher percentage of HYVs on the small amounts of land they operated than richer income groups. There was also little evidence in Fonogram of intra-village tenancy arrangements that would lead to sale of land. Despite this, it did appear that poorer households were being forced to sell land to the higher income groups at an alarming rate. And any gains were very small in comparison to the benefits that had flowed to the rich in the village. The rich took advantage of their larger landholdings and the power structure in the village was firmly imprinted on the surrounding landscape.

In the years after the green revolution, two households in particular, whose head of household were members of the *samity*, had perceptibly increased their wealth, although others in income group 4 and the upper levels of group 3 had also done so. The first of these, Jyonal's household, has already been mentioned as a lorry owner. Jyonal was also the main purchaser of land during the fieldwork period, and had bought a motor bike which was a conspicuous symbol of his wealth.

The second household was that of Romesh, and I have noted above his household's purchase of two hectares of land (before the field work period) and two lorries, and his access to large amounts of urban credit, as well as his brother's poultry business which involved urban connections. He had also repaired his house, but did not engage in any other conspicuous expenditure. He was rarely at home, spending most of his time in the local town conducting his various business affairs, most recently the sale of bricks, tiles, earth and sand for building purposes.

Four other households in income group 4, whose heads were four brothers had all also benefited substantially; the eldest of these brothers, Daoud, came from the richest household in the village and was also a member of the *samity*. Daoud was involved in the division of land into housing plots near to Fonogram, as well as in the sale of building material for this housing, from all of which he was likely to reap substantial profits, and which necessitated urban links. Daoud's family had also recently

107

purchased a hand tiller which would not only cut costs but was a symbol of status. He and the second oldest brother had bought land in Fonogram from their friend the factory owner and absentee landowner G., and were at the end of 1989 both completing, at the entrance to the village, the building of large brick houses on the land which cost at least 50,000 rupees each. These were in stark contrast to the shack of leaves and palm fronds owned by one of the poorest households in the village that lay in front of their new houses at the entrance to the village. This was a potent symbol of the increased differences in wealth between very rich and very poor.

The benefits from the STWs were only one reason for increased resources flowing to these *samity* households and their relatives; the development of their businesses involved them in contacts in the towns around Fonogram, with government offices and other businessmen, and borrowing of capital from local banks and moneylenders, as noted above. As others have commented (Howes, 1985; Van Schendel, 1981), increased wealth from the green revolution may be invested outside of the village, especially if the land market is competitive, as it was in Fonogram. The cases above show that higher profits meant greater consumption by the richest, and movement of capital into business enterprise outside of the village. Rich absentee landlords were the other group that received significant benefits, and there were ties between these landlords and wealthier Fonogram households. Chambers (1983) has written of 'integrated rural poverty', or an interlocking set of factors that 'trap' the poor in deprivation. In Fonogram 'integrated rural wealth' was also found, with power, wealth, good health and contacts, particularly urban contacts that could be extremely lucrative, integrated to ensure, for a select few households, control of village resources.

The idea of 'partial proletarianization' is supported by the evidence from Fonogram. This is mainly because poorer cultivators and agricultural labourers were gaining absolutely at the same time as losing relatively in comparison with their richer neighbours. This absolute gain did not appear sufficient to halt the sale of substantial amounts of land by poorer households. It is possible to concur with a number of other studies from the region that have come to similar conclusions concerning benefits to the poor from the HYVs within a situation of increasing inequality (Boyce, 1987; Howes, 1985; BRAC, 1983; Hartmann and Boyce, 1983; Van Schendel, 1981; Arens and Van Beurden, 1977).[19] Given this finding, the financing of irrigation facilities in isolation from other development programmes that provide support to the poor must be questioned.

---

[19] Wade's (1988) detailed study of farmer groups in south India also shows that wealthier farmers are able to organize to control irrigation resources. It should be noted, however, that some forms of mechanized irrigation may be more equitable than others (see Glaeser, 1988; Boyce, 1987: 228–245; Howes, 1985; Jones and Ahamad, 1985: 24; Wood, 1984).

The claims by RDC concerning the success of the irrigation project are unfounded. The project had the opposite effect to that intended by its funders, which included the Government of West Bengal, because of a failure to understand the nature of the rural socio-economic structure or of irrigation technology. This form of external intervention into the village was a failure as far as delivering major benefits to the poor was concerned, although some benefits did seep through.

Dasgupta's conclusions from a survey of all-India data were also found to hold in Fonogram (1980: 379):

> Rather than undermining the existing rural institutions by bringing about a radical transformation in the agricultural scene, the new technology has strengthened those and the groups in control of those institutions. Whereas it was a difficult political task to antagonize the rural elite before, it is even more difficult today as the former is now deeply entrenched in power in the Indian countryside.

The original aims of the propagators of the green revolution of maintaining the status quo in villages has been met in Fonogram.[20]

Although governments may be increasingly unwilling to antagonize rural elites, antagonism has come from other sources. Boyce (1987: 241) cites a reference to the sabotaging of deep tubewells in Bangladesh. This also occurred in Fonogram. Three STWs were stolen during my fieldwork, one from a plot of land owned by Romesh's household just before they were to begin irrigation (all were insured and subsequently replaced). The power lines that brought electricity to Fonogram were also stolen, which meant delays in irrigation. That this was an antagonistic act rather than simple theft can be seen from its regular occurrence every *boro* season during my fieldwork, rather than at other times of year when the STWs were hardly in use. The perpetrators of these acts remained anonymous. There had also been several attempts at theft from Romesh Ali's house, and during one of these attempts at night the perpetrator had broken the wooden slats in a window and put a hand through and grabbed the first thing that came into it – which happened to be Romesh's wife's hair – a story that circulated very quickly in the village. The building of brick houses by richer Fonogram households was for protection as well as for comfort or to display increased wealth. As discussions with them showed, richer household members were frightened of theft and violence.

It would be both naive and ahistorical (given the discussions in chapters three and four concerning peasant protest) to suggest that the relative

---

[20] Webster (1989), in a ten year re-survey of three villages in Birbhum District, West Bengal, found no increase in polarization from 1977–8 to 1987–8 between different categories of landowners. Webster connects this to the Left Front government's policies avoiding structural change (ibid.: 41).

polarization of income of richer and poorer households noted in Fonogram would be likely to cause increased violence between the rich and poor in the village. What it did appear to be leading to was continued bitterness among the poor, and more 'everyday forms of poor people's resistance', part of the friction that was integral to everyday village life. It is this friction that I will look at more closely in the next two chapters, after examining the effects of the land reform programme in the two Midnapore villages.

Land reform in the Midnapore case study villages

As noted in chapter four, the redistribution of land owned by families with more than the maximum allowed and 'vested' in the government, was one of the policies central to the Government of West Bengal's reform programme. To recap, the declared policy of the government was (Government of West Bengal, 1986: 2–3):

> to reduce, as far as possible the disparity and irregularities in the rural economic structure by bringing about a change in the ownership of land . . . With this end in view a comprehensive multipurpose programme has been undertaken to distribute surplus lands among the landless . . . The objective of the present government is to vest as much as permissible surplus land above ceiling in the State within the existing legal framework . . . The help of the Panchayat is also sought to search out surplus land above ceiling.
>
> Regarding distribution of vested lands Government's policy is to distribute at least a fraction of land to each landless (sic) enabling him to become self reliant . . . up to 31st December 1985, 8.13 lakh acre vested land has been redistributed among 16.40 lakh peasants. Special mention may be made of the fact that 55 per cent among them belong to scheduled castes and scheduled tribes community.

Two issues make an evaluation of distribution of land relevant here. Firstly, it is a rural development programme aimed specifically at the landless, into which category many of the poorest are likely to fall. Secondly, it aims to include a high percentage of scheduled caste and tribe households, which made up a large proportion of the poorest in the Midnapore study villages.

The few studies that have evaluated the land reform programme show mixed results. Redistribution is discussed in a 14-village study from throughout West Bengal by Bandyopadyay (1983), where the programme is accorded moderate success. Westergaard, from a four-village study throughout West Bengal, including one village in the south east of Midnapore, concluded that: 'if we look at data on land distribution in the four villages, this land reform has been insignificant.' (1985: 81). Bose and Bhadoria's study of 40 villages throughout Midnapore District commented that (1987: 32):

110

The state government's vigorous pursuit of targets of vested land distributions seems to have been very effective because this item has proved itself to be the most important factor (among all forms of government support) in generating additional income, particularly for the poorer strata.

The same authors conclude however (ibid.: 74): 'The class and caste-wise distribution of aids (i.e. government support) also reveal a tendency to concentrate more on the articulate sections.' To these views of redistribution I now add an analysis of how far the government has met its aims and how resources were mediated through village power structures in the two Midnapore villages.

In theory, land reform in West Bengal is the responsibility of the *panchayat samity*, the block level middle tier between village and district levels. In practice in the Midnapore study villages decisions as to which land was to be redistributed and who was to receive it appeared to be made at village level by the *panchayat* chairman. The *panchayat* chairman under whose jurisdiction Bithigram and Keshipur fell had been elected in 1988. He came from a wealthy household from a village about 4 km from Bithigram. I interviewed him twice, once in his home, and once in his 'office' in Bithigram, the latter a small room in the house of the wealthiest Bithigram household, whose head had been *panchayat* chairman before the present incumbent, further evidence of control of *panchayats* by the powerful. The present chairman did not yet appear to have a good grasp of his duties, perhaps because of his newness in the post. One of his methods of selection of beneficiaries for government programmes became clear during the interview in his office when discussing the various schemes that the *panchayats* were undertaking. When he came to IRDP he turned to an acquaintance (who did not appear to be poor) who was waiting to do business with the chairman, and told him that he was the right sort of person to be taking out an IRDP loan. This approach seemed to be taken partly out of the exasperation of trying to meet a 'quota' and not having sufficient time to make a more considered choice of beneficiary.

As outlined in chapter five, land operated by Bithigram and Keshipur households was divided between about half *danga* (or high land) and half *sali* (or lower *aman* paddy land). This was significant for the land redistribution programme in the villages, as relatively large quantities of the lower quality *danga* land, used for grazing livestock and *aus* paddy, were available for redistribution in the area. Another local political feature was the historical dominance of *zamindars* or large absentee landowners. Large amounts of *zamindari* land should in theory have been available for redistribution, but absentee landlords were still powerful locally in 1988–9, and hired out their land to villagers in villages near to Bithigram; any land that they had given up in the past would most likely have been *danga* land.

111

As part of the first-round survey, household members in the two villages were asked if they had received any *patta* land (or land redistributed under the land reform programme), how much, and the type of land they had received. The following analysis is therefore based on respondents' replies and is not as accurate as the findings on land operation in Fonogram. Nevertheless, the discussion below does give a good indication as to which groups have benefited from this government programme.

Bithigram respondents reported receiving some 26 hectares of *patta* land, or 30 per cent of land operated in the village, while in Keshipur the figure received was a more modest 18 per cent of village land operated, or eight and a half hectares. These figures can be compared to the six hectares received on average by each of 40 villages in Bose and Bhadoria's Midnapore study (1987: 28); probably the figure in Bithigram is larger because of the large amounts of *danga* land re-distributed there, and possibly because the former *panchayat* chairman lived in the village and had been able to direct more land towards his neighbours. Also, households may have counted as *patta* land which they had operated in the past but to which they had no formal right. Respondents reported taking land before receiving *patta*, but with the consent of the *panchayat* chairman, by *dockol* (or right to hold or possess), which presumably meant that in some cases they had established use rights to the land previously.

Table 6.5 gives *patta* land received by Bithigram households and the use they made of it, and Table 6.6 gives the same details for Keshipur.

Benefits from this programme can be seen to have been spread more evenly across the income groups than those from the irrigation scheme in Fonogram. Income groups 1 and 2 (made up mainly of scheduled caste and tribe households) received 63 per cent of total land in Bithigram and 54 per cent in Keshipur, whereas in Fonogram (which had no land reform programme), it was the wealthier two income groups which received about 80 per cent of the benefits from the green revolution (Table 6.2). It is in this

Table 6.5 *Patta* **land (decimals) received in Bithigram up to 1988–9 by income group and use of land**

Income group	Aman farming[1]	Aus farming	Under trees	Not in use	Total	
1	141 (19)	155 (19)	495 (16)	487 (27)	1278	(20)
2	333 (44)	452 (53)	1299 (42)	704 (39)	2788	(43)
3	124 (16)	238 (28)	337 (11)	176 (10)	875	(13)
4	156 (21)	–	979 (31)	448 (24)	1583	(24)
Total[2]	754 (12)	845 (13)	3110 (48)	1815 (27)	6524 (100)	

[1] Figures in brackets for the first four rows give rounded percentages of the amount of land received by each income group.
[2] Figures in brackets for the fifth row give rounded percentages of the amount of land under each type of land use.

Table 6.6 *Patta* land (decimals) received in Keshipur up to 1988–9 by income group and use of land

Income group	Aman farming[1]	Aus farming	Under trees	Not in use	Total	
1	–	109 (24)	167 (15)	193 (35)	469	(22)
2	–	100 (21)	212 (20)	361 (65)	673	(32)
3	–	200 (42)	153 (14)	–	353	(17)
4	–	62 (13)	546 (51)	–	608	(29)
Total[2]	–	471 (23)	1078 (51)	554 (26)	2103 (100)	

[1] Figures in brackets for the first four rows give rounded percentages of the amount of land received by each income group.
[2] Figures in brackets for the fifth row give rounded percentages of the amount of land under each type of land use.

comparative light that the land reform seems impressive, and indeed the programme has provided greater benefits than many development programmes for the poor in India. The success is qualified by a relatively large percentage of benefits having trickled up to the wealthier income groups.

The success of the programme is also qualified by the quality of the land received by recipient households. The two tables show that the quality of the land received overall was poor – only land listed under '*aman* farming' in the tables was better quality *sali* land; the rest was *danga*. In Bithigram 11 per cent of land was better quality *sali* land, while no land received in Keshipur was *sali*. The uses to which the land was put shows that in many cases only reduced benefits would accrue to its new owners. Eighteen per cent of total land in Bithigram and 26 per cent in Keshipur was not in use, either because of the inability of the household which had received the land to cultivate it, the poor quality of its soil, or the distance of the plot from the village. In Bithigram 66 per cent of this land belonged to groups 1 and 2, and in Keshipur all of the land in this category belonged to the same two groups. Yield from land under trees (i.e. eucalyptus, planted under the government social forestry programme) might be of high value, dependent on the market price of eucalyptus. However, about half of the land under eucalyptus owned by income groups 1 and 2 in Bithigram was being rented out to a company called Palport, which planted the trees, guarded them and would give the landowner 50 per cent of yield after 14 years. In Keshipur it was mainly the upper two income group households that had planted trees. The *amount* of land under eucalyptus shown in the tables also hides the fact that on average the higher income groups planted more trees per *bigha* of land. Equally, land under *aus* was likely to be planted only every alternate year, and to produce poor yields. Overall, then the quality of land received, especially by the poor, tended to be of low quality.

One further point needs to be made concerning this programme. Poorer households receiving land did not just consider the material benefits it might bring. Some viewed their receipt of low quality *danga* land which they could not cultivate with a certain amusement. As one tribal woman from Bithigram put it: 'The government has given me stony land on which nothing will grow. So I will eat stones.' To others, particularly poor tribals in Bithigram, the land they received signified the possibility of escaping from dependency on the wealthier families and moneylenders in the village. They could now produce paddy for their own consumption, and even eight decimals of paddy land could be a significant amount for a poor household. Farmed intensively during the *aman* season, when the main input was household labour, households were reporting yields of 4–5 *maunds* of paddy from this amount of land (or 160–200 kg), the equivalent of two full months of wages from agricultural labour. In comparison to the Fonogram programme, tribals in Bithigram receiving land did have a sense that the government was attempting to support them even if in a small way, which gave them a psychological boost.

The government's aim of distributing 'at least a fraction of land to each landless' household can be seen to have been almost met, particularly in Bithigram. The wider aim of reducing 'disparities and irregularities in the rural economic structure by bringing about a change in the ownership of land' was not met. The quantity of land distributed was high, but much of it was of poor quality, and either could not be cultivated or would produce limited benefits. The upper two income groups continued to dominate in terms of land operation, and, particularly in Keshipur, also to receive at least equal benefits from the redistribution programme as the two lower income groups.

Conclusions

The analysis in this chapter of two rural development schemes 'targeted' at the poor shows that resources entering the study villages did not pass into a political vacuum. Resources were mediated through the power brokers in the two villages – the *panchayat* in Midnapore and the *samity* in Fonogram. Use of these resources reinforced the patterns of integrated rural wealth and poverty. In Fonogram it was clear that the introduction of irrigation facilities was distorting socio-economic structures in favour of those who already had much power in the village, and who were likely to gain both more power and wealth.

In comparison, the land reform programme was more equitable but distribution of benefits still mirrored the existing socio-economic structure. Neither programme was likely to bring about major changes in the social structure, although the psychological boost given to land recipients in Bithigram and Keshipur should not be under-estimated. Furthermore, both government-backed programmes were implicitly 'targeted' at the world of men, agriculture and farming without recognizing in any way this gender bias.

114

The analysis in this chapter, particularly the section on agriculture in Fonogram, is probably more detailed and more accurate than most evaluations of development projects. The conclusions I draw from the evaluations support the evidence from other studies presented in chapter four which suggests that rural development initiatives in West Bengal have been of only moderate success. External intervention by the government would seem to be at best ameliorating the condition of the poor, and doing little to change their relative position of powerlessness *vis-à-vis* the rich. The analysis also shows that a good understanding of village agro-ecology and its relation to socio-economic structures is essential for the formulation of rural development programmes. In Fonogram, failure to understand this on the part of the implementing agency meant that most resources flowed, like the mythical river in the *Mahabharata*, upwards.

This chapter, in combination with the previous two chapters, has given a picture of the constraints under which the poor in the study villages live their lives. Their access to village resources is severely limited, and what support they can expect from government or other external intervention is likely to be both small and diverted to their wealthier neighbours. These structural constraints were central to what poverty meant for the poor. I turn next to the question of what poor people themselves do to improve the quality of their lives, how they manipulate and at times are crushed by the constraints they face, and to their experience of poverty.

7   Surviving against the odds in the case study villages: Everyday strategies and priorities

Introduction

The previous chapters have been something of a prologue to the information I will present now as to how the poor experience poverty and go about improving their quality of life. I argue that, in contrast to historical and contemporary representations, poor people are active and ingenious, particularly so given the structural constraints they face. This has implications for policy, for, as seen in chapter two, the view taken of the poor will partly determine the direction and content of policy.

There is now a small literature focusing specifically on theorizing survival strategies in the context of 'developing' societies (e.g. Taylor, 1992; Lieten and Nieuwenhuys, 1989; Schmink, 1984; C. Wood, 1981). However I would argue that the most sound existing theoretical tradition for a study of poorest people's survival is the work on people's history discussed in chapter three, which has attempted to show how poor people have been active participants in the making of their societies. In particular, I use Thompson's concept of the moral economy, where poor and rich negotiate, bargain and struggle over natural and social resources within a ring of mutual need and antagonism, as an interpretive device for understanding the experience of the poor in modern day West Bengal. As they struggle for resources and for a better quality of life, the poor are forced at every turn to confront the realities of their poverty, their strengths and weaknesses, and the dominance of their richer neighbours, a dominance they contest at both practical and ideological levels.

Survival strategies can be taken to mean activities of poor people in times of stress which they see as crucial to the continued running of their household. I argue in this and the next chapter that indigenous methods already in place in rural societies, negotiated over time and via class and socio-economic structures, might provide useful media through which governments and NGOs could support the activities of the poor. These are the 'soft spots' in the rural economy which Chambers (1983) refers to as possible intervention points – areas which benefit the poor but do not harm the rich. To build on these strategies might therefore be a useful complement to existing development programmes, and would involve acknowledgement of the strengths of the poor. This recognition would appear to be crucial in the formulation of a humane, sensitive, and possibly more successful form of rural development. This and the next chapter therefore look critically at some attempts that have already been made, in particular by NGOs in the Bengal region, to build on indigenous methods of combatting poverty.

116

This chapter is organized as follows. First I discuss 'characteristics' of poor people, and outline the method of selection of poorest households in this study, and the next sections deal with poorest people's use of the natural resource base, and with poorest people and food. I then discuss an indigenous method of livestock redistribution from rich to poor that is widespread throughout Asia, comparing the effectiveness of this to the government-sponsored IRDP programme. Finally I cover poorest people's use of assets.[1] To return to the typology formulated by Anderson and outlined in chapter three, the strategies discussed in this chapter are for the most part 'private' and 'public', in that they are short term and work within the existing socio-economic framework, although they do have longer-term consequences. In chapter eight I will turn to longer-term or 'collective' strategies of the poor that challenge the status quo.

In contrast to chapter six, which concentrated on the formal village economy, agriculture, irrigation, and the world of men, this chapter is mainly concerned with the village 'informal economy', which is operated to a large extent by women. This is not to suggest any absolute division between the public and private as far as gender roles are concerned (for a discussion on the 'public–private' debate, see White, 1988). But it is to acknowledge that repressive patriarchal structures operated in the study villages and these restricted severely the extent to which women could influence events outside the household and caused them to direct their activities towards their immediate locality.

Who are the poorest?

Students of poverty in India, as B. Harriss (1987) has noted, have used a wide variety of indicators to track poverty down and determine who the poor are, in particular wealth and capability (the latter for example in terms of mortality, morbidity or literacy).[2] Using these indicators various authors have analysed data from rural surveys in a way that is relevant to defining poverty groups and comparable to the findings I will present here. For example, Agarwal (1986) has noted for all India that the poor are likely to be found in agricultural labourer households, have large households and high dependency ratios and low literacy rates; Chen and Dreze (1992) and Dreze (1988b) have noted the high percentage of widows amongst the poorest in villages throughout South Asia; Hossain (1987) has commented

---

[1] Throughout, comparative material is used to draw out the representativeness of my findings, and the two agro-ecological study regions are compared. There is now a large literature on survival strategies, much of it on Africa. Most of this literature has concentrated on famine rather than everyday forms of coping.

[2] The shortcomings of the paradigmatic base of both of these indicators has been discussed in chapter two.

on lack of homestead land as an indicator of ultra-poverty in six villages in Bangladesh; and Greeley (1982) has noted that poorest households in Bangladesh have female household members participating in the wage labour market.[3]

I will not at this point attempt to outline further comparative material, useful as that exercise might be. The focus here is not on who the poor are but what the poor are capable of. My use of the work 'capable' is in contrast to the narrow definition of 'capabilities' used by Sen (1985) (see chapter three), where capabilities are discussed in terms of indicators such as mortality or literacy. Sen's choice of indicators would suggest that he is more interested in people's *lack* of capability than their abilities. Much work on poverty does the same, focusing on incapabilities of the poor such as ill health or mortality. For example, here is Lipton's negative portrayal of the poor (1983b: 10):

> The poorest are usually likeliest to be ill . . ., to lack extended family to help with childcare . . ., to be casual employees . . ., and to be subject to seasonality . . . Hence a downturn in ASPRs (age- and sex-specific participation rates) around the level of ultra-poverty . . . would be perfectly normal economic behaviour.

I have no criticism of the substance of these findings (in fact all except the last are widely known and were found in my own investigations). My criticism is that such concentration on the inablity of the poor neglects human agency. Such definitions continue to take an attitude towards the poor as passive victims (of illness or 'subject to seasonality'), who need to be targeted by development policymakers.

Having made these criticisms, it remains necessary to know who the poorest are to discover their capabilities, but this should be a means to an end rather than the end in itself. The method of selection of poorest households in this study and who they were is therefore described below.

During my fieldwork, poorest households were selected for interview using a combination of different indicators. As I required a purposive sample, random sampling techniques were not used. I needed to interview an adequate number of households to be able to discuss in general terms poorest people's agency, and a 20 per cent sample appeared to be manageable. In Fonogram my local knowledge made access and selection more easy. The two Midnapore villages had been selected for study partly

---

[3] The most comprehensive attempt to differentiate the poor from the poorest (or what he calls the 'ultrapoor') has been that of Lipton (1983a, b, c and 1985). Lipton's papers discuss the relation between poverty, nutrition, land, demography and labour. There is no scope to discuss the very detailed findings of these papers here, some of which are highly controversial (for a brief summary, see Chambers 1988: 6–7).

because of their Scheduled Tribe and Caste Populations, and most of the poorest respondents in those villages came from these populations. Physical indicators used in selection were lack of assets and income (calculated from the first-round interviews), the state of housing and the health of household members. Other 'indicators' were the loquaciousness of respondents, and their willingness to go through what at times could be highly emotional discussions. Some households were excluded even though by any indicator they were the poorest in the village. This was because household members were unable to answer detailed questions because of ill-health or mental incapacity. A further technique used was to ask each poorest household to name five other poorest households in the village. The same names came up regularly enough to suggest that this technique could overcome 'respondent bias' and be useful in identifying the poorest.[4]

The distinction between poor and poorest here is necessarily arbitrary. The purpose of the selection procedure was not to pinpoint accurately the 'bottom' 20 per cent of households in each village, but to estimate who the poorest were as a means to discussing with them their experience of poverty. But to contextualize the following discussion on poor people's abilities, I will describe here the 'characteristics' of respondent households. When carrying out the interviews I spoke to whoever was present in the household at the time(s) of visit, which, as intended, meant that more women were interviewed as they tended to be present more often. In Fonogram I spoke to fifteen women, three men and seven families (wife, husband and/or children), in Bithigram four women, eight men and seven families, and in Keshipur eleven women, four men and one family (in total 30 women, 15 men and 15 families). As mentioned above, interviews in Bithigram often turned into group interviews. Respondent households included seven female-headed households in Fonogram, three in Bithigram, and six in Keshipur (all headed by widows). In contrast, there were three widowers in the sample. Class and gender structures interlinked with the result that it was households headed by single women with young children, or independent elderly widows, that were most likely to be poor.

Asset holdings of respondents are discussed below. Respondent households came from income groups 1 and 2. Twenty-four out of twenty-five came from group 1 in Fonogram, 10 out of 19 from group 1 in Bithigram, and 12 out of 16 from group 1 in Keshipur (income group 1 being much smaller in the Midnapore villages). By primary occupation, Fonogram respondent households included 14 agricultural labourers, four lorry labourers, one maid servant, one van driver, one petty trader and one beggar; Bithigram households included 17 agricultural labourers and two contract

---

[4] Dreze (1988b: 24) came to similar conclusions about villagers' ability to determine who were the poorest from a study in Uttar Pradesh.

labourers, and Keshipur households 11 agricultural labourers and five contract labourers. Respondents depended almost exclusively on their unskilled labour to earn income. All respondents except one were illiterate, and in only six cases were their children attending school.

Having discovered who the respondents were, I will move on now to discuss the informal economy they operated and the way in which they survived.

Access to the natural resource base and common property resources

Most literature on common property resource (CPR) use in India focuses on the arid and semi-arid, hill, and forest fringe regions of the country (for a review, see OFI 1991). Little literature has discussed CPRs in West Bengal, and has done so mainly in the context of forests or social forestry programmes (e.g. Shah, 1987; an exception is Nesmith (1990) who covers both social forestry and other natural resource use in West Bengal).[5] Part of the reason for the relative lack of attention on CPRs has been the focus in the region on formal aspects of agricultural development. Also, West Bengal does not have the relatively large areas of 'common' land that are found in other less densely populated regions of India. For example, an estimate of private as opposed to common land gives an all-India figure of 64 per cent private land and 36 per cent common land, but for the district of Mushidabad in West Bengal, an estimate of 98 per cent private land and 2 per cent common land (Agarwal and Narain, 1989: 41). Of total land in the state, about 60 per cent is classed as cultivated, with about 25 per cent classed as wasteland and 12 per cent as forest area in 1985–6 (Singh and Bhattacharjee, 1991). Of the 'common' land that exists, the trend is towards 'privatization' through the land redistribution programme that places land held by the government in the hands of villagers (discussed in the last chapter). So even in the western part of the State, for example the districts of Purulia and Bankura, western Birbhum and Midnapore, where there are relatively large areas of so-called waste land, common land is increasingly being transferred to individual villagers.

In much of West Bengal, therefore, common property resources are not the grazing lands or forests found in other parts of India. Access to many natural resources in village West Bengal is not clearly defined legally but depends on a process of negotiation, bargaining or conflict between poor and rich, and on a system of customary rights. While some resources are open access (for example stubble left after harvesting or wild foods that

---

[5] There is a more extensive literature on CPR use in Bangladesh, discussed below, e.g. Sadeque (1990), Howes and Jabbar (1986), Briscoe (1979).

grow in drainage ditches), other important CPRs (such as gleaned grains or fallen fruits) should be defined as products that are found mainly on private land controlled by richer villagers, and to which the poor have customarily negotiated access. It is this latter resource-use system that is likely to become more dominant, for reasons discussed below. While from the perspective of the rich these latter resources may be privately owned, from the perspective of the poor they are common in that the poor have attempted to maintain a right of access to them. To define these resources as private property misses an important point, as how a village resource is defined will depend on whose perspective is being considered.[6]

Perhaps because it has focused on the more equitable areas of India, the inter-class element of CPR use is largely absent from its current analysis. For example, it is not mentioned in either a World Bank review (OFI, 1991), Jodha's much quoted articles (1990; 1986), or a major work on water and trees in India (Chambers, Shah and Saxena, 1989). 'Class' analyses have looked at differential access of sections of the rural population to CPRs (e.g. Jodha, 1986), but not the relations between the different sections of the rural population concerning CPRs.[7] However, as will be seen below, control and conflict over such resources was closely tied to power relations in the study villages.

Although most rural households in India make use of CPRs, collection of CPRs is more important the poorer a household becomes (Jodha, 1986). This section describes an 'everyday' strategy of the poorest that is intensified in times of stress or disaster. The areas that will be discussed here are the importance to the poor of gleaning, gathering of fuel, and gathering of other wild products.

Gleaning

Paddy grains that fell during harvesting were collected by poorest household members after the *aman* harvest in all three study villages, but access and type of gleaning differed. Respondents were asked who gleaned, when they did so, how much they gleaned, and whether this activity was subject to any restrictions.

In Fonogram 20 out of the 25 respondents questioned reported gleaning whenever there was time, and that it was an activity carried out mainly by children. In the other five households there were either no children or respondents were out at work all day and unable to glean. The amount gathered was partly dependent on the overall yield of the crop. Respondents' replies were therefore coloured by the consecutive poor *aman*

---

[6] For a more detailed discussion of delineation of types of local resources in West Bengal, see Beck, forthcoming.

[7] An exception is Briscoe (1979), writing about common property use in a Bangladesh village.

harvests in Fonogram; the floods in 1986–7 for example meant that very little grain was available for gleaning.

The amounts collected varied depending on household make up and who had time to glean. Respondents reported that on average children went out for an hour a day in the 15 to 30 days when the crop was harvested and collected in total between 10 and 15 kg of paddy. The average collected by the 11 households who gave clear estimates was 13 kg in one season. The highest estimate was 25 kg for the season. These amounts can be favourably compared to the 2–3 kg of wheat received by most respondent households after the 1986–7 floods from the government as relief.

Three of the twenty gleaning respondents said bitterly that farmers refused access to their fields, a point that was also made in informal discussions with other poor household members not included in the 'formal' survey. As one poorest woman put it: 'If the crop is good the rich let us in, if not they don't.'

In Bithigram 18 of the 19 respondents reported gleaning. Gleaning was usually carried out by women and children. Up to 5 kg could be gathered in a day by one person (the equivalent of two female agricultural labourer's wage). For the gleaning 'season', total estimates varied between 15 and 80 kg. Only one respondent reported restrictions on gleaning. She said that she was only allowed to glean on the land of the farmer whose paddy she harvested. Otherwise respondents could glean as they wished.

Seven Lodha respondents also reported another form of gathering of paddy grains – from rat holes. Rats made deep, long holes under the narrow *auls* (or partitions) between the fields. One respondent estimated that 10 rats could store a maximum of 100 kg of grain in a single hole. The Lodhas dug up these holes, killed the rats, and took the grain. This work was very hard, which limited the numbers of those who could take part, and took a whole day. Snake bites were also a potential danger. The average amount collected in a day's work by two men was about 6–7 kg, although sometimes no grain was collected.

Unlike gleaning, collection from rat holes was an activity that benefited both farmers and collectors. Farmers benefited because rats were cleared from their fields, and the collectors benefited from receipt of grain, as well as obtaining the rats which they killed and ate. Lodhas wishing to undertake this activity had to request permission from the landowner to do so, which was usually granted. This activity can therefore be labelled as one of negotiated mutual benefit rather than one of conflict.

Grain collected by gleaning and collection from rat holes made a substantial contribution to poorest households' subsistence in Bithigram. One household reported gathering a total of 100 kg a season in this way, the equivalent of the wages from about 30 days of male agricultural labour. Respondents who gave clear estimates of the amount of grain collected in one season gained an average of 29 kg per household for gleaned grain and 32 kg for grain collected from rat holes.

It was in Keshipur, the village just a couple of kilometres from Bithigram, that most restrictions were faced concerning gleaning. Only one of the respondents reported gleaning, and this was a respondent whose household owned land on which paddy was grown. None of the other households gleaned because no farming household permitted access to their land. Typically, one respondent said indignantly: 'No one lets us glean from their land, people glean from their own land. They never let us go and glean.' Another put it this way: 'We are not allowed to glean. They won't let poor people glean.' This clear separation between the rich and poor ('them' and 'us') was encountered in all three villages, and was a clear expression of class conflict manifesting itself over access to resources. It was clear from the bitterness in the comments of Fonogram and Keshipur respondents that they saw gleaning as a right that was being denied.

Each of the three villages had therefore developed different regulations concerning gleaning. In Fonogram it was permitted with some restriction, in Bithigram encouraged (particularly collection of grain from rat holes) or allowed without any restriction, and in Keshipur it was not permitted. Why was it that Lodhas were able to gain almost unrestricted access to their employers' fields, while their neighbours in scheduled caste households in Keshipur, who were equally poor, could not gain similar access? The answer lies partly in intra-village dynamics and partly in state politics. The Lodhas as a separate ethnic group partly defined their own identity in opposition to the Hindu Mahatos. This ethnic coherence had a long history, founded in oppression and exploitation of the colonial and post-colonial periods, an exploitation justified in the colonial period by labelling the Lodhas as a criminal tribe. As a strong ethnic group they bargained vigorously with their employers over wage levels every transplanting and harvesting season, as well as over other rights. I will discuss this in more detail in the following chapter, looking as well at the effects of state politics, but for now I note that the Lodhas' coherence as a group gave them a significant advantage over their scheduled caste neighbours as far as access to local resources was concerned, and this advantage stretched to their access to gleaned grains.

Gleaning can be seen as an activity that expresses poor and usually landless people's symbolic claims on the land. While the poor in the study villages saw gleaning as a natural right, the owner of the land on which gleaning took place in some cases found such gathering as an infringement of ownership. There is, as I pointed out in chapter three, a direct parallel here with the case of gleaning in nineteenth-century Britain. I recall again Thompson's comments (1986: 239): 'Those petty rights of the villagers, such as gleaning, access to fuel, and the tethering of stock on the stubble, which are irrelevant to the historian of economic growth, might be of crucial importance to the subsistence of the poor.'

How important is gleaning to the poor of the Bengal region? A number of studies have commented on its occurence. Sengupta (1978: 7) has noted of landless labourer families in Birbhum District:

> Immediately after the harvest, the children of their families would rush to the fields and collect handfuls of grains that are left on the fields. Each landless family could collect 30 to 40 kg in the process. Santal (tribal) children are adept in collecting grains from rat holes where rats would store their day's collection.

Cain (1977: 219) mentions gleaning and the opening of rat holes as an activity carried out by children in a Bangladesh study village, and Howes (1985: 41) notes for his study village, also in Bangladesh, that: 'children from poor households, and the occasional widow, search for rat holes from which small quantities of grain may be retrieved.' The collection from rat holes mentioned here is probably not on the scale found in Bithigram. Siddiqui (1982: 358) also mentions children, old men and women gleaning, and collecting up to 1 kg of grain a day each. Begum (1985: 235) has noted differences in gleaning, from a four village study in Bangladesh, between Comilla District, where gleaning was the source of nearly 20 per cent of female labour earnings, and Modhupur District, where it made no contribution to female earnings; this regional difference can apparently be accounted for by differences in rice varieties grown. However, none of these studies covers restrictions placed on gleaners. Therese Blanchet has also commented that she saw hundreds of gleaners at work during the harvest in the *haor* (or semi-permanently flooded) areas of Sylhet in north-eastern Bangladesh (personal communication, 1992). These references, while far from conclusive, suggests that gleaning remains of importance to the poor throughout Bengal.[8]

I also noted in Birbhum District a pre-harvest collection of grain known locally as *jhora*. This involved the removal of unripened stands of unwanted paddy from a farmer's fields by poor people; this took place for example where there were poor quality stands that the farmer wanted to remove so that the seed stock for the following year would be kept pure. The poor person collecting the grain had to ask the farmer's permission to do so, as the collector might damage the crop surrounding that to be collected. This is another example of negotiation for mutual benefit between the landless and landowners over resources on the owner's land.[9]

---

[8] The class aspect of access to fields for gleaning purposes is also discussed in some detail by Scott (1985: 256–7) for his Malaysian study village.

[9] I am grateful to Dr M.G. Ghosh for pointing out this practice to me; he suggested that the practice might be widespread in Birbhum District.

A further point to be made concerns gleaning after HYV crops. As mentioned in chapter six, Fonogram respondents said that it was not possible to glean after the *boro* harvest. Respondents from Bithigram also said that HYV paddy grains only fell if there was hail or heavy rain. This finding is supported by Greeley (1987). Greeley and Huq (1980: 14) comment that it is the longer straw of *aman* paddy that ensures lodging and therefore more fallen grain, as opposed to the shorter statured HYVs. Given the importance of gleaned grains to the poorest, attempts to develop varieties of rice that drop less grain will, as Lipton has noted (1989: 255), 'damage nutrition among the poorest gleaners.'

Fuel

More attention has been paid to the importance of the collection of fuel by poor rural households throughout South Asia than to gleaning (for a review of literature on India, see OFI, 1991; and various other studies discussed below). I asked respondents who gathered fuel, where it was gathered from, how much was sufficient to meet household need, if there was increasing difficulty getting fuel, and if collection was seasonal.

The situation concerning fuel was the same in each of the study villages. Poorest households met nearly all of their dry season fuel requirements through CPRs. This was mainly in the form of fallen leaves and *gobar* (cow dung), but twigs, crop residues and any other burnable materials were also gathered. These materials were gathered from homesteads, fields, paths and ponds and wherever else they were available, for example in Fonogram from the graveyard that was allowed to overgrow and where everyone was permitted to collect dry wood and leaves, and from a nearby large garden owned by an absentee landlord. Gathering was done in either *juris* (bamboo baskets) or *bastas* (sacks, usually kept for storing rice). Gathering was done almost exclusively by women and children.

A common remark in the villages was that one person could gather enough leaves or *gobar* in a morning (about three hours) to last for two days. A *juri* of *gobar* (about 8–10 kg wet or 3–4 kg dry) or a *basta* of leaves (about 5 kg) was considered sufficient to last for a day's cooking. Two respondents in Fonogram whose household members did not gather fuel were unable to do so in one case because both of the members (two widows) were out all day at work, and in the other because both of the parents worked and the children were too small to gather. These households spent 1–2 rupees a day on jute sticks or low-grade coal.

All respondents noted that it was not possible to gather fuel during the rainy season, a seasonal dimension of rural poverty that does not seem to have been often noted (but see Jodha, 1986: 1174, and Briscoe, 1979). Gathering was not possible because leaves did not fall in this season, and cattle were kept in the homestead to protect both them and the paddy crop for the monsoon season. It seemed likely that the new HYV paddy crop in Fonogram would mean less cattle being grazed during the *boro* season and less cow dung available. For the monsoon period households stored *guti* (dried *gobar* made into cakes) gathered in the dry season, and also used jute sticks which were stored around the homestead or in the eaves of the roof of the house. Making of *guti* was women's work. Labourers cutting and retting jute often received jute sticks as part of their payment.

Respondents in the three villages also noted that collection of fuel, particularly twigs and wood, was becoming progressively more difficult, which meant that households were occasionally having to buy small sacks of *guti*. As one Fonogram woman put it:

> If we don't collect wood or leaves how will we cook. If there isn't any fuel we have to cut the amount we eat and buy a sack of *guti* that costs 10 or 12 rupees. We can't get any *gobar* as the cows aren't allowed out into the fields. There aren't any mango gardens in Fonogram, we have to cut wet wood and dry it. Wood is getting more and more scarce, and things will get worse.

This scarcity causes particular problems for women and children, who were the main gatherers of fuel, but also increased stress on the household as a whole, which had to divert money to buying fuel formerly gathered for free. A similar decline in the natural resource base has been noted throughout India (for an overview, see Agarwal, 1989a, b).

Despite the increasing scarcity, respondents in Fonogram or Keshipur did not mention restriction of access to fuel, as its collection was a traditional and unspoken 'right'. In Bithigram some restrictions did occur. The relative lack of local biomass surrounding Bithigram was partly compensated for by the fact that the village economy depended to a greater extent than that of Fonogram on livestock, and by the government sponsored social forestry programme which supplied resources that were formerly found in local forests. Collection of fuel had been made much easier, as the eucalyptus groves planted under the programme were within easy walking distance from the villages. However, access to these groves was not assured. The percentage of poorest households which had planted trees was lower than for the whole village (42 per cent as against 54 per cent). Eight of the nineteen poorest respondents had planted trees. As might be expected, it was two households that had not planted trees that reported restricted access to this resource. Those other villagers who had not planted but were able to gather leaves had to negotiate this use in an informal manner with their fellow villagers. A study by Nesmith (1990) of the West Bengal Government social forestry programme in three villages contiguous to those discussed here, examines in detail how the access of poor women to eucalyptus groves was restricted on a widespread basis. It was there-

126

fore not only declining resources, but also restricted access in some cases to these resources that meant the poor lost out.[10]

Comments from wealthier Mahatos in Bithigram suggested that trees were a source of village class conflict. The Mahatos claimed that the Lodhas broke branches from eucalyptus trees owned by them, and on occasion stole trees. Who committed such thefts was often not substantiated, but was bound up with the class friction that existed between Lodhas and Mahatos, and also in keeping with the Lodhas having formerly been a 'criminal' tribe. It was still possible to hear comments from Mahatos about the Lodhas such as: 'They have always been thieves and always will be.' 'Theft' in this case was closely tied to specific definitions of property rights. I also came across an example in Fonogram of a landless labourer cutting down the trees of one of the wealthiest villagers during the night in revenge for what the labourer viewed as maltreatment. After being accused and admitting his guilt the next day, the labourer was 'pardoned'.

The findings presented here as to the importance of the natural resource base to poor people for fuel is supported by evidence from studies throughout the Bengal region. Rohner and Chaki-Sirkar (1988), Warrier (1987) and Mayoux (1982) report very similar findings from Purulia, Midnapore and Birbhum Districts of West Bengal. Howes and Jabbar (1986: 23) also mention that women and children spent 2–3 hours every day gathering fuel from a four location study in Mymensingh District, Bangladesh.[11] Jodha's (1986) finding that poor households in 21 districts of seven states of dry western and southern India met 66–84 per cent of their fuel requirements from CPRs is mirrored in the material from case study villages presented here.

Jeffery et al. (1989a) have broadened the discussion of 'dung-work' by locating it within relevant feminist theoretical debates, as well as connecting it to debates concerning the 'modernization' of Indian agriculture. They make the point that because gathering of gobar and production of guti is women's work its value to the household is not recognized by either male villagers or development programmes and programmers. As they put it, in a statement that has particular relevance to rural development in Fonogram (1989: WS35):

> All the efforts of the government and industry in expanding credit, fertiliser, seed and water supply have undoubtedly commercialised important aspects of agriculture and increased the output of grain and

---

[10] Comparison can be made with Dasgupta (1987: 109), from a study of a village on the Delhi-Haryana border, which noted that because of perceived shortages, collection of dung was restricted to the owners of the cattle.

[11] See Hossain (1987), Dasgupta (1987: 106–7), and Jeffery et al. (1989a) for other regions of South Asia.

cash crops, while equally important areas of economic activity in which women's roles are more significant have been ignored.

'Wild' foods and other common property resource uses

'Wild' foods means here those foods consumed but not cultivated by poorest households. These were generally gathered from the sides of paths, ponds, swamps, and the 'jungle' or overgrown areas that were found in patches around the villages and accessible forests. They were therefore resources that could be gathered free and for the most part without restriction. I asked respondents questions about wild foods similar to those concerning fuel.

In Fonogram 23 out of the 25 respondents said that they gathered wild foods as a way of getting by in times of stress, and such foods were eaten regularly particularly during the rainy season, when agricultural employment was limited, and the price of rice was highest. Gathering was done whenever and wherever possible, a point stressed by several respondents. It was difficult for respondents to give clear estimates of the amount gathered. Some of the foods, for example *kochu* (probably *Colocasia indica*) stalks, were eaten all year.[12]

During the four months of the rainy season (approximately June to September), when agricultural employment was limited, respondents said that one person could gather or catch daily one or part combinations of the following:

○ 200 grams to 3 kg of various kinds of fish, e.g. *puti* (*Barbus sophora*), *pekal* (*Clarius batrachus*). The market price of these fish varied from 4–15 rupees per kg;

○ 200 grams of prawns (market price 30 rupees per kg);

○ 500 grams of jute leaves (not sold);

○ 1–2 kg of *kochu* stalk (not sold);

○ 5 kg of watercress (market price 2 rupees per kg);

○ 500 grams of *shojne* (a kind of horseradish, market price 8 rupees per kg).

A number of authors (Crow, 1984; Greenough, 1982; Currey, 1981; Rahaman, 1981) report the consumption of *kochu* by poor families in famine conditions in Bangladesh and Bengal. This plant was at the beginning of this century grown as a field crop (O'Malley, 1914, refers to it as *kochu* yam), but has since then been 'relegated' to a wild food.[13]

---

[12] Sources for the plant and fish types were the Samsad Bengali-English Dictionary (Calcutta: Calcutta Printing House 1980); Kelly (1985: 23); and Tindall (1983).

[13] It is ironic, given its importance in the poor person's diet, that the Bengali phrase *kochu khaowah* (or literally 'to eat *kochu*') should mean metaphorically 'to eat or get nothing', or 'to be disappointed'. Similarly *shakh pata*, also consumed by the poor, which literally means 'edible leaves', has a figurative meaning of 'extremely poor food'. *Kochu* is still marketed as a cash crop in Birbhum District of West Bengal.

There were limits to the amount of certain kinds of wild leaves that could be eaten because of their detrimental effect on the digestive system if consumed too often. Fried *neem* (*margosa*) leaves were also eaten. Figs were eaten all year round, and were now being sold in the market when previously they had only been consumed within the village. On one point all respondents agreed, that the wild foods available locally were continuing to decline as more land was put to agricultural use, and the wild foods were either marketed or more villagers tried to collect them. The following comment from a Bithigram respondent was representative: 'Ten years back all of the foods mentioned were found locally all around but now it's difficult to get them. We have to go a long way to get them now, going out in the morning and coming back at four or five in the evening.'

Within Bithigram it was poorest Lodha households that made most use of wild foods. Wild foods were also more important to them than to the poorest in the other villages, signifying a cultural difference and the traditional importance of 'minor' forest products to tribals. It took some persistence to gather information concerning these foods, as some respondents were reluctant to admit that they ate them (out of shame or embarassment (*lojja*), as one respondent put it). Table 7.1 gives the average amount of individual items that could be gathered in a day by one adult, although some, such as the monitor lizard and the tubers, could only be caught or dug up occasionally. The table also gives the monthly price of bought rice for purposes of comparison.

Table 7.1 shows that most of the foods were gathered in the pre-*aman* harvest period when seasonal factors combined to the disadvantage of the poorest, and the price of rice was highest. Wild foods therefore substituted when rice became too expensive. Let me describe in a little more detail the quantities and importance of the different kinds of foods gathered.

Fish could be caught throughout the year, in ponds or the canal. Every household except for one reported fishing, and Table 7.1 gives a representative amount caught each day. Usually half of what was caught was eaten by the household and half sold. In the monsoon crabs sat in pools of water and were easy to collect. Local Santhal women sold red ant eggs at 25 *paisa* for 3–4 grams which were used to catch fish. Fishing was done mainly by men. Molluscs were available in large quantities on the sides of ponds.

Mohua had in the past been in plentiful supply but was now difficult to find in any large quantity. As one respondent said: 'Before we used to get a lot more from the jungle, but the *jotedars* cut it all down, so not so much is available.' Liquor was produced from it. The fruit was also boiled and eaten with spices like meat. The flower was dried in the sun, broken on a *dheki*, mixed with *chira* (flattened rice) or fried rice and made into a round sweet.

Various tubers and potatoes (including some not mentioned in Table 7.1 as their genus was not identified) were dug up from the local forests by

129

Table 7.1   Wild foods gathered by Bithigram poorest households

Month[1]	Type of food	Amount gathered (kg/day)[2]	Market price (rupees/kg)	Market price of rice (rupees/kg)
Boishakh	Mollusc	1	?	3.50
Joistho	Monitor lizard	One lizard is 10	12*	4.00–4.20
	Bairon leaf[3]	0.25	–	
	Sorrel	0.25	–	
	Mohua fruit[4]	?	?	
	Mohua flower	0.20	1	
Ashad	Bairon leaf	0.25	–	4.00–4.20
	Sorrel	0.25	–	
	Sweet potato	2	3*	
	Prawns	0.5	10	
	Various fish	0.5–1	5–10	
Srabon	Bairon leaf	0.25	–	4.00–4.20
	Sorrel	0.25	–	
	Sweet potato	2	3*	
	Crab	0.3	2	
	Prawns	0.5	10	
	Various fish	0.5–1	5–10	
Bhadro	Khudro[5]	0.2–0.5	8†	4.50
	Sweet potato	2	3*	
	Crab	2	8	
Ashin	Sweet potato	2	3*	4.50
	Crab	2	2	
Kartik	Churka aloo[6]	2–3	–	3.50
	Sweet potato	2	3*	
Agrahan	Churka aloo	2–3	–	3.50
	Ikra rat	0–1		
Pous	Churka aloo	2–3		2.75
	Ikra rat	0.2–1		
Magh	Shaluk[7]	10	–	2.75
	Ikra rat	0.2–1		
	Pigeons	0.25	3	
Phalgun	Shaluk	10	–	2.75
Choitro	Shaluk	10	–	3.50

[1] The Bengali calendar runs from 15 April, i.e. Boishakh month lasts from 15 April to 14 May. The main part of the rainy season is in Ashad, Srabon and Bhadro (i.e. 15 June to 14 September).
[2] Average amount that could be gathered by one person.
[3] Not identified. Eaten boiled.
[4] Madhuka latifolia or Bassia latifilia.
[5] A gourd, possibly Coccinia cordifolia.
[6] A kind of yam, possibly Solesnostemon rotundifulius.
[7] A kind of water lily.
* Sold in the village.
† Exchanged for rice.

130

children, women and men, but were also becoming increasingly scarce. Some of these tubers were estimated to be found 3–4 feet underground, so that it took a whole day to dig them out. Most respondents carried out this kind of collection. One respondent said that when rice was very scarce equivalent weights of *khudro* and rice were exchanged between farmers and Lodhas, which meant that the Lodhas received 'much less than the market price.' Honey could also be found 'if you looked hard enough for it.'[14]

Hares, rabbits, tortoises and pigeons, cranes and other birds were also caught in the dry season. Hunting was done by men and children from most households. The monitor lizard, or *goshap* as it was known locally, the skin and meat of which was sold within Bithigram, was reported as common by O'Malley in the early 1900s (1914).[15] O'Malley also noted a variety of wildlife in western Midnapore including deer and wild pig. He suggested (ibid.) that 'aboriginal tribes' were 'destroying indiscriminately' game, including partridges, quail, geese and ducks, a remark that reveals the colonial administrator's ignorance of the importance of such game to the subsistence of local tribals.

Despite their increasing scarcity, the knowledge of location and methods of preparation of wild foods still existed, and as one man put it: 'People may deny that they go and gather these foods out of shame, but just you wait until they get hungry, they certainly know where they are and go and find them.'[16]

In Keshipur much less use was made of wild foods by poorest households. The main wild foods eaten were various kinds of fish, which were caught mainly in the rainy season, along with crabs and prawns. *Noteh shakh* (a kind of spinach) was also gathered locally.

Keshipur respondents did make use of other CPRs. In seven of the sixteen respondent households women went to the local forests to gather *sal* (*Shorea robusta*) leaves for platemaking. These women said that they had to avoid the Forest Department guards to collect the leaves, but continued to go regularly to the forests. The main period when it was possible to collect the leaves was in the spring. The leaves were gathered, carried home, dried, and sewn together with small twigs from the *neem* (*margosa*)

---

[14] *Churka aloo* has been described as a totemic object for the Lodhas (Bhowmick 1963: 53).

[15] *Go* is the local colloquial term for cow, and *shap* means snake. The *goshap* apparently sucked the milk of cows, hence its name. This lizard is also hunted by the Hill Pandarams of South India (Morris, 1982: 76) and by nomadic groups in Maharashtra (Malhotra and Gadgil, 1988: 397).

[16] Davis (1983: 56) and Bhowmick (1963: 30–1) mention the importance of CPRs to the Lodhas. Bhowmick (1963: 41) also comments that access to farmers' fields by Lodhas for fishing was restricted; such restrictions were not found in Bithigram.

131

tree. These plates were sold in the market by the women themselves (who had to walk the 10 km there and back) on Sundays. For about 3–4 days work up to 10 rupees could be earned. The following comments from a female respondent were representative:

> I go to get *sal* leaves from eight to three. I can only get a few leaves – do you think there are any leaves left in the forest? Before I could go and gather leaves all day long. We used to make plates with many more leaves than we can now. I go during the week, when I can, and sell the leaves on Sunday. I make about 6–8 rupees a week doing this, women who are a bit younger make a bit more.

This access by women from the Keshipur households can be contrasted to a *lack* of similar access by women from Lodha households from Bithigram. Women from Lodha households made it clear that they did not go to gather *sal* leaves as the Forest Department guards would beat them if they tried to do so. This lack of access was linked to two factors. The first was that tribals were often perceived by the Forest Department as destroyers of the forest, and as the Lodha's ethnic identity was obvious from their appearance it is probable that the forest guards not only stopped them entering the forest but also harassed them if they tried to do so. Secondly, the label with which the Lodhas had been branded by the colonial authorities – a criminal tribe – had remained until the present day, which meant that they remained a target for present day authorities, despite the efforts of the West Bengal government.[17] The ethnic coherence noted above in relation to access to farmers' land for gleaning was of little use outside of the village when individual Lodha women were faced with threats from local forests guards.

Not mentioned above but used or collected in all three villages were other free resources to which the poor customarily had access. These included fruit which fell from trees (especially mangoes in the summer, plums, and tamarind); these were collected in particular by children.[18] Some of this fruit, for example figs, was now being sold in the local markets. In Fonogram children from poorest households also collected snails to feed to poultry. Date palm leaves were left on the side of ponds with most of the leaf submerged, and the snails crawling onto the leaves could be gathered easily. Snails were also found all over the paddy fields after the monsoon rains. Of particular importance to poorest households was their ability to graze their livestock either on fallow fields, on the *aul* dividing fields, or in ditches and by the sides of ponds, for six months of the year (the same practice as 'tethering of stock on the stubble' to which

---

[17] Harassment and exploitation of tribals by forest guards has been noted throughout India (Agarwal, 1989b: WS57; Morris, 1982).

[18] Sengupta (1978: 9) describes 'landless families living on jackfruit or mango' in Malda and Coochbehar Districts of West Bengal.

Thompson refers in the quote above). One Fonogram household member also said that in the rainy season up to 30 kg of grass could be collected from *auls*. In the Midnapore villages where livestock were more important to the village economies, much of the *danga* or higher infertile land was used for grazing, some of it all year round.[19]

The value of CPRs to the poor

It has been demonstrated that in contemporary West Bengal claims on 'common' land and customary usages are important to the subsistence of the poor. How much are these claims and usages worth in monetary terms? Lodha respondents in Bithigram estimated that they gained the equivalent of 400 rupees a month from all CPR activities; they included in this figure the opportunity cost involved in gathering CPRs, as well as the market value of the CPRs themselves. Using this calculation, CPR activities provided more income per year for them than the six months' agricultural wage labour they earned in an average year. A more conservative estimate of the value of CPRs from across the three villages, excluding the opportunity cost, would be 50–100 rupees worth of rice gleaned a year, 1 rupee a day worth of fuel gathered, and 1–2 rupees of wild food gathered a day. This gives a figure of between 780 and 1195 rupees a year. Given that on average total household income from all formal sources (including market transactions) for a respondent household was some 4, 000 rupees a year, collection of CPRs was worth between approximately 19 per cent and 29 per cent of the household's income. This accords roughly with Jodha's survcy from western and central India which concluded (1990: A66): 'CPR products collection is an important source of employment and income, especially during the period when other opportunities are non-existent. Furthermore, CPR income . . . accounts for 14 to 23 per cent of household income from all other sources in the study villages'. It is unfortunate, given this importance of CPRs to the poor in West Bengal, that the literature on CPRs has largely ignored the State.

Common property resources and policy

It is possible to draw three general conclusions from the data presented above. First, that, despite the lack of local 'common land' as found in other parts of India, CPRs are vital to the subsistence of poorest households and that CPR activities take up a substantial part of respondents', and particularly children and women's, time. An informal economy exists that

---

[19] Much of the literature on gathering of wild foods deals with Africa, and concerns famine situations. For a list of famine foods, see Watts (1983: 43–23), and for a more detailed discussion in Ethiopia, Rahmato (1988: 8–10). For a review of other literature on India and Africa which shows that such gathering is widespread, see Longhurst (1986).

is largely invisible to economists and planners, but vital from the perspective of the poor. It is perhaps because it is mainly the work of women and important to the poor that CPR use appears to have been largely ignored by policymakers who are generally out of touch with the perspective of such groups.

Second, the most important CPRs for the poor in the densely-populated deltaic regions of West Bengal and Bangladesh are not the grazing lands or forests so important in other parts of India but plants, fuel, fish and gleaned grains, even though grazing lands and forests remain more important in semi-lateritic Midnapore than in north 24 Parganas. Access to CPRs is decreasing in both of the study regions because of increasing agricultural development, commoditization of formerly open access natural resources, and increases in the numbers dependent on CPRs. The situation in the study regions would appear to fit within a wider pattern throughout India. The declining access to CPRs in West Bengal is likely to have a grave effect on the quality of life of the poor. Protecting the access of the poor to the 'invisible' CPRs in West Bengal may prove more difficult than protecting access to the more visible grazing lands in other parts of India.

Third, class conflict over CPR access has been largely ignored, mainly because, once again, the perspective of the poor is usually not taken into account when CPRs are discussed. Conflict over this access takes its place in the overall class friction, struggle or bargaining between poor and rich over the distribution of village resources and village ideology. From the above analysis it is possible to divide CPR access in West Bengal into two types; firstly CPRs such as fuel or wild foods that are at present gathered for the most part without restrictions but on which restrictions are likely in the future because of increasing scarcity and commoditization; and secondly CPRs such as gleaned grains and minor forest products the access of certain groups to which is presently restricted, and on which restrictions are likely to increase as well. Further agricultural development and commoditization of the economy, making further 'encroachment' into what the poor see as common rights, is also likely to increase class conflict over access to CPRs in West Bengal.

The discussion above also shows that an analysis of CPR use based on availability or type may be simplistic. For example, in the two adjacent villages of Bithigram and Keshipur one group of the poorest were enthusiastic gleaners and the others were not permitted access to post-harvest fields, while the same two groups faced an opposite situation when it came to the collection of *sal* leaves. Respondents in each of the villages were angry that their access to these resources was restricted by the rich or the government, and declining in front of their eyes. Their anger was an expression of the poorest to their traditional 'right' to such free produce, and part of the general conflict between rich and poor. Access to CPRs not only contributed substantially to household subsistence, but also meant less

134

dependence on the rich for loans or other kinds of support. The combination of class and gender structures meant that it was poorest women who faced restrictions and antagonism while trying to glean or collect *sal* leaves, and these petty restrictions were integral to their experience of poverty and lack of power.

Could government agencies or NGOs intervene to support the poor in their use of CPRs in West Bengal or similar ecological regions to those covered in the fieldwork? Given the problems with making land reform work and the complex land operational patterns in the region, it is difficult to envisage how local government institutions could intervene to support the poor in their efforts to gain access to local CPRs. But it is possible to draw some select conclusions for policy purposes.[20]

1. The expansion of HYV crops may adversely affect the access of the poor to CPRs, because land that was formerly 'common' and fallow for one season is now double cropped, and because HYV paddy provides little grain for gleaning.

2. Clear rights concerning access to forests and trees if carefully planned will assist the poor in income generating and food gathering activities, although in much of Bengal there remains little forest land. It is of note that the Government of West Bengal has attempted such a policy, which has included the setting up of local Forest Project Committees (FPCs). This programme covers about 240,000 hectares of land, or about one-quarter of forest land in West Bengal, primarily in the lateritic areas to the west of the state. About 1,800 FPCs have been organized to date (Roy, 1992). The Forest Department has offered 'to provide preferential rights to certain tracts of degraded forests in return for villagers taking responsibility for their protection.' (OFI, 1991: 46). This programme awaits a detailed evaluation, but appears to have achieved some success in protecting and providing clear access to forests (see Roy, 1992). However, it is easier to develop programmes where there is a clear geographical resource to be covered, which is not the case with many CPRs in West Bengal.

3. In areas such as north 24 Parganas there is little direct scope for public intervention to support poor people's uses of CPRs on private land. However, research on wild foods could improve varieties that are important to the poor (Chambers, 1989). If scientists have come up with HYV paddy and wheat, why not HYV *kochu*, or other wild foods, as well?

---

[20] These conclusions will not deal with social or community forestry programmes which have been evaluated in detail elsewhere for the Bengal region (see Nesmith, 1990; Singh and Bhattacharjee, 1991; White, 1991). These programmes are for the most part based on external interventions rather than strategies that the poor have customarily used, which is the focus here.

4. The most important point about policy to be made here comes from the comparison between the ability of the poorest in Bithigram and Keshipur to gain access to farmers' land for purposes of gleaning. The conclusion that can be drawn from this is that supporting the poor in their attempts to gain what they see as customary rights may be the most effective rural development initiative outsiders can undertake. I deal with this point again in the next chapter.

Poorest people and food

The rich and well-fed have written extensively about the eating habits of the poor, as evidenced in chapter two. Latterly, hunger and food have become a near obsession for development researchers, and the complex and esoteric discussions of how much the poor eat and how much of that food they turn into energy is closely related to the need of the academic community to set a poverty line. Again, the consequences of objectifying the poor by turning them into a set of nutritional statistics were discussed in chapter two. On the other hand, very little research has been done that explores poor people's perceptions of food. The aim of my questions relating to food was to find out poor people's priorities concerning food, and how poorest people coped with food shortages. I asked respondents what foods filled their stomach most when they were hungry; which types of food were eaten in times of stress; who decided on allocation of food and who went hungry if there were inadequate supplies; the amount of food needed by the household in a day, and the amount of shortfall.

It was not always easy to discuss food. Questions about the amount people ate and shortfalls of food were being asked to people who were regularly hungry. Some respondents made it clear what they thought about such questions, for example by using the interrogative form when replying, showing a mock contempt of the questioner, a common use in Bengali. In addition, estimates below of food consumption should be taken as such. As one man put it: 'We don't measure how much food goes into our stomachs.'

Poor people bought food mainly from the local shops, and from the local markets. Food had to be bought every day, as the cash was not available to buy in stocks at cheaper prices. Little of respondents' food requirements came from ration shops. Ration rice, which was about 20 *paisa* cheaper than rice bought locally with cash, was taken by all except three Fonogram respondents when it was available, but the ration shop was open only once a week, the supplies erratic and the quality of the rice very bad. In Bithigram rice was available but only two households took it, and in Keshipur it was not available. Ten Keshipur respondents and 14 Bithigram respondents said they took ration sugar (at 100 grams per household member) on a regular basis. All other food had to be bought on the open market, although some wages were still paid in grain in the Midnapore villages.

136

Consumption and its regulation

In reply to questions about the amount of food needed by the household, most respondents referred to the shortfalls of the particular day or week in which the interview was conducted. As the interviews took place during the post-harvest period, shortfalls were lower than at other leaner times of year (although the poor *aman* harvests in Fonogram meant more than usual hardship). Respondents were also asked to estimate their daily expenditure on food.

A representative daily shopping bill, from a Bithigram household with two adults and two children under six, is given below. This shows the amount the household members estimated they would need to suffice for one day, and fits closely with other estimates, when adjusted for household size.

Item	Amount	Price (rupees)
Rice	2 kg	6.50
Potatoes	1 kg	1.40
Oil	50 g	1.20
Chillies	25 g	1.00
Lentils	100 g	1.00
Spices		1.50
Mustard oil		.50
Tea leaves		.40
Pan		1.00
Kohni		.20
Salt		.20
Vegetables		1.00
Total		15.90

If both parents worked, the woman earned eight rupees a day and the man ten rupees, so that they would have enough to meet their daily needs. However, employment was available for only half the year at most, so they and other respondents had to resort to cuts in consumption and supplementing their diet by wild foods. It was not a surprise to hear that this household, along with fifty-six of the other fifty-nine households replying, spent more or less all their daily income on food on a regular basis. Only three households out of sixty said that they were getting an adequate amount of food. For the others, their estimated shortfall in grain ranged from 10 per cent to 33 per cent, with an average in Fonogram of some 25 per cent. These findings therefore fit in with a general nutritional pattern that has shown that poorest people spend 80 per cent or more of their income on food but still only meet 80 per cent of their nutritional requirements (Lipton, 1983a: 35). The implications of this for nutritional research are discussed below.

137

In this situation of regular shortfall respondents had little choice but to regulate food consumption, to borrow food from neighbours or to take loans to buy food, often from the local grocer shops. The latter they did circumspectly, as taking a food loan meant paying a higher price than if goods were purchased with cash, a psychological burden concerning repayment, and dependency on the shopkeeper.

Even though possible action concerning consumption was severely circumscribed, respondents did have strategies by which they tried to alleviate the often desperate situation in which they found themselves. One tactic which saved energy was for household members to stay at home and fast while sleeping or lying down (noted also by Lipton, 1983a; and by Hartmann and Boyce, 1983 and Harari and Garcia-Bouza, 1982, for poor households in Bangladesh and India). Respondents also decided to spread their hunger rather than meet immediate needs. As Fonogram respondents put it when describing how they got by after the 1986–7 floods: 'We made one meal stretch into two.' or: 'We ate one day and fasted the next.'[21] That this was a conscious decision was clear from the response to the question of what respondents would do if they had a little more money. Thirty-nine (out of forty-three who replied) said they would buy rice. Of these, eight of the nineteen respondents in Fonogram volunteered the information that they would buy rice, but this would not be eaten on the day it was bought but rather kept for a future date. Respondents were therefore willing to live with a degree of hunger in order to safeguard themselves against future problems, and this became more apparent when asking about strategies for retaining or buying assets (see below).[22] Such cuts in consumption were therefore attempts to stave off future hunger and having to take loans from shopkeepers or employers, which would increase dependency. However much they might like it, respondents were not spending extra income irresponsibly in the purchase of fish!

Cuts in consumption did not fall equally on all members of the household. Intra-household distribution of food is a controversial subject (see Harriss, 1990a, b; Agarwal, 1989b; Agarwal, 1986; Wheeler and Abdullah, 1988). In the three study villages it was clear that it was adult females, who were usually both mother and cook, who ate last (and by proxy, least) in every respondent household, and this tied in to many women's internalizing of the norms of the patriarchal system that operated in the villages.

---

[21] Such regulation of consumption has been widely noted in South Asia. See Van Schendel, 1989: 163; Jansen, 1989: 3; Dreze, 1988a: 7980; Cecelski, 1987: 46; Caldwell, et al., 1986: 688; Jodha, 1978: A38–39; 1975: 1620, fn 15. Dreze (1988a) notes that richer households may also use this strategy during periods of hardship.

[22] For similar findings from Howrah District in West Bengal, see Bharati and Basu (1988: 423).

However, access to food is only one indicator of deprivation, and this apparent acceptance of patriarchal norms in the matter of food allocation was in contrast to other areas of life where some women protested about their husband's actions. For example, responses concerning control of money from the thirteen women interviewed on their own where the subject was relevant (that is, excluding seventeen women who were widowed or no longer married), made it clear that wives did not accept their husbands' complete control over money; in six cases women complained that their husbands took the money they had earned for their own use or said that they were unable to spend money without their husband's permission.

There was also one case of regular violence by a man against his wife, particularly when the man had been drinking, which his wife complained bitterly about (and possibly other cases I was not told about).

Regulation of consumption may therefore be a strategy that harms some members of the household more than others.[23] Households as a whole, however, did get by making one meal stretch into two, and by fasting and tolerating a degree of hunger. They also used some other strategies to stave off hunger, described in the next section.

Food preparation and food types
During the discussions on what fills the stomach most when hunger comes, respondents in all three villages mentioned different types of food preparation that helped to stave off hunger. There was common agreement that it was only rice, the staple grain, that would 'make the stomach happy'. 'The stomach won't understand unless it gets rice', as one respondent put it. When a sufficient quantity of rice was not available, three respondents in Fonogram and five in Bithigram said that they would take the water left over from boiling rice (*bhater phen*), which would fill the stomach and was usually fed to livestock.[24] Several respondents in Fonogram also said that they ate broken grains of rice known as *khud*.[25] When a 40 kg sack of rice was shaken or sieved, about 1 kg of *khud* would fall out. This was sold only within the village and between women; one male respondent said contemptuously that it was sold by the wives of rich farmers to save up money

---

[23] Wheeler and Abdullah (1988) have shown, however, that the perception of all villagers in a Bangladesh village that women need less food may not translate into actual discrimination.

[24] Greenough (1982: 226, 233) notes that beggars during the Bengal famine in 1943 went from house to house asking for *phen*, and connects this to the cultural significance of rice in Bengali culture, as *phen* contains little of nutritional value; it may also have been connected to the fact that *phen* appears to stave off hunger pains. This tactic of drinking *phen* was also used by a poor rural family in Korea during the Korean war (Yun Heung-gil 1989: 79).

[25] *Khud* literally means a fragment or grain of rice. *Khudkura*, which literally means huskings and particles of rice, figuratively means very humble or bad food.

139

to buy jewellery. *Khud* cost about half of the market price of rice; it could be boiled, and fried with oil and salt and alleviated hunger pangs. One Fonogram respondent also said that when hunger was severe or extreme they ate parts of the chaff left over after the threshing of paddy.

If money fell short for the day's food requirements, most households opted for purchasing rice before anything else. Among the rice varieties, 'fatter' ones were preferred as these 'gave more energy'. However, a substantial minority (ten out of twenty-five respondents in Fonogram and eight out of nineteen in Bithigram) said that they would buy 500 grams of flour and make *gola routi*; this was flour mixed with water and fried like an omelette, which was said to be more filling than *chapati*. It was interesting to find *gola routi* eaten both by Muslims in Fonogram and Lodhas in Bithigram (no Keshipur respondents reported eating it), although I have found no other references to its consumption in the literature on village Bengal.

Fifty-two of the sixty respondents also reported taking tea with salt in it as flavouring, as a means of staving off hunger. The reason for this was that for most of the poorest households sugar or *gur* were not available; salt was cheaper, as one Fonogram respondent said: 'You can't ask your neighbours for sugar or *gur*, but they will let you have salt.'

Respondents said that they resorted on a regular basis to appetite suppressants (for the widespread use of these in developing countries, see Leakey, 1986). In Fonogram respondents, both female and male, regularly took *pan* (betel leaf), which was also eaten by other villagers, as well as smoking *bidi* (cheroot). Bithigram and Fonogram respondents also bought *pan*, as well as cheaper forms of tobacco known as *khohoni* and *dokta*, which were all also taken by women and men. One man in Bithigram expressed the importance of such substances: 'If we didn't take *pan* we would die of hunger.'[26]

Food and self respect

The quote from Dasgupta in chapter four as to the relative importance of food and honour for tribals during the 1886 famine in Midnapore would suggest that self respect has been important to the poor for some time, even during times of extreme hardship. Chambers (1988: 16) has suggested that self respect has become increasingly important for poor people in India. As part of my attempt to find out which were the areas that poor

---

[26] Male respondents also drank village liquor, from the date palm or other trees. It was a subject of some amusement when I asked about it in the villages, and no attempt was made to investigate the quantity taken or the amount spent on liquor.

people themselves prioritized, I asked respondents about the relative importance to them of food and self respect.[27]

Across the three villages, of the fifty-eight respondents replying, forty-nine said that they valued self respect more than food. As one Fonogram respondent succinctly and typically replied: 'If I don't have self respect, will food go into the stomach?' Bithigram and Keshipur respondents said much the same; for example one man in Bithigram replied: 'Even if there isn't any food in the house, if I can speak with other people in the village it is better as then I have self respect.' Of the other nine respondents, six said that they needed food more, and three that they needed both equally. Of the latter, one Fonogram woman said: 'If I don't have food what use is self respect. But if I have food and people insult me, that is no good either. I need both.'

The wider implications of these replies and the importance of social status for the poor will be discussed in the next chapter. Limiting the discussion here to the relation between food and self respect, the preference of most of the poorest respondents suggests that the concentration on nutritional minima by poverty measurers misses poor people's experience of poverty, which meant that, despite their regular hunger, most poorest people in the study villages felt it was more important to be treated with respect than gratify immediate needs.

While the information on poor people's strategies for staving off hunger adds to the general argument of this book that poor people are capable and plan for the future, there would appear to be little scope for policy interventions based on such short-term strategies. Action of the poor in this area is one of the most circumscribed by the socio-economic nexus in which they find themselves. State intervention, such as the effective establishment of public distribution ration shops as part of a wider nutritional intervention programme including school lunch programmes, feeding programmes at nurseries for infants and pregnant and lactating women, has been successful in Kerala in terms of alleviating undernutrition (Franke and Chasin, 1991; Dreze and Sen, 1989). But such interventions necessitate both political will on the part of the government as well as its control over local political institutions. Such a situation does not appear to exist at present in West Bengal.

The findings that self respect was more important to the poor than food, and that poor people can give reliable estimates as to their dietary intake and shortfall has implications for future nutritional research. First, it must certainly be worthwhile consulting poor people concerning food intake, as subjects rather than objects of nutritional surveys, rather than just carrying out anthropometric or food intake surveys, which now seems to be the

---

[27] The actual phrasing of the question was 'Which do you value more, food or self respect?' (*Aponi konta moolaban mone koren, khabar na saman?*).

141

norm. Second, surveys that focus exclusively on nutrition are likely to receive an extremely narrow picture of what hunger is and means, and any policy prescriptions will be equally narrow.

As I mentioned earlier, many studies have been carried out by the well-fed on the hungry. What do the hungry think of the eating habits of the well-fed? In the interviews such views came up. Here are two examples. When being asked about which foods filled the stomach most, Hamedchha, my assistant from Fonogram, said that he thought those doing manual labour needed to eat a fatter grain than *babus* (gentlemen) who sit in offices all day (wearing wristwatches and trousers) and prefer thinner varieties of rice. A similarly ironic comment was made when asking Murjina, a widow from Fonogram, how she managed to stay so healthy when regularly missing out on meals. We had been discussing poverty and wealth at some length. Murjina began talking, mimicking the rich and poor people she described:

> When rich people sit down to eat, they have a big plate in front of them and five or six smaller dishes around it with different types of food in them, full of meat, fish and vegetables. They take a little bit from one dish and say 'Oh, that's too spicy', then a little bit from another dish and say 'Oh, that's too sweet.' Complaining like this, they don't end up eating very much. But when a poor person sits down to eat, they just eat whatever is put in front of them as quickly as they can, even if it a whole plate of jungle greens, and get by in that way.

Murjina was a good mimic of the dainty eating habits of the rich, and this type of mimicry is an example of her resistance to her deprivation, and I will discuss the implications of this and give other examples in the next chapter. Looking at eating habits from the perspectives of Murjina and Hamedchha, consumption relates closely to power relations and eating habits are one aspect of class conflict. Studies that focus exclusively poor people's eating habits will continue to inform outsiders about poor people's weaknesses, missing both poor people's attempts to deal with food shortages as well as the social nexus into which hunger fits as an integral part.

Sharerearing of livestock

This section will analyse a system of rearing of livestock by which the poorest in Fonogram gained livestock. This system is of considerable interest because livestock were crucial assets for the poorest, as they could be sold in times of crisis or need, and the income from such sales could mean, literally, the difference between life or death for household members. I should note at the beginning of this section that some of the following will be conjectural and preliminary, and some of the conclusions I draw are tentative. I make these disclaimers because I am dealing with a subject that has been commented on previously only in passing, even though it would appear to be of great importance to the poor, and the widespread nature of this system and its existence in different places and across cultures does not appear to have been previously recognized. For example, I draw together references to thirty separate studies below, in something akin to detective work; but many of these references do no more than mention sharerearing in passing or footnotes. Sharerearing might therefore be one of a number of unrecognized and semi-discovered systems of village resource redistribution which exist and from which the poor gain benefit.

Livestock ownership in the study villages

Before discussing the sharerearing system I will introduce the section with an analysis of livestock use and ownership in the three study villages. Second to land, livestock was the most important source of income from household resources in all three study villages.[28] Livestock were grazed on fallow land, or fed with gathered grass or other CPRs, and hence for the poor rearing of livestock was mainly free. Livestock were looked after by children and women, and it was a common sight to see children driving out cows or goats to the fields in the morning as they went to gather fuel, and bringing the animals back at sunset, on their heads baskets filled with cow dung or crop waste to be used for fuel. Animals were also frequently the subject of dispute, with cows and goats eating standing crops and ducks and chickens wandering into courtyards and eating grain or disturbing women trying to cook.

Table 7.2 gives the number of adult plough animals, milk cows and goats owned in the villages.[29]

Table 7.2   Number of livestock owned in the case study villages, 1988–9[1]

Village	Type of animal		
	Milk cows	Plough animals	Goats
Fonogram	45 (0.3)	76 (0.5)	70 (0.5)
Bithigram	130 (1.3)	115 (1.2)	50 (0.5)
Keshipur	99 (1.7)	69 (1.2)	50 (0.9)

[1] Figures in brackets give the number of livestock per village household.

[28] For example, a pair of plough animals if hired out provided a household with about 1,600 rupees a year, while milk cows provided a profit of about 500 rupees a year. By comparison, the profit from a *bigha* of paddy land for the *boro* season in Fonogram was about 800 rupees.

[29] Bithigram and Keshipur villagers owned buffaloes and sheep, but these have not been included in the table as they were not kept in Fonogram. The value of animals owned differed depending on age and quality, but most plough cows were valued in the range of 750–1,000 rupees, milk cows in the range of 300–600 rupees, and goats in the range of 100–150 rupees. The price estimated by respondents did not vary greatly between the villages.

The table shows the greater importance of cattle in the Midnapore villages, reflecting the need to diversify sources of income because of the less fertile nature of land operated, as well as the large amount of *danga* grazing land available locally. Table 7.3 shows distribution of livestock across the four income groups for the three villages, compared to land operated.

Table 7.3 Ownership of livestock and operation of land by income group in the three study villages, 1988–9 (percentages)

Village					
			Income group		
	1	2	3	4	Total
Fonogram					
Milk cow	13	31	27	29	100
Plough animals	11	20	45	24	100
Goat	28	44	17	11	100
Land operated	7	15	33	45	100
Bithigram					
Milk cows	2	19	18	61	100
Plough animals	3	34	23	40	100
Goat	10	48	10	32	100
Land operated	8	26	22	44	100
Keshipur					
Milk cow	–	21	5	74	100
Plough animals	3	19	19	59	100
Goat	6	28	16	50	100
Land operated	11	25	19	45	100

Table 7.3 shows that, as with land, it is the higher income groups that control livestock, although livestock is more equally distributed among income groups in Fonogram than operated land, and a higher percentage of goats in Fonogram and Bithigram are owned by the two lower income groups, which shows that the poor have greater access to small livestock. Also, higher percentages of livestock as compared to land operated were found in income group 1 in Fonogram.[30]

Sharerearing of livestock
While enquiring about ownership and sale of livestock, poorest respondents in Fonogram told me about a system known locally as *poussani* (meaning to rear), which involved the sharerearing of animals.[31] Cows, goats,

---

[30] I have not included in the analysis of ownership of livestock ducks and chickens, although poorest respondents persistently raised fowl as a way of increasing their resource base, even though the mortality rate of fowl was very high.
[31] See opposite.

ducks or chickens could be taken on loan in this fashion. The most common arrangement was similar to some sharecropping arrangements. The sharerearing-in or borrowing household would rear the animal, taking responsibility for feeding it. In the case of a female, after the animal had given birth twice the rearing-in household kept the second born and returned the mother and first born. In the case of a male animal the proceeds after sale would be divided equally between rearer and owner. In the case of fowl, eggs were shared equally between the two parties. Some variations of the system also operated, but these did not vary differently from the description above.

Subsequently, I asked each household in Fonogram whether they were involved in sharerearing. In Fonogram in 1988–9, 26 households (some 18 per cent of village households, a similar figure to those sharecropping land) were involved in the *poussani* system. In all there was a total of 34 cases of rearing-in of animals (with six households rearing-in more than one animal from different parties). The intra-village income group distribution of sharerearing is shown in Table 7.4.

Table 7.4 Income group distribution of instances of sharerearing, Fonogram 1988–9

Income group	Giver of animal				
	1	2	3	4	Total
1	4	2	3	5	14
2	1	–	–	3	4
3	1	–	–	–	1
4	2	–	–	1	3
Total	8	2	3	9	22

Two trends can be located in the table concerning exchanges within the village. The first is that the general direction of rearing was from a higher to a lower income group, or between members of the same income group (about 80 per cent of all transactions). The second was that, while income group 4 households lent out the most animals, it was income group 1 households who were most involved in this system, loaning four animals to

---

[31] Such a system is officially known as 'agistment'. The Oxford English Dictionary gives agistment as: 'To take in livestock to remain and feed, at a certain rate.' First usage of the word in Britain was in 1224, which suggests that agistment has a long history. For example, Thomas Blount's Law Dictionary of 1691 gives the following definition: 'This word Agist is also used for the taking in of other Men's Cattle into Any Man's Ground at a certain Rate per Week.' Cruz de Carvalho (1974: 205) notes that agistment arrangements in Angola resemble those of Portuguese customary law.

other groups, receiving ten animals from other groups, and transferring a further four animals within their own group.

Apart from the twenty-two intra-village cases, there were another twelve cases of rearing-in. Eight of these involved receipt of animals from absentee landlords or others outside the village, and the other four involved rearing-in of animals from a close relative outside the village. Eight of the households rearing-in from outside the village were from income group 1, and three from income group 2.

Loaning and borrowing of livestock within the village met a variety of purposes and needs. The numerically most significant transfer was from income group 4 households and absentee landlords to income group 1 households (13 out of a total of 34 intra- and extra-village transactions), and in total income group 1 households reared in 65 per cent of all livestock borrowed. These transactions followed closely the organization of village power structures. Lending livestock was also used as a means of supporting poorer relatives, and seven of all the transactions involved close relatives. There were also four transactions within income group 1, where poorer households were either unable to raise the livestock themselves or gave livestock to other poorer households to help them out. Discussion with respondents made it clear that it was women who organized *poussani*, and it was their role, along with children, to rear the animals. This system can be seen to parallel the system of sharecropping, organized by men. Like sharecropping, it was a system negotiated by two unequal partners where both gained, if unequally, from the transaction. That rearing of livestock is women's work is perhaps another reason why the *poussani* system has received little systematic attention.

The animals reared were 10 cows, 31 goats and 11 chickens. Income group 1 households reared-in a large proportion of these for – example, five milk cows, 18 goats and one plough animal, which amounted to some 38 per cent of milk cows and 64 per cent of goats owned by income group 1 households. In contrast, the animals borrowed by the other income groups made up a much smaller proportion of their total animal holding. The point to be reiterated is that the sharerearing system was much more important to poorest households than to any other Fonogram households.

Sharerearing by poorest Fonogram households
When interviewing the Fonogram poorest households, I discussed share-rearing arrangements and transactions with them in some detail. Of the 22 poorest respondents asked about sharerearing, 20 had livestock, the other two having insufficient space to keep animals. Of these 20, seven had borrowed livestock in 1986–7, and five others had sharereared-in in the previous 2–3 years. Two other households wanted to sharerear but could not because of unavailability of animals.

146

Sharerearing arrangements could be quite complex. For example, one of the poorest Fonogram villagers, Nurjahan, who was an elderly widow, had lent out a milk cow to Rupajan, who lived in one of the richest households in the village, as she was unable to look after it herself because she went out to work every day. At the same time, Nurjahan's daughter-in-law, who lived in the adjacent house to her, had taken a goat from Rupajan's sister-in-law.[32] There was a long-standing connection in terms of livestock between these two sets of households; Nurjahan had a few years before sold the offspring of a cow reared-in from a further household to Rupajan, in order to raise money to pay for medical expenses.

For another poorest widow, sharerearing was an important source of income. She sharereared-out a milk cow to another poorest woman, and a goat to an income group 4 household. At the same time she sharereared-in a goat from the poorest person in the village (another elderly woman who was ill) and a chicken from one of the richest households. These examples show the complex web of relations that governed this enterprise, as well as the enterprise that the poorest showed in fuelling the system to gain assets for themselves.

It appeared from my discussion with poorest respondents that, among other things, working the *poussani* system was a further way in which the poor attempted to redistribute resources within the village, a kind of unspoken but continuously renegotiated claim on property that was in the hands of their richer neighbours. I interpret this as a kind of symbolic claim on livestock, similar to the way in which gleaning is a claim on the land. Only more research into this neglected subject can ascertain this with clarity, but *poussani* did appear to be part of the overall process of negotiation, friction and struggle between poor and rich. Here are some examples of what I am describing.

One poorest respondent (a man, employed as a petty trader), whose household sold the offspring of one sharereared goat after the 1986–7 flood in Fonogram to raise money for food, talked generally about livestock and sharerearing:

We have taken *poussani* goats in the past from B. (an absentee landlord) but they died. If the goats or cows go into anyone else's property it causes a lot of problems. Five to seven years back there was more *poussani*, but people don't give animals now because of spite and jealousy (*hingsha*). Rich people won't even sharecrop out their land, they would rather let it lay fallow than give it out to the poor.

---

[32] This paralleled the sharecropping system where some households both hired-in and hired-out land.

This picture of increasing scarcity of available livestock was echoed by other respondents, as was the animosity towards the rich (see the next chapter). One man put the increasing scarcity down to the increase in the price of milk which made people reluctant to rear out cows. Other respondents said that the rich were not giving out animals, and therefore the poor had to do so. As one woman put it: 'Rich people don't give animals for sharerearing – if poor people have to give, do you think rich people are giving?' It was implicit here, and in the quote above, that the poor saw it as their right to borrow livestock from the rich, and that if the poor wanted to rear animals from the rich they would have to be forceful in demanding this right. The failure of the rich to provide animals was an area of complaint for the poor, complaints which they presumably hoped would spur their richer neighbours to greater generosity.

Another more subtle example of this process comes from a description of her experience of sharerearing by another poorest widow, Sundari, a maid-servant who lived with her relative Raila who followed the same occupation. Sundari described her and Raila's ventures into sharerearing as follows:

> I've taken a *poussani* bullock from Lokibabu (her employer), when it is bigger we will get half and Loki will get half. We've also taken some hens from Raila's daughter who is married outside the village – they will have to be returned. If the hens lay eggs no-one will touch them even though we are both out all day, because we are poor people. We used to have a cow that died from dehydration – I used to cry all the time about that, then Loki's mother told me to take the cow we've got now. I also used to have a *poussani* goat from the shop-keeper, but that died as well.

On the one hand, this quote can be taken as describing a straightforward set of transactions between employer and employee, where the employer patronisingly gives his poor employee livestock under *poussani*. But perhaps there is also an element of complaint in Sundari's comment that she used to 'cry all the time' until she received another cow. In this sense, her comments fit with the other demands that servants make on their masters and mistresses – for higher wages, time off, or clothes. I read Sundari's complaint, and the comments of the other poorest villagers about *poussani*, as examples of demands made on the rich by the poor.

Was the indigenous system more successful at getting livestock to the poorest than the government-sponsored IRDP?

In the Midnapore villages *poussani* rarely took place, and as will be seen, this makes them somewhat unusual. The *panchayat* chairman told me that such arrangements had taken place up until about the early 1980s, but now no-one wanted to give out animals as they were in shorter supply than previously, although a few people still gave goats.[33] In Bithigram and Keshipur cattle were looked after on a different basis, known as *chorano*, which involved their grazing by a cow boy who took the livestock out for the day and returned them to their owners at night. Each cow boy took about 20 animals, and was paid for the number of animals tended, usually either 30 kg of paddy per cow a year, or seven rupees a cow per month.

I hypothesize here that the absence of the *poussani* system possibly accounts for the lower percentage of livestock owned by income group 1 households in Bithigram and Keshipur (Table 7.2). The Integrated Rural Development Programme (IRDP) did operate in the Midnapore villages. IRDP has from the late 1970s been India's major anti-poverty programme, aimed at providing loans for the poor for the purchase of assets or setting up small businesses, and about half of the funds under the programme have been used for the purchase of livestock. Evaluations of the IRDP have come to different conclusions about its success (see Swaminathan, 1990; Seabright, 1988; Kurian, 1987; Rath, 1985; and for a review of relevant literature, Dreze, 1990). However, it seems likely that a substantial proportion of assets intended for the poor under IRDP have benefited the non-poor. As the IRDP scheme did not operate in Fonogram as far as loans to buy livestock were concerned, but such loans were taken in the Midnapore villages where *poussani* was not taking place, it is possible to compare the effectiveness of the IRDP and the *poussani* system in terms of getting assets through to the poorest.

The very small number of milk cows owned by households in income group 1 (Table 7.3) in the Midnapore villages shows that villagers with the least income (who were the target group of the IRDP) had not received major benefits.[34] In total, only six households in Bithigram had received IRDP loans for buying livestock, and these households were spread throughout the four income groups; two were from income group 1, two from group 2, and one each from groups 3 and 4. One of the households from group 1 had sold their IRDP cow after two years at a loss of 50 rupees. In Keshipur a further six households had received loans to purchase livestock; the distribution was better than in Bithigram as far as IRDP's aims were concerned, as two recipient households were in income group 1, and four in group 2. Even given the smaller percentage of households in income group 1 in the Midnapore villages, which in any case is balanced by the greater importance of livestock in the villages, the IRDP

---

[33] Evidence of Lodha households engaged in sharerearing in 1952 can be found in Bhowmick (1963: 40). This took place near Jhargram, which is close to the study area described here. One household in Keshipur was in 1988–9 rearing-in two goats from someone outside the village.

[34] IRDP has been more successful in other regions of West Bengal. See Swaminathan (1990).

performance did not match the ability of the sharerearing system in Fono-gram in terms of transferring assets to the poorest. In addition, as seen in Table 7.3 and discussed above, livestock were distributed more equitably in Fonogram than in the two Midnapore villages, and more equitably than land in Fonogram, and this was a direct effect of the operation of the sharerearing system. Policy implications of this are discussed at the end of the section.

The literature on sharerearing
Livestock have been crucial assets for the poor in rural societies for cen-turies (for examples from different societies, see Guha, 1989; Thompson, 1983; Hufton, 1974), so it is perhaps unsurprising that intra-village systems for livestock redistribution should have developed. What is surprising is that the widespread contemporary importance of this system has not pre-viously been commented upon. A large number of studies from throughout India and elsewhere have noted the existence of *poussani*, and I deal with them at some length precisely because the importance of the system has not been recognized. I will first discuss historical evidence from Bengal, and then consider findings of studies from West Bengal and Bangladesh, and from other parts of Asia, and Africa. Because of the large number of relevant studies, the discussion is confined to noting the widespread nature of the system, and who is involved in it in terms of class and gender. As I mentioned above, information about the system is not always clear, and in many of the studies I refer to it is commented upon only in passing. In the studies discussed the nature of the system in terms of division of animals is as described above unless otherwise mentioned.

Cooper (1984: 80), referring generally to Bengal in the 1930s and 1940s, discusses sharerearing as a form of exploitation:

Animals required (by share-croppers) for cultivation were loaned in various ways. A landlord could supply the cattle and the sharecropper bear the costs of maintenance, while the cattle continued to belong to the landlord. Alternatively the sharecropper looked after a cow for a landlord and the first calf that was born would belong to the sharecrop-per, but subsequent calves belonged to the landlord. In these ways the landlord ensured that the sharecropper was provided with the means of production without actually bearing the costs of raising the livestock, even increasing his own stock.

Historically, therefore, sharerearing was carried out between landlords and sharecroppers, and fitted into an exploitive system of sharecropping that dated back at least to the nineteenth century (ibid. : 26).[35]

---

[35] Sunil Sengupta has told me that *poussani* operated in Bengal for several genera-tions before the 1940s.

More recent evidence from West Bengal shows that the system remains pervasive throughout the state. Danda and Danda (1971: 42–6), writing about fieldwork carried out in a village in Burdwan District in 1967–8, refer to landowners 'sometimes' developing a *paalaa* (also meaning to sharerear) relationship involving cows, goats and hens, with male daily and annual wage labourers, farm servants, and female paddy huskers and domestic servants. P.K. Bose in two studies (1984; 1985), the first in three villages in Birbhum District and one in Purulia District, and the second in ten villages in Purulia, Midnapore and Birbhum Districts, describes sharerearing arrangements, mainly for sheep and goats, in all villages studied. In the second of these studies Bose comments that: (1985: 79): 'In the . . . system prevalent in the [ten] villages an owner of livestock loans one or two of them, to another – mostly to poor peasants – who looks after them and in return gets half of the progenies.' Sharerearing is mentioned in passing by A. Dasgupta (1981: 72) in a study of a Jalpaiguri District village where the: 'animal *adhi* (sharing) system between a *jotedar* (landowner) and *adhiar* (sharecropper) (is no longer followed), but the arrangement is still followed by kinsmen and neighbours.' Rohner and Chaki-Sirkar (1988: 28) also comment, from a study of a Birbhum District village, that young untouchable boys reared-in cows and goats, although (ibid.): 'Few boys are lucky enough . . . to have such "adopted" animals.'[36]

Further extensive evidence is available in studies from Bangladesh. Van Schendel (1981: 112) for a village in Rangpur District mentions the great importance of the system to rearing-in households, and also discusses the risk involved for the borrower if the animal died, as the owner would claim compensation. Siddiqui (1982: 35) found 20 poor households (out of a total of 156 village households) in a Jessore District village rearing-in calves or kids. Jansen (1986: 44) from a village in Dhaka District noted that nine out of 62 village households reared-in livestock, with the transfer being from rich to poor. White (1988: 298–301, 394) discusses *poussani* in more detail from a study village in Tangail District, where sharerearing-out of goats, but not cattle, by women from richer households was common, placing it in the context of the overall village social and patriarchal structures. White notes that (ibid.: 300–1): 'Socially, share-tending contracts express the good relationship between the two parties . . . married women commonly share-tend out in their natal village to retain some independence of their husband's household.[37]

---

[36] I also came across sharerearing from landowners to the poor in one other village in Birbhum District.

[37] Evidence of similar sharerearing arrangements in Bangladesh can be found in Cutler *et al*., (1989: 54); Katona-Apte (1988: 45); Howes and Jabbar (1986: 24–5) (where dung rather than animals was kept by the rearer-in); Akhter, Lily and Karim (1984); Chen (1983: 148, 163); Hartmann and Boyce (1983: 163); and Abdullah and Zeidenstein (1982). The last four of these studies and that by Katona-Apte note that it is women who arrange sharerearing.

151

It should be clear from these references that the *poussani* system is common throughout West Bengal and Bangladesh, and that it also occurs across the different agro-ecological regions, and Muslim, tribal and Hindu villages represented in the studies quoted. What appears to have happened to the sharerearing system over time in the Bengal region is that while the arrangements for lending have remained unchanged, the 'partners' to the arrangement may have changed, although the scanty evidence of past arrangements makes this comment hypothetical. Rather than being between landlord and sharecropper as evidenced in the quote from Cooper, the arrangement now seems to be between rich and poor, and, particularly in Bangladesh, between rich and poor women. Six of the eleven studies referenced from Bangladesh comment that it is women who organize sharerearing. This can be related to the fact that in contemporary West Bengal and Bangladesh it is mainly women who raise livestock.

Outside Bengal, Breman (1979) gives an interesting perspective on *poussani* from his field work in Gujarat. In 1962–3 he noted in one study village that *Dublas* (or lower castes) took in cattle from *Anavils* (upper castes). He describes this (ibid.: 192) as: 'an excellent means of bonding the farm servant who no longer lives on his master's land.' He also noted (ibid.: 193): 'Of the eight Dublas who have managed to pay off their debts, six did so by rearing cattle for their masters.' Returning to the same area between 1977 and 1982, Breman remarked (1985a: 270–1): 'The farmers are no longer interested in what is literally called "sharecropping of cattle". . . . Now that milk production is commercialized the farmers are interested in improving the quality, to the cost of agricultural labourers, who are not in a position to provide appropriate feeding and stalling.' This loss of a source of income for the poorer lower castes is placed by Breman in the context of the decline of the extra-economic links between employers and labourers. Breman notes the double-edged nature of the system: a means of bonding the farm servant from the perspective of the employer, but also a means of repaying debt from the perspective of the Dublas. This situation is somewhat different, therefore, to that in Bengal where *poussani* still exists in a different form to its original one, although it is interesting to note that the commercialization of milk was the reason given by one Fonogram household for the increasing unavailability of livestock to rear in the village.

The importance of the sharerearing system to the poor has also been noted by individual studies throughout the rest of India. Jodha concluded (albeit in a footnote) from an eighty-village study in western India that 'the practice of 'salvaging' [i.e. sharerearing] unproductive animals was observed in practically all the study areas. Large farmers gave their unproductive animals to the poor . . . In areas like Gujarat and Rajasthan such herding was an important source of income for the rural poor.' (Jodha, 1986:1180–1, fn. 10). Heyer (1989: 37) from a village study in Tamil Nadu also notes that many agricultural labourers rear in livestock on a share ownership basis. Instances of sharerearing from rich to poor have also been noted in village studies in Uttar Pradesh (Dasgupta, 1987); Gujarat (Chen and Dholakia, 1986); Karnataka (Epstein, 1983); and elsewhere in south India (Hill, 1986).

Table 7.5 gives further details of seven cases of sharerearing, three from Asia, and four from Africa, outlining who rears-in and out, and the type of animal involved.

Table 7.5 Sharerearing of livestock in Asia and Africa[1]

Study	Place	Rearer in	Rearer out	Type of animal
Blaikie et al. (1979: 64)	W. central Nepal	Poor h/h	Patrons	Livestock, oxen
Tura Institute (1981)	Thailand	Poor h/h	Development project	Buffaloes
Grossman (1984: 160–3)	Highland Papua New Guinea	58% of h/h raising pigs	Patrons	Pigs
De Carvalho (1974: 205)	Angola	Relatives/ friends	Relatives/ friends	Cattle
Swift (1981: 86)	Mali	Poor pastoralists	Rich h/h	Livestock goats
Cashdan (1985: 462)	Botswana	Poor h/h	Wealthy cattle owners	Cattle
White (1986: 24)	Mali	Poor h/h	Richer h/h	Cattle
Rahmato (1988: 16)	Ethiopia	Peasant h/h	Peasant h/h	Livestock

[1] In addition, the study by De Carvalho notes that similar mechanisms are widespread among African pastoral societies, and refers to a further four studies from Africa where the system is mentioned.

The thirty studies I have quoted and referenced, as well as my own field work, shows that the *poussani* system is replicated in a wide range of rural societies where livestock are important to the poor. Where a trend in the direction of lending is discernible, this is from rich to poor. While few studies specify which gender organizes the *poussani* arrangement,[38] the Bengal evidence suggests that it is mainly women who are involved in *poussani* transactions.

Indigenous systems of livestock redistribution and policy making
The mainstream focus in development planning has been on the poor as

---

[38] In the studies noted after Breman's, only Epstein *et al.*, and Cashdan specify this, referring to a woman making the arrangement in the former and men in the latter.

'beneficiaries' of public policy. This is one reason, I would argue, why subjects such as sharerearing of livestock have received so little systematic attention. Why attempt to find out what the poor can do themselves if it is believed that development agencies or the state can solve the problem of poverty? This is *not* of course to argue against state involvement, only to suggest that state planners should be more open to and aware of indigenous systems of resource redistribution.

The example of IRDP shows this quite clearly. The performance of the IRDP has been at best mediocre in India as far as poverty alleviation is concerned. There are a number of reasons for this, mainly involving 'leakages' to the non-poor and inflated prices and poor quality of animals lent (see Dreze, 1990 for a literature review). Ironically, the original intention of the programme was '. . . to provide poor families with an income generating asset that will conflict as little as possible with their other economic activities.' (Seabright, 1988: 7–8). But as is clear from the discussion above, the IRDP has run parallel to an indigenous system of livestock redistribution of which the planners of the IRDP presumably were not aware. It is also possible that the IRDP has damaged the *poussani* system by increasing the commoditization of livestock, making livestock less available for sharerearing.

Even if the sharerearing system is more effective at providing livestock for the poor than the IRDP, there are difficult questions about *poussani* that need to be asked about its organization, and which can only be partly answered given the present information available. For example, *poussani* is a system built upon inequality of resources. Yet there appears to be little scope to introduce the kind of legislation concerning *poussani* that the Left Front Government have introduced in West Bengal concerning sharecroppers' rights to land. This is because the *poussani* contract is so informal, and so little is known about it. The *poussani* system is also a potentially exploitive one, dependent of course on one's definition of exploitation. It involves surplus extraction of poor people's labour, and the transfer of quite limited resources to the poor. For example, the borrower in the arrangement may have to rear the animal borrowed for two to three years before two offspring are born. The return from this labour – one of the offspring – is probably well below market value. However, the borrower of the livestock must think this 'exploitation' is worthwhile, or the system would not have survived. I do not find a contradiction here; in many situations individuals continue to operate within systems that exploit them, and even attempt to perpetuate these systems, if they either have no alternative, or consider that their gain is worth the exploitation, or do not consider that they are being exploited.

In addition to providing low returns to labour, the *poussani* system is also one which may leave poor rearers open to claims of compensation if the animal borrowed dies. This is mentioned in the studies by Van

154

Schendel (1981) and Swift (1981). Both authors comment that if the share-reared animal dies this can have serious consequences for the household rearing-in, in terms of claims for compensation. The evidence on this subject is fragmentary; whether or not compensation is claimed would seem to depend on the relationship between borrower and lender. For example, no Fonogram villagers mentioned the possibility of compensation claims, and the one example I have of an animal dying while in the custody of the borrower (the case of Raila, described above) did not lead to any retribution nor to a closure of lending on the part of Raila's employer. However, given this added inequality in the *poussani* contract system, it might be asked what opportunities this indigenous system could provide for policy intervention?

In this respect, it is of considerable interest that a major NGO in Bangladesh, Proshika, have adapted the sharerearing system in their development programmes. Proshika was founded in 1976, and its central aim has been to improve the quality of life of the poor in Bangladesh by organizing groups numbering about twenty poor women or men, who then become involved in consciousness-raising and income-generating activities. Proshika now operates in about three thousand villages and has formed about 20,000 groups of the poor, and has achieved substantial geographical coverage. Loans for livestock rearing is the second largest activity for Proshika in terms of numbers involved and money lent, and rearing was carried out by about 30,000 poor women and men in 1990 (Proshika, 1991; 1990). Proshika developed their livestock-rearing programme in response to requests by the poor, and particularly poor women, for loans to raise livestock.

Proshika organizes sharerearing in the following way. Firstly, a request is made by one of Proshika's groups for a loan for livestock. A feasibility study is then carried out with the group members. If the loan is approved, the group next decides which of its members will take the animal on loan from the group as a whole. Any profits from the livestock are divided as follows: the rearer recoups the cost of rearing and any further profits are then divided among the group. This avoids the extraction of surplus labour that exists in traditional sharerearing arrangements, where the rearer receives below market value for his or her labour. Proshika also provides insurance for the livestock to the group as a whole in case the animal dies, which avoids possible claims for compensation, although the groups do not always take out this insurance because of its cost.[39]

Proshika have therefore adapted the sharerearing system and turned it from an unequal (and possibly exploitive) system to a co-operative one. In

---

[39] I am grateful to Md. Shahabuddin, Proshika's Principal Programme Co-ordinator, for providing information on their livestock programme. He also informed me that several other NGOs in Bangladesh have taken up similar schemes.

other words, they have built on and improved an indigenous form of resource management that was already well established and understood by poor people. Proshika's livestock programme awaits a detailed evaluation, although Proshika's Principal Programme Co-ordinator noted that an economic evaluation of the programme would only partly show its success or failure, and that the programme needed also to be understood in terms of its contribution to the development of co-operative action among the poor (Md. Shahabuddin, personal communication, 1992). The wider lesson here is that planners should make themselves aware of indigenous systems of resource management by the poor, and why these might have persisted, before intervening in the rural economy with grand development programmes. One may question for example whether the IRDP would have gone ahead in its original form if planners had been aware that a widespread indigenous system already existed concerned with transferring livestock to the poor. It is clear that *poussani* continues to function in many societies because it is a system that is negotiated within and takes account of village socio-economic structures, a system that both poor and rich can live with.

Poorest people and assets

Physical assets that can be sold or mortgaged, such as land, livestock, trees or jewellery can be crucial to poor people's survival in times of stress. Their importance has been mentioned in a number of studies (quoted in Chambers, 1983). However, Chambers and Leach have noted (1989: 330): 'scholars and practical analysts (have not) often treated contingencies and asset disposal as central concerns.' Among the reasons the authors give for the subsequent general gap in knowledge about poor people's use of assets is the neglect by professionals of: '. . . things that matter to the poor.' (ibid.: 331). There has been a limited amount of field work carried out concerning sale of village land in South Asia (see BRAC, 1984: 7–10; Siddiqui, 1982: 141; and in particular Cain, 1981). Chambers and Leach (1989) themselves discuss the importance of the sale of trees in meeting contingencies. This section aims to add to the limited knowledge on this subject, examining assets through the eyes of their owners.

It became clear during the interviews that assets, debt, illness, and power were closely interlinked within 'integrated rural poverty'. But the importance of illness was not fully recognized until after the interviews with poorest households had been completed in Fonogram, so information from that village on the relation between illness and sale of assets is partly lacking.[40] Below I describe the assets people owned, sales, and poorest people's views about assets.

---

[40] An extra question on illness was included for the Midnapore villages.

Assets owned by the poorest
B. Harriss (1987: 11) has commented after a review of micro-level literature on poverty in India that:

> The domestic asset position of the poor describes the consequences of
> inability to accumulate in almost identical terms in a large number of
> micro studies. The poor have one or two sets of clothing 'in which they
> stand and sleep', a few mats, a mud stove and mud cooking pots, grind-
> ing stones, a few simple lamps, elementary agricultural tools.

The evidence from the case study villages supports this finding concerning
domestic assets. Very few household members had more than two sets of
clothing; one woman in Fonogram told me that she only had one *sari*,
which she had worn for the last year, and confided that she rarely washed
the *sari* as that way the cloth lasted longer.

Poorest households in Fonogram did own (in 1986–7) a number of other
productive assets, and the quantity of these had not been substantially
affected by the flooding in 1986. Between them, the twenty-five Fonogram
poorest households owned: 171 decimals of farm land (not including homestead land – which five households did not own), one plough animal, six
milk cows, and nine goats (mostly sharereared in), a number of chickens
and hens, 25 fruit trees (mainly mango, plum, tamarind and *bel*), as well as
banana trees. None of the households had any jewellery, although one had
a nose-pin in mortgage.

Bithigram's nineteen poorest households in 1988–9 owned more assets,
mainly because of the government programmes in the village. Between
them they owned a little under two hectares of *dhan* land, and about four
hectares of *dahi* land, all of which had been received under the government
patta (land redistribution) programme. On the *dahi* land between them
they had planted 8,650 eucalyptus trees. They owned very few other trees
and no jewellery. They also owned five plough animals, six goats, and four
sheep (none of which had been received under IRDP). Apart from their
agricultural tools, Bithigram households had almost nothing else – no cots
and usually only one or two thin blankets. Keshipur's sixteen interviewed
poorest households owned six hectares of *dahi* land and only five decimals
of *dhan* land, about half of the *dahi* land being *patta*. On the *dahi* land they
had planted 5,900 eucalyptus trees. They also owned five plough animals
(one of which had been bought with an IRDP loan), one milk cow, four
goats and eleven sheep.

Comparatively, Fonogram poorest households owned seven decimals of
land each, Bithigram households about 30 decimals of *dhan* land and 60
decimals of *dahi* land, and Keshipur households about 100 decimals of *dahi*
land. The *patta* land received by Bithigram and Keshipur households had all
been received in the few years prior to the survey, and could not be sold
under government regulations, although respondents said that it could be

157

mortgaged. The limited quantity of assets owned by poorest households meant that their ability to manage these assets resourcefully was severely restricted.

Management and sales of assets by the poorest
Respondents were asked if their household had sold any land in the last five years, or any other assets in the last two years, the reason for the sale, who bought the asset, and the price. The intention was to gather information on how poorest people manage assets and to see how this management might be supported by external intervention.[41]

There were a large number of sales in all three villages under varying circumstances. Tabular mode has been chosen as the most concise form in which to represent the data, although detail is sacrificed for concision using this method. Chambers (1983: 114–118) has suggested a five-fold typology for documenting the purpose of asset sales, which includes social conventions (such as marriage or funerals), disasters, physical incapacity, unproductive expenditure, and exploitation. This typology, with two additions, productive expenditure and miscellaneous or unknown, was found to be a useful one as most of the reasons for sales could be subsumed within it, and is used in the tables below. Information in the tables is based on recall, and where respondents were uncertain about dates or prices this has been indicated with a question mark.

In terms of sales of particular assets, the tables show the importance of livestock to the poorest. Out of the total of 31 cases of individual sales, 22 involved livestock (making up some 50 per cent of monetary value where this could be identified). In Bithigram all except two were livestock sales. Land was sold in four cases, for the marriage of a daughter or son in three, and for the repayment of a large debt in one, suggesting that land was reserved for large-scale contingencies such as these. Only three sales of trees were reported, which may reflect the ease with which it is possible to sell livestock as opposed to trees, and the very few homestead trees owned by Bithigram respondents. This latter finding suggests that Chambers and Leach's (1989) hypothesis as to the relative importance of trees as savings banks for the poor may need further empirical investigation.[42]

In 22 out of the 26 cases where the purchaser of the asset could be identified, the sale was either in the market or outside the village. There

---

[41] Land sales by income group for Fonogram has been discussed in some detail for the 1986–7 to 1988–9 period in the previous chapter, where it was seen (Tables 6.3 and 6.4) that during that period income group 1 households (into which category all except one of the poorest Fonogram respondents fall) sold only 33 decimals of land.

[42] However, Conroy (1992: 2385) notes the importance of sale of trees to poor tribals in Gujarat: 'It is clear . . . that the sale of trees is by far the most frequently used option for obtaining cash to cope with contingencies.'

Table 7.6 Sale of assets by Fonogram poorest households (land 1982–7, other assets 1985–7)

Asset	Buyer (income group no.)	Price (rupees)[1]	Date of sale	Reason for sale
Social convention				
2 jack-fruit trees	?	? (good)	1986	Marriage of daughter
10 decimals of land	Absentee landlord	800	?1985	Marriage of daughter
2 cows; 2 goats	Market	?(good)	?1986	Marriage of daughter
1 bigha land	Distant relative	?	1984	Marriage of son
Disaster				
Cow	Nephew (group 3)	150 (good)	1986	Post-flood expense
Cow	Market	?	1986	Post-flood
Goat	Market	150	1986	expense
Physical incapacity				
Van	Outsider	700(poor)	1986	Sickness
Unproductive expenditure				
10 decs land	Brother (group 4)	2000	1985	Repayment of debt
3 trees	?	?(good)	1986	House repair
Productive expenditure				
1 cow	Outsider	1200	1986	Purchase of land
Miscellaneous				
2 goat kids	Outside village	? (poor)	1986	?

[1] 'Good' or 'poor' indicates respondents' views as to whether or not they received adequate money for the asset.

were periodic markets relatively near to the three villages, and villagers were obviously getting a better price for their assets outside of the village. Respondents were not generally unhappy about the prices they received for their assets,[43] although there were clear examples of dissatisfaction, for example the case of the sale of the van in Fonogram by a household with a very sick male adult (see chapter nine for more details on this case). This sale of assets outside of the villages was in contrast to sales of land which took place mainly to other villagers (see chapter six for reasons for this).

The reason for sale differed across villages. In Bithigram the reason given was sickness in 11 out of 14 cases, and if other cases of sale of assets

---

[43] I asked about this only in Fonogram.

Table 7.7   Sale of assets by Bithigram poorest households (land sales 1984–9, other assets 1987–9)

Asset	Buyer	Price (rupees)	Date of sale	Reason for sale
Social convention				
Bullock	Market	1500	?1987	Marriage of daughter
Physical incapacity				
400 roof tiles	Outside villager	500	1988	Sickness
7 sheep	Market	700	1987	Sickness
2 goats	Market	180	1988	Sickness
Bullock	Market	400	1989	Sickness
1 goat	Market	120	1989	Sickness
2 goats	Market	200	?1988	Sickness
1 goat	Market	120	1989	Sickness
Bullock	Market	400	?1987	Sickness
Hens	Market	250	1988	Sickness of
Sheep	Market	500	1988	h/h member
2 bullocks	Market	1400	1988	
Unproductive expenditure				
2 sheep	Market	150	1988	Repayment of loan
Exploitation				
600 roof tiles	?	550	?1987	Court costs

Table 7.8   Sale of assets by Keshipur poorest households (land sales 1984–9, other assets 1987–9)

Asset[1]	Buyer	Price (rupees)	Date of sale	Reason for sale
Social convention				
4 *bighas* land	Outside villager	8000	?1984	Marriage of daughter
Cows/goats	Market	?	?1987	Marriage of son
Physical incapacity				
Bullock	Market	700	1988	Sickness
2 bullocks	Market	1700	1988	Sickness/ death
1 *chola* tree	?	150	1988	Sickness
Productive expenditure				
2 sheep	?	250	?1988	Household expense

before 1987 are taken into account, almost every one of the 19 Bithigram respondent households had sold assets because of major illness in the household.[44] Across the three villages, seven households also sold assets to marry off a child.

Only one of the sales has been listed under 'exploitation'. However, asset sales should be seen within the context of 'integrated rural poverty'. For example, many of the households selling assets were in addition taking loans, sometimes on exploitive terms. The illness of household members, combined with powerlessness, and lack of alternative means of getting money, meant that it was extremely difficult for the poorest to retain any productive assets and therefore improve their standard of living.

Respondents' perceptions and management of assets
Respondents were initially asked about the sequence of sale of assets in times of stress, in order to discover which assets were more important to households and why. This line of enquiry was not followed because of the small number of households reporting more than one sale. Instead Fonogram respondents were asked in which order they would sell during a period of stress five equally priced assets (jewellery, chickens, goats, trees and land). As this mode of questioning usually received only incomplete replies, Bithigram and Keshipur respondents were asked the preferential order in which they would take five items, again of equal value (a cycle, a cow, goats, jewellery or cash). Some respondents thought that they might actually get some of the items mentioned, and others were unable to answer. One Bithigram respondent said ironically: 'I'll take all of the things that you've mentioned, thanks.' However, respondents' replies, even where incomplete, did give some idea of the relative importance to them of different assets.

Of the 13 Fonogram respondents who replied about the order of selling assets, chickens were the item to be sold first in six cases, and trees in four cases. Jewellery was no longer sold in the village, but only mortgaged. Land was in all cases the last asset that would be sold. As one respondent said: 'If we sell land we will never get it back, but we can plant more trees or get more hens.' Interestingly, three respondents also said that they would sell trees or mortgage jewellery first because: 'there was a certain attachment to living things.' (e.g. livestock).

Of the eight Bithigram respondents replying about the order in which they would take assets, all opted first for a cow (in seven cases) or goats, and four had goats or a cow as their second choice. Of the 14 Keshipur respondents, nine first chose goats and five a cow, with livestock again

---

[44] Chambers (1983: 127) notes that: 'Sickness emerges as a common cause and form of poverty ratchet.' Tuberculosis was rife in the Lodha *para* of Bithigram.

being the main second choice. Respondents in these two villages therefore chose productive over non-productive assets (and cash). This was clear from the rationale volunteered for their choice by two Keshipur respondents who said: 'If we had a cow we would have some income – what use is jewellery?' This finding ties in to the desire that even poorest people had for independence. It also suggests that the rationale of the IRDP in providing livestock for the poor was not displaced as far as poorest people's priorities are concerned (an issue not considered in the literature on the IRDP). However, firm conclusions cannot be drawn from such a small sample. More detailed discussion of poor people's priorities as far as assets are concerned awaits a wider survey.

Respondents in the three villages made clear the importance of maintaining productive assets, even if this meant cutting back on their own consumption. This was particularly the case with larger livestock where feed had to be bought for a part of the year. This connects to the importance of such assets in meeting contingencies, as seen in the tables above. Having an asset of one's own might mean not having to go (further) into debt when problems invariably arose, and therefore less dependence on the local money lender or employee. In addition, it meant that households could meet their social obligations. It was also clear from my discussion with them that poorest households managed their assets with acumen and sold them in the market where possible, and only when they thought absolutely necessary.

However, the cost of maintaining assets may not be met by all household members equally. If households cut food consumption to maintain assets, then in a situation where patriarchal ideology and daughter disfavour prevails, women and girls may lose out as their food consumption may be cut most.[45] While I did not explore this linkage in the study villages, it may explain the findings of a study over five years in the Kosi hill area of Nepal, where, in response to a development programme, land sales decreased but nutritional status did not improve (Cassells *et al.*, 1987). If such a linkage does exist, the question as to whether or not to provide assets or cash to poor households to support their livelihoods remains one that is extremely problematic.

Conclusions

Any rural development initiative is likely to have both positive and negative elements. Each of the strategies I have described in this chapter benefit

---

[45] As noted above, the intra-household distribution of hunger is a controversial subject. It is discussed in some detail in Dreze and Sen (1989), with reference mainly to famine situations. It is clear from almost all studies that adult women in rural areas in developing countries fare worse in times of crisis. How well children make out, whether boys or girls, is more ambiguous.

the poor to some extent but may also harm their interests over the long term. For example, gathering of CPRs is crucial to poorest households' subsistence in the short term, but may damage their interests in the long term if there is a depletion of the natural resource base. Similarly, share-rearing of livestock may be exploitive, and interventions to support poor people's use of assets may harm poor women. As with loan taking, what is useful today may turn out to be disastrous in a year's time.

The evidence from this chapter shows that great caution should be taken when attempting to formulate rural development programmes. But it has shown as well that poor people's knowledge of their natural and social environment is a great resource and one which they use to improve their quality of life. I have given the examples of knowledge and collection of CPRs, bargaining over gleaned grains and livestock to rear, and management of assets. Each of these areas is one where the poor negotiate, bargain and struggle with their rich neighbours for a share of village resources. They are strategies that the poor, and in particular poor women, have developed themselves from their experience of their local environment. Nor are they confined to the case study villages or regions. The literature I have referred to in this chapter show that such activities are commonly used by the poor throughout India. Such strategies deserve the attention and support of outsiders who intend to intervene in the rural economy.

163

8 'The rich don't help the poor, and they never did': Power and the poorest

Power relations are, arguably, the most important organizing feature of village society in West Bengal, and power and powerlessness were central to poor people's experiences of poverty. Chapters four to six have shown that in each of the study villages resources and power were held by a small group of households, the group I call middle farmers and which the poor identify as 'the rich'. Their lack of resources, their lack of external contacts, their exclusion from important decision-making within the village, and their need for credit to make ends meet, meant that the poor were locked into a position of dependence on those who exploited them. Remarkably, they still found room for manoeuvre. This chapter will continue the discussion of how poorest people negotiated better positions for themselves within village power structures, what they did to resist their subordination, their opinions of other poor people and rich people, their views on politics, and the importance to them of self respect.

It is worth recalling at this point the comment by Breman (1985b: 34): 'In India there is a great scarcity of literature in which those living in the lowest echelons of society themselves speak out.' The reasons for this are not difficult to find. As Scott (1990) makes clear, the subordinated are often forced to hide their 'transcripts' or readings on the working of the world as a means of self-preservation. If they do not their livelihoods, and quite possibly their lives, are endangered. Even though the poor may keep their true feelings hidden as a survival tactic, there has also been a negligence on the part of researchers who have ignored the poor for political or methodological reasons. This leads to the kind of unsubstantiated theorizing about the characteristics of the poor that I have earlier criticized.

Scott also refers to the situation where (ibid.: 18): ' . ... .offstage, where subordinates may gather outside the intimidating gaze of power, a sharply dissonant political culture is possible.' The aim of this chapter is to contribute to an understanding of how the poor experience power, and to hear them speak out about the sharply dissonant political culture to which Scott refers, albeit through my interpretation. Respondents across the three villages usually spoke in similar terms, sometimes using the same words and phrases, about their experiences of exploitation and power; below I have selected representative comments of individual respondents to express these commonalities, while at the same time including the views of those who dissented from the majority.

Poorest people and politics

Respondents were asked how well the affairs of their village were being run, if they were members of or supported any political party, if they knew government sharecropping or minimum wage legislation, and whether they thought the Left Front was doing good work for the poor.

None of the sixty poorest respondents were members of political parties. In Fonogram no poorest respondent knew the minimum wage rate and only two respondents knew the terms of sharecropping regulations. Respondents there did tell me that recently less land was being hired out because the owners feared the land would be taken over by the sharecropper. The situation in the Midnapore villages was little different, although there was more knowledge about the distribution of *patta* land, as so many of the villagers had received it.

The Communist Party of India (Marxist), or CPM, the key member of the Left Front that has ruled in West Bengal since 1977, was the dominant political party in all three villages. Of the thirty respondents who gave a definite answer as to which party they supported, twenty-seven said the CPM. Replies concerning party support were partly determined by the government's programmes in particular villages. In Fonogram there was an overall disillusionment and cynicism about politics; in general respondents thought that the CPM were doing little for the poor. They continued to vote for the CPM as the best alternative, and not because they were happy with the party's perfomance. As one woman put it, describing how she decided to vote:

> I will vote for anyone who helps us, and decide for myself. There is no use in voting for any party, but in any case we vote. The party people say they will take us to the voting place by van but we have to walk back anyway, so we say we will walk to the voting place and vote for who we want.

The reference here is to the common practice in both study regions of political parties providing transport for rural voters to take them to polling stations. Other respondents were also determined to be independent in their voting. Another respondent expressed his cynicism by noting that it was possible to tell when there was to be an election because this was the time when the road leading into the village was repaired. Clearly, there was no intoxication with what Frankel (1971: 185) has called 'Marxist political propaganda'.

Support for the CPM was most enthusiastic in Bithigram. All fourteen respondents replying there favoured the CPM, or, as three of them called it, the 'poor people's party'. This enthusiasm was closely tied to the psychological boost involved in the receipt of *patta*, and to their present security from violent attacks (see below). On the other hand there was a realism

165

about what had been accomplished, as noted in the response of one tribal woman I quoted earlier to receipt of poor quality land: 'The government has given me stony land on which nothing will grow. So I will eat stones.' Almost all respondents from Bithigram attended mass rallies held by the Left Front in Calcutta and Kharagpur. Attendance was an expression of solidarity with the CPM, but also a day out. Respondents could remember what they were given to eat at the rallies, but not the speeches. For example, one Bithigram respondent said about a rally in Calcutta:

> We were so far away from the speakers at the meetings that we had no idea what they were saying. We don't know reading or writing so what can we understand?

Women also attended CPM women's meetings locally, but could remember little of what had been said at them, although some respondents did recall that the issue of setting of labourers' wages was discussed.

Six of the Keshipur respondents were CPM supporters; in general their views were closer to those of Fonogram respondents than their Bithigram neighbours, despite their receipt of *patta*. Women in particular in Fonogram and Keshipur were less interested in formal politics than men. In Fonogram female respondents who worked in the homestead said that they did not go outside, and so knew nothing about politics. Respondents were not therefore 'political' as far as political organization was concerned.

There was near unanimity of opinion across the three villages concerning the work of the local leaders, the *samity* in Fonogram and the *panchayat* in the Midnapore villages. One Bithigram woman summed this up:

> If a sari comes for a poor widow then the *panchayat* takes it, if wheat comes we don't get it, paddy seeds come but *panchayat* people say they have come for themselves. *Panchayat* people are taking everything, and becoming rich themselves. They have been able to buy scooters with the money meant for us. But this is not the fault of the CPM government.

Two points are noticeable about these and other similar comments I heard. The first is that the poor considered the village authorities as unscrupulous enough to steal a sari intended for a poor woman, and they were therefore viewed with great suspicion and as thieves. The second is that respondents quite often separated local political leaders from state leaders. Of the twenty-one respondents in Fonogram replying, eleven said that they did not know if the government was supplying anything but it wasn't coming to them, and ten said they thought the rich were stealing government aid that was intended for the poor. The other direction in which two respondents from each of the Midnapore villages and four from Fonogram thought government support went was to other local villages. As Hamedchha (my Fonogram guide) put it: 'The CPM is certainly supplying things for the poor but it isn't getting through to us.' This faith in the CPM as a body that directed aid to the poor was no doubt one of the reasons respondents continued to vote for it.

A respondent in Fonogram linked this inablity to receive aid to the powerlessness of the poor:

A lot of rich people are getting loans, but no goods come to the poor villagers. We don't have anyone who can tell us if these goods are coming or anyone who can go in a group to collect them.

This can be contrasted to the ability of the Lodhas in Bithigram to go 'as a group' and make demands, as we will see below.

Exploitation, violence and organization

Debt and exploitation

Different forms of exploitation were encountered in the study villages, but in all cases the system of exploitation was founded on control of resources by the wealthy, on credit lent by shopkeepers and employers which poorest people were forced to take due to their lack of resources, on low wages, on patriarchy, and ultimately, on violence. It was when men from wealthy households abused or beat poor women that the worst features of the social structure in the villages came to the fore.

To gauge the level of credit relations, respondents were asked about debts, the reason for taking these, and whether they had to pay interest on them. Exploitation was most noticeable in terms of debt relations. I would argue that debt is not inherently exploitive, but becomes so when, as in the case study villages, credit reinforces a system that marginalizes a large group of the population at a standard of living well below subsistence. As noted in chapter five, most debts in Fonogram were with local shopkeepers. The nineteen poorest households interviewed in post-flood Fonogram in 1986–7 who provided definite figures had some 9,900 rupees of outstanding debt, or the large amount of some 500 rupees per household, the equivalent of about forty days of agricultural labourer's wages. Of this total amount a little under 45 per cent was owed to one shopkeeper who lived in the village, and a further 15 per cent owed to three other shopkeepers, two of whom lived outside the village. Only 8 per cent of the total involved other intra-village loans. The shopkeepers sometimes acted as moneylenders, but loans with them were usually for food taken on credit, and were regularly 'chalked up' over several months, particularly in the pre-harvest period. In a normal year they would be repaid after the harvest from the earnings from daily labour. Shopkeepers did not charge interest on these loans, but rather charged 10 per cent more for items taken on credit, on top of their existing profits. Poorest households were rarely able to repay fully such a large sum as 500 rupees, so being in debt became, literally, a way of life as well as a heavy responsibility. Respondents' own views of debt are given below.

In the Midnapore villages in 1988–9 respondents had smaller outstanding debts, some 100 rupees per household in Bithigram and 300 rupees per household in Keshipur. Almost all of this debt was to moneylenders, banks or employers. These figures are, however, unrepresentative, because interviews were carried out almost immediately after the *aman* harvest. Under the *dadan* system which operated in the villages, loans were taken in the pre-harvest lean period, and repaid with labour during *aman*, generally at half the market rate. This tied labourers to working for the landowner from whom they had borrowed money, ensuring labour for the landowner during peak agricultural periods, and making bargaining for wages by the labourers more difficult. Respondents realized that the *dadan* system was exploitive (for examples, see below), but had little choice but to take part in it if they were going to survive the pre-harvest period. Pre-harvest borrowing from farmers had already been repaid with labour at the time of the interviews, and respondents would only begin to accumulate debts again from February or March, unless there were major contingencies such as illness. All respondents working as labourers took *dadan* loans, so if interviews had been carried out four months earlier their debt would have been much higher. Loans from the local shops were restricted in that they had to be repaid within a week, presumably to ensure no competition with the *dadan* arrangement, and shopkeepers charged between 10 and 20 per cent higher rates for items bought on credit.

Violence

The dependency that developed from unequal control over village resources and subsequent borrowing by the poor was itself ultimately dependent on physical violence or threats of violence perpetrated by the wealthy or their supporters, the aim of which was to ensure the acquiescence of the poor to their exploitation. While violence against the poor (and among the poor) was common in all three villages, in Bithigram this violence had the most unpleasant history. I was told several stories by Lodhas of routine violence against them in the past by *zamindars* and their henchmen. The following is an account from a group interview with six Lodha women and men who spoke of the violence from pre-Left Front Government days:

> A lot of land used to be owned by people in the village. It was taken 40–50 years back by the *zamindar*. Before, if anyone did anything wrong, even something quite small, they would be tied up on the ground by the *zamindar's* henchmen and big stones placed on their chest, and left in the sun all day until four o'clock in the afternoon, when they would be released. Sometimes they put on sugar [on the bodies of those tied up

like this] so that red ants would come. Some people died from being left like this. The *zamindars* used to take our livestock. When we gathered from the forest we would have to give them half. They burnt down two houses of people still living in the village. They used to beat us very hard, but we could take it because our bodies are so strong. They cut G.L.'s body and rubbed in chillies, they beat him up very badly so that we had to take him to hospital. Then G.L. had a cycle and a radio, that is why they beat him so he wouldn't get above his station. They used to accuse the men of stealing standing paddy, and if they couldn't find the men they used to come with cloths over their faces and beat the women. The police used to come with them. Since the CPM time this has stopped, and the police are no longer coming.[1]

Two points can be noted here. There is the brutality of the methods used. The violence was not just arbitrary, it was a means of keeping the poor in their place and stopping them getting above their station, and it was perpetrated by the landlord's thugs and police in conjunction; but there is also an element of bravery in the claim that 'we could take it'. There is also the near cessation of violence after the CPM came to power, which contributed to the enthusiastic support the Lodhas gave to the CPM. This was so even though there were still instances of violence towards villagers. For example, a young Lodha man had been taken into police custody in 1985, accused of stealing electric power lines. After a week the man had died; the police claimed he had hung himself, but the villagers did not believe them. The parents of the man who died, with the support of other villagers, wrote a letter to Jyoti Basu (the West Bengal State Prime Minister) asking for an enquiry, but received no reply.

The Lodhas also still faced problems from absentee landlords. One respondent had argued with one of these landlords about a loan he wanted to take three years before the interviews:

He said I could take the loan but then he told me I would have to work as a labourer for five rupees a day, but I told him that I couldn't run my household on that. Then that year at the fair he and his *goondahs* started a problem and blamed it on me, and got the police to take me to jail. He started a court case, and eventually I had to give 550 rupees to pay off the lawyers and the police. I had to sell 600 roof tiles to do this.

Such a confrontation and its outcome might spell disaster for a poorest household, given the large sum of money involved. The message here is a clear one – stay in line and work for low wages, or intimidation will be the result.

---

[1] A more recent example of violence by the police and local élite against poor tribals in Bangladesh can be found in BRAC (1986).

The Lodhas appeared to be a particular target because of their past as a 'criminal tribe', and their ethnic separateness. There was also obvious tension between the Lodhas and local farmers, and I heard farmers talking about Lodhas in insulting terms. It was little wonder that the Lodhas were now keen supporters of the CPM, which had stemmed violence against them by absentee landlords, even if exploitation still continued.

In Fonogram and Keshipur violence was concentrated within the villages. One example of violence, organized by the *samity*, took place against a Fonogram poorest respondent, Asgar, because he had gone against village social norms. This incident is described in the next chapter. A good example of the meeting of class and patriarchal oppression comes from Keshipur. During the field work period, relatives of the *panchayat* chairman were intimidating their neighbours, two women who lived in one of the respondent households. The women claimed that their neighbours were trying to drive them away so that they could take over the women's homestead land and expand their own homestead. The women said that drunk men from their neighbours' house came at night and abused and beat them. They went on:

> We don't have any men in our family so the people next door want to take our homestead land. They have everything and we have nothing. They drink and come and cause a problem. They say they will come back and beat us some more. They have cut down our trees and taken them for themselves and bought wristwatches with the money they got.

The wristwatch here, as in Hamedchha's comments about *babus* who wear trousers and wristwatches and prefer thinner varieties of rice, is a symbol of power and oppression. One could not have a clearer example of exploitation that took place within the villages – the wealthy taking the resources of the poor and using them for their own benefit. The day after I interviewed these two women, a chicken belonging to them was killed (not a small matter for those living on the edge of survival). In the early morning I watched one of the women plucking the chicken and while she did so she shouted in the direction of her neighbours, whom she was accusing of killing the chicken and trying to take their land. She continued shouting for some time, as her only weapon at that point was the power of her voice that was informing all the village of her case. In such cases, a loud voice can be a powerful weapon. She was attempting to shame her neighbours, and the presence of an outsider may have added force to these attempts. To some extent she was successful, because the *panchayat* chairman, who was also the school teacher, came to talk to me and explained that poor people got into such trouble because they were ignorant. A good case, perhaps, of blaming the victim.

It is difficult to know how widespread such violence was, and how to interpret some clashes, as there were constant arguments and occasional fights in all three villages between various parties, including between poor people. It was clear however that for the poorest to be involved in an open conflict with more powerful neighbours or outsiders was potentially disastrous, and also that the threat of violence or violence itself was integral to the experience of power relations and poverty.

Organization
At first sight, there appeared little that poorest households could do openly in response to exploitation and violence. I have described earlier some of the 'everyday forms of resistance' to exploitation, such as cutting down trees of the rich, and theft. Insulting the rich (albeit usually behind their backs) or trying to shame them was another form of protest, and I will give examples of this below.

It was in Bithigram with its separate *paras* and different ethnic groups that there was most open organization among the poor. The group of Lodhas who told me about past violence during the pre-Left Front Government period also told me of the response by Lodha and other villagers after the Left Front came to power:

> A mass of people from about thirty villages went to the *zamindar's* house and tried to break it down. We couldn't do it because it was made of brick, but the *zamindar* ran away. Slowly the house was ruined as it was left empty after that.

This was presumably during the first period of Left Front Government in 1967–70, when there were major confrontations between the poor and landowners throughout West Bengal.

In 1988–9 and for several years prior to this Lodha households had organized as a group concerning bargaining for wage rates for work on the *aman* harvest. A female respondent described the bargaining process in this way:

> There are women's meetings (arranged by the CPM) before the harvest and we are told not to work for too little pay. We decide on 3 kg of rice or ten rupees for a day's work. Then there is a meeting in the village every pre-harvest time – the *panchayat*, farmers and poor people come together to decide the rate, then the *panchayat* gives the order concerning the amount. It we don't get the right rate after that then we stop work in protest for a day, or until we get the right price.[2]

Another respondent told me that the Lodhas went in a group of up to sixty people (which would mean representatives from every Lodha household) to the Mahato *para* in order to discuss and negotiate wage rates for transplanting and harvesting.

---

[2] A similar process of bargaining over wages was described to me in Sahajapur village in Birbhum District.

171

There was much less organization in Fonogram and Keshipur, and labourers were not able to act in a group as they did in Bithigram. In Fonogram the wage rate for agricultural labourers was already comparatively high, although wages in the local factories owned by absentee landlords were very low. Village meetings, called by the *samity*, did take place to decide on the rent for sharecropped land during the *boro* season, and other important issues that affected the whole village. Respondents in Fonogram thought poor people could not get organized in the way that rich people did for two reasons. The first reply (in twelve cases) was because of jealousy (*hingsha*) of the poor for each other, which was caused by lack of resources, and meant there was no unity among the poor. The second (in three cases) was because of powerlessness, or as one respondent put it: 'The rich won't let poor people form a union. If they did then they wouldn't be able to cheat us so much.' Being an all-Muslim village, with many complex kin linkages between rich and poor, also inhibited organization by the poor, as landowners and labourers might be close relatives. In Keshipur I also found very little evidence of open organization among the scheduled caste groups. The Lodhas' ethnic separateness and their location in a separate *para*, as well as the support they were receiving from the CPM, were the forces behind their ability to organize.

Poorest people's views of the rich and the poor, and the causes of their poverty

To understand how respondents' experienced poverty, I asked them why they thought they were poor, whose fault this was, what poor and rich people were like, whether the rich helped or cheated the poor, and if the poor helped or cheated each other.

In chapters two and three I discussed 'moral economy' theory and how it has been used to explain both the supposed passivity of the poor and, during its breakdown, protest against the decline of a system that provided subsistence to the whole rural population. Some academics still view moral economy arrangements as central to village society. Greenough (1982: 183) for example claims that the: ' . . . .moral bonds of patronage were, and are, a principal mechanism of cohesion in Bengali society' (and see also Davis 1983: 36, 46, on village Midnapore). Given that agriculture in the Midnapore villages was mainly based on the *aman* season, and there were fewer market linkages than in Fonogram, it might have been expected that 'moral economy' relations would have been found in the more 'traditional' settings of Bithigram and Keshipur. However, there was much common ground in responses in all three villages as to their views of poor-rich relations, and in their rejection of the notion of a 'moral economy', with villagers talking about the relations between poor and rich in very similar terms; respondents' replies across the three villages are therefore discussed together.

172

Causes of poverty

As to why they thought they were poor, responses were fairly standard. Respondents gave a number of different reasons, but these centred around lack of assets, and fate.[3]

Forty-one respondents out of the total of sixty said specifically that they were poor because they had either lost or not inherited any land; most of the others thought it was because they couldn't work, because they had no education, or were less intelligent than the rich (in the case of three of the Lodhas), or could not say why. When asking whose fault respondents' poverty was, most thought that this was their own fault, or caused by their fate. For the latter explanation they used the popular colloquial Bengali phrase 'I have bad luck written on my forehead' (*Amar koppal upore lekha kharap*), meaning that they were intended by fate to be poor. Respondents were quite explicit about this. As a woman in Keshipur said: 'It is not right to say that because other people have land we are poor. It is our own fault we are poor.' A woman in Fonogram said more or less the same: 'We are poor because we don't have anything – I don't blame the rich for my poverty. I have bad luck.' When I reasoned at length with two respondents that they were poor precisely because others in the village were rich they agreed, but with little conviction.

In contrast, seven respondents in Bithigram blamed the rich for their poverty. In four cases this was because their ancestors had been cheated out of their land by the *zamindars*, and in one case because farmers did not give out land to the poor for sharecropping. The other two respondents linked together present-day exploitation and their poverty, the only ones among the sixty respondents to do so. One was the Lodha man mentioned above who had lost money after being taken to court by an absentee landlord. The other was a Lodha man who was extremely bitter about the Mahatos in Bithigram. He said: 'It's rich people's fault we are poor, even now rich people in our village are trying to keep us poor.' When I asked him where he got these ideas from he said: 'We haven't heard this from anybody, it comes into our own minds.'

Views of the rich

Although for the most part respondents did not blame the rich for their poverty, they were clear about what they thought of the rich. Forty-three respondents, thirty-nine of whom came from Fonogram and Bithigram, thought that the rich *cheated* the poor. Fourteen respondents did not reply or could not answer, and only three said that the rich did not cheat the poor. The main forms of cheating as far as respondents were concerned were either, in most cases, paying too little as salary for the amount of work

---

[3] Siddiqui (1982: 235) reports similar findings from a Bangladesh study village.

173

done by respondents (under the *dadan* system or otherwise), or, in fewer cases, paying too little for assets bought.

Only six respondents thought that the rich *helped* the poor. Three of these were in Fonogram, and were receiving benefits from a 'patron-client' relationship. Fifty-three respondents (with one non-response) were emphatic that the rich did not help the poor. A woman in Fonogram claimed bitterly (the best refutation of simplistic moral economy theorizing I have come across, and why I have used it for the title of this chapter): 'The rich don't help the poor and they never did.' Rather than helping the poor, the rich tried to harm their interests, as the following representative quotes show:

Man in Fonogram:
Rich people beat and eat the poor (*gorib mere khai*), they hit poor people and earn their profit.

Widow in Fonogram:
Rich people don't give any help, they try and hurt the poor more.

Woman in Fonogram:
If we borrow ten rupees from a rich person, we have to repay twelve rupees. If I died a rich person wouldn't even give me the earth to be buried in.

Man in Bithigram:
Rich people have everything they need, they don't give us anything, they cheat us 100 times, we have to work for them for three rupees. Rich people would never help us, even if we were dying they wouldn't give us ten rupees.

Woman in Keshipur:
Rich people don't help the poor, they hate us, they can't bear to look at us.

Widow in Keshipur:
If I go to rich people for help they will say we have no rice. When there is no food in the house if we go to rich people's houses to ask for food they won't even talk to us.[4]

At a superficial level it is not difficult to interpret such comments. Not only did respondents consider that the rich were cheating them, they also accused them of complete lack of charity and heartlessness – 'Even if we were dying they wouldn't give us 10 rupees.' The second woman in Fonogram I

---

[4] Compare this quote from a poor person noted by Scott (1985: 12–13) in his Malaysian study village: 'The rich are arrogant. We greet them and they don't greet us back. They don't talk to us; they don't even look at us!' Several of the points I make in this chapter overlap with Scott's analysis. Very similar comments by the poor about the rich in Bangladesh can also be found in Yunus (1984: 42) and Chen (1983: 151).

quote goes even further, using black humour as a means of attacking the meanness of the rich – 'If I died a rich person wouldn't even give me the earth to be buried in.' But there is also tied in with these comments a question of social prestige, a bitterness that the poor are not treated as human beings by their fellow villagers. These comments came from scheduled caste women in Keshipur who had all their lives suffered the indignity of having been born outcastes and shunned as morally inferior by the higher castes. Even in this village where little 'modernization' had taken place and which had been largely untouched by agricultural change, poorest illiterate women were quite clear about the rich – ' . . . . they hate us, they can't bear to look at us.' Let me recall at this point Frankel's comments which I quoted in chapter two (1989: 1):

> Village studies show that . . . . asymmetrical obligations among unequals were oriented toward ensuring subsistence for all members according to their ceremonial and productive functions. . . . .. As a result, it is arguable that commands by the dominant castes were perceived as legitimate and evoked a high level of predictable compliance for the lower castes towards whom they were directed.

It would be difficult to describe a situation that was more different from the one found in the study villages. One can only conclude that Frankel and the authors of the studies she mentions have seriously misread the perceptions of the 'lower castes' in this case.

As the quote from the man in Bithigram suggests – 'Rich people have everything they need, they don't give us anything . . . .' – respondents saw their poverty in terms that were relative to others living on the village. Economists might debate about poverty lines and whether or not there is an absolute core to poverty, but respondents' comments show the narrowness of academics' preoccupation with income or nutrition measures. An elderly widow in Keshipur put this most clearly and simply: 'If I live next to someone who is a bit better off, who manages to eat and I don't, then I feel poor.' There were many other such comments, most of which noted the disparity of ownership of assets between rich and poor, and some of which specifically compared the different lifestyles of the two groups. Of the latter, the following are colourful and also representative:

Woman in Fonogram:
Rich people don't look after the poor at all – even if we were dying and we called them they wouldn't come. Jyonal is going by motorcycle, Romesh by lorry and Daoud by cycle. I am going by foot, shoeless. In the rainy season rich people will eat good food, the poor will eat fig leaves, get sick and have to go to the doctor.

175

Man in Bithigram:
In the summer rich people can stay inside out of the sun, they will shout down at us from their houses: 'Work harder, cut my trees', but if we were hungry they wouldn't give us a piece of *mouri* (puffed rice).

Woman in Bithigram:
All our land was taken a long time back by *zamindars*. They took the land of the poor, and now they say 'Poor people can die, what do we care?' If we had 4–5 *bighas* of land we could live like human beings, but we don't have that. Look at the colour of our skin, we take salt tea and have to go out in the heat of the summer, so we are dark. The daughters of rich people stay indoors and keep fair complexions. Rich people have land, rice, nice houses, they eat lots of vegetables. They have no problems.

Again there is disdain at the heartlessness of the rich ('. . . .even if we were dying they wouldn't come.'), the same insults, and the same interest in social prestige. There is also use of humour in stressing the miserly quality of the rich – '. . . .if we were hungry they wouldn't give us a piece of *mouri* (puffed rice).' But in these quotes there is also an ambivalence in the comparisons between the lifesyles of rich and poor, and an element of envy. Rich people, claimed the poor, have good food, land, and no problems, they even have fair complexions (a sought-after characteristic in some circles in India). They can sit in the shade at home and watch poor people work. This complaint was more noticeable in Bithigram as the wealthier Hindu Mahatos did not work on the land themselves, but supervised hired labourers, often sitting all day on the edge of the field under the shade of an umbrella. It is not surprising that the poor envied the rich. The wealth of the rich dangled tantalizingly in front of their eyes on a daily basis, and this goes some way towards explaining as well the hatred that the poor felt for them.

The abusive comments I have quoted were one 'weapon of the weak'. Insulting rich people and making fun of their lifestyle as these respondents were doing was one way of attacking the rich. In this one area respondents were well off – their ability to use language to abuse or mock the rich.[5] In the closed village society where gossip was a favourite pastime, all villagers were keen to protect their reputations. Again and again respondents attacked the reputations of their rich neighbours, accusing them of a lack of humanity, not being willing to help if poor people were sick or even dying. The standard format of their complaints ('the rich are only too happy to see us die') suggests that these had become a kind of ritualized assault on the character of the rich, a strategy that the poor used as they negotiated for better conditions for loans or other village resources such as livestock to

---

[5] Compare Scott (1985: chapter one).

rear. This was despite the fact that the main sources of credit, employment and other village resources were the richer households. In Fonogram villagers' hostility was linked to the fact that in the eyes of respondents, and in the wake of irrigation development, the gap between poor and rich was growing even greater. Respondents there, as the woman quoted above, usually accused the three main members of the village *samity* as benefiters from an unfair and immoral economy.

The situation thus existed (peculiar perhaps to outsiders' eyes) that the poor were virtually unanimous in their dislike of the rich, compared their lifestyles with those of the rich, but at the same time did not in the majority of cases blame the rich for their poverty. There is perhaps here an internalization of dominant norms about fate, or what Marxists might refer to as false consciousness, especially given that some Bithigram respondents did recognize the connections between their poverty and others' wealth. I would, however, argue strongly against the idea that because the majority of respondents did not recognize what I would consider the main cause of their poverty, they therefore accepted what the political scientists I criticized earlier have called 'traditional forms of dominance.' This should be clear from the various comments I have quoted above which show that the poor were certainly not subservient to the rich. That they did not appear to need to know the real causes of their poverty (as I perceived them) did not mean that they passively accepted the status quo. It is quite clear that they were resisting the rich in any way feasible. Their outrage came from a sense of exploitation rather than an understanding of the structural socio-economic causes of poverty. And perhaps the 'failure' of the majority of respondents to make this causal link is no more peculiar than the fact (and despite the ready availability of information on such matters) that the majority of people in developed countries would not be aware of the importance in these countries of interlocking directorships between the boards of multinational corporations, or the large exchange of personnel between business and government, arrangements that in the long term have as important a consequence on their lives as does the socio-economic dominance of small groups of élites in developing countries on the lives of the rural poor.

Mutual support among the poor
In marked contrast to their feelings towards the rich, there was a large degree of perceived solidarity among the poorest in all three villages. The poorest were united as a group by the commonality of their experience of power relations and poverty. Another commonality was that the poorest were often related, and tended to help their relatives (although they were also related to richer villagers, particularly in Fonogram). While most respondents did not think that the poor could *work* together, fifty-three of the sixty respondents replying thought that the poor *helped* each other, with six saying that they did not and one non-respondent. This help was

mainly in the form of small loans of rice, oil, salt or money. Small sums of money were frequently transferred between poorest households, and almost all of the fifty-three households were or had been involved in such transactions. Sums of money or amounts of goods lent could also be quite large if the need arose; for example, in Bithigram and Keshipur respondents reported lending up to 200 rupees and 40 kg of paddy to another poor or poorest household. Other forms of help commonly mentioned were looking after children or livestock if a household member was ill, and taking sick people to the hospital or doctor.

Small loans were common enough to be unremarkable. They worked on the basis that households shared with others in need what they had, and borrowed when they were in need themselves. This reciprocal borrowing was often negotiated between women, particularly in the case of small amounts of food. Respondents stressed that despite the difficult situation other poor people were in, they still helped out when they could. As one woman in Fonogram said: 'If poor people have anything they will loan it to each other.' Even if the quantities were small, these reciprocal arrangements were very important to respondents as they showed a solidarity among the poor. However much time had passed since the loan, respondents said that a loan from another poor person had to be repaid as a matter of honour.

Respondents were clear about the meaning of such mutual support. A woman in Fonogram put it this way:

> Poor people help each other, if we didn't help one another then we wouldn't get help in times of need. I get salt, oil, rice and money from other poor people.

Others expressed this sentiment in almost the same terms. These loans among the poor were particularly important in times of illness or if there were other major contingencies, again in contrast to the perceived stinginess of the rich in these circumstances. Two respondents also expressed the feeling of the common experience of the poor.

> Widow in Keshipur:
> Rich people say: 'If I give money to a poor person I won't get it back', but a poor person will lend to me, they understand my sorrow.

> Woman in Fonogram:
> Rich people are bad, they never give any help. Poor people understand each other's poverty so they help each other.[6]

Respondents differentiated in a telling fashion loans from the rich and those which they received from their fellow poor. Although loans from the

---

[6] Similar remarks made by poor people in Bangladesh concerning their solidarity are reported in White (1988: 321) and Hartmann and Boyce (1983: 98).

rich were usually much larger than loans from the poor, the former were not seen as help (*shahajo*) but as a form of contract in which the poor were cheated. In contrast, loans among the poor were seen as help. It was the quality of the relationship between lender and borrower that mattered to the poorest more than the size of the loan.[7]

In South Asia, the literature on mutual support networks has been placed in the context of the moral economy debate, and the increasing importance of networks among the poor as former client-patron networks break down (e.g. Van Schendel, 1989; Platteau, 1988; Breman, 1985a). Whether or not this breakdown is taking place, there is agreement among a large number of authors of the importance of such networks to the poor for their survival. These studies describe similar networks to those found in the study villages here (e.g. Dasgupta, 1987: 114; Caldwell *et al.*, 1986; Howes and Jabbar, 1986: 25; Chen, 1983; Siddiqui, 1982: 48. For an overview of the literature on networks among women in South Asia, see Agarwal 1989a: 25–8). While authors have considered the extent and erosion of such networks, very few have considered them from the poor person's perspective.[8]

Given these findings about the widespread nature of solidarity, it is worth questioning the following view proposed by Sen (1983: 161):

> In a poor community . . . . the perception of poverty is primarily concerned with the commodity requirements of fulfilling nutritional needs and perhaps some needs of being clothed, sheltered and free from disease. This is the world of Charles Booth or Seebohm Rowntree . . . . and that of poverty estimation, say, in India. The more physical needs tend to dominate over the needs of communal participation.[9]

---

[7] This was the perceived reality of most residents. I heard of many past and present disputes in the study villages within poor households and families, and between women and men, particularly over land. However, in response to my questions almost all respondents presented a picture of solidarity rather than friction.

[8] See also the literature review on phenomenological studies of poverty in chapter three, many of which note the same systems of mutual support. Bandyopadhyay and von Eschen (1988), on the other hand, found very little networking of any kind in a 2-village study of West Bengal in 1972–4. There is also a substantial literature on mutual support networks among the poor in Africa which may be comparable to that from South Asia (dependent on agro-ecological and social context). Much of this has focused on famine rather than poverty. See, for example, Rahmato (1988: 7), Longhurst (1986: 30) and Toulmin (1986: 66), and for a review of relevant literature, Dreze and Sen (1989: chapter five).

[9] See also Lipton (1983a: 66), for a similar view. It may be 'the world of Charles Booth and Seebohm Rowntree', but it is not the world of the poor people in their surveys. As Booth and Rowntree note, there were networks for mutual support among the poor in the societies that they studied. See chapter three for specific references.

The poor in the study villages would certainly not subscribe to such a statement. To the contrary, the 'needs of communal participation', the need for social prestige, for respect, and to be seen as supporting other poor people in the village ranked at least as highly as commodity requirements. By extension, the absolutist approach to poverty Sen espouses is also called into question by such findings. Does poverty really have an absolute core when even those on the very margins of society, who are regularly hungry, feel that they are willing to forego food in order to gain respect? The implications of this are that poverty involves much more than lack of food, shelter and being subject to illness; it also involves the experience of being subordinated and oppressed, and resisting this where possible. And this is why mutual support, the 'needs of communal participation', were perceived as so crucial by the poor.

From a policy perspective the type of intervention needed to support such mutual support systems can come in at least two forms. The first can be found in the work of NGOs that have proliferated particularly in Bangladesh over the last ten years or so. Some of these NGOs, for example Proshika and BRAC (see Wood and Palmer-Jones, 1991; Chen, 1983), have been successful in building on mutual support systems by setting up formal groups of poor men or women and funding income-generating activities, education and 'consciousness raising'. Their success has been achieved by ensuring that the groups are homogenous, and by staff training and staff commitment. Hundreds of thousands of the poor are now members of such groups throughout Bangladesh. The problems that have arisen with NGO work have been those of scale and of depth. NGOs cannot take on the role of the government, that is, their work will always cover a small minority of the population. This is an intractable problem while governments in developing countries continue in their present form. The question of depth relates to how far NGOs can either improve solidarity among the poor, or change socio-economic structure. A recent survey of NGOs in Bangladesh (White 1991) makes the point that NGO programmes may do little to undermine the causes of poverty, and also may not increase solidarity among the poor because the onus in their credit programmes are on the individual. In another study of six major NGOs in Bangladesh, Hashmi (1989) has noted that NGO consciousness raising programmes may be superficial attempts at social change because they turn into sessions where poor group members repeat slogans, chanted by NGO staff, which they do not understand.

The second policy intervention to build on mutual support networks among the poor is one that has been almost completely ignored in the development literature and by anti-poverty programmers – that is, supporting agricultural labourer unions. In all of the literature on participation of the poor in development programmes I have read I have not come across one reference to labour unions. Given the present emphasis on the market

180

in development thinking, it is unlikely that there will be much focus on unionization. Yet whatever the state of unions in developed countries today, unionization in the past has been the main method by which poor workers have pooled resources to improve their working conditions and overall quality of life.

The literature on unions in the agricultural sector in India has tended to focus on peasant organizations. But there has as well been considerable attention paid to the success of agricultural labour unions in Kerala (see Alexander, 1989; Tharamangalam, 1981). Labourers in Kerala, with the support of the communist parties there, have organized to achieve better working conditions, wages, ownership of homestead plots, and freedom from exploitation. This organization has been one of the main methods whereby the population of Kerala has improved its quality of life (Franke and Chassin, 1991). Clearly aid agencies and most NGOs have veered away from supporting unions, but they should certainly be seen as one vehicle by which outsiders could support agricultural labourers in their bargaining over wages and better working conditions. Recent studies by Lewis (1991) and I. Sen (1990) have described local attempts of the poor in India, some from within unions, to organize with the support of outsiders. Their studies show both the difficulties faced in such organization, particularly the problems of maintaining solidarity among different sections within the poor, as well as the potential that such a development 'model' offers in helping the poor make demands on the state or their employers.

Poverty and self respect

The antagonism that the poor felt towards the rich was further complicated by the importance respondents placed on self respect. I noted in the last chapter that self respect was valued more highly than food by forty-nine out of fifty-eight respondents. Respondents were well aware that, no matter how poor they became, they needed to live as social beings, and to receive respect from others to maintain their own self respect. As a Fonogram woman said: 'Self respect is more important than food; no matter how poor you are you want to keep some self respect.' An incident that happened to Sundari, the widow and maid servant I have mentioned in the last chapter as a user of the *poussani* system, will illustrate the strength of this feeling. Sundari and her relative Raila who lived with her were certainly among the poorest. They had nothing except what their daily labour in other people's houses brought in and what they could entice other villagers to give them. They owned no homestead land, and lived in the dilapidated corner of the house of a relative. Sundari had for some time been shopping at the local store owned by the wealthy landowner who lived in the village and to whom most village credit was owed. This man's son, Abdul, ran the shop. Sundari had gone to do her daily shopping and had been kept waiting

181

by Abdul; when she had tried to attract his attention he had snubbed her verbally. As she told me of this incident, Sundari relived it, becoming angry at the memory. She said: 'I refuse to be treated like that by anyone.' She had then raised money in the village (no easy task) and paid off her credit at the shop, and then moved her custom to another shop. A minor incident perhaps, but just one of the many incidents that take place everyday when the powerful make the subordinated aware of their power in this fashion. Sundari used the only two weapons she had at this point – that of consumer, and storyteller in repeating the incident from her point of view and insulting, as she did so, Abdul.[10]

Their need to be respected meant that respondents were keen to adhere to the norms of village life, including religious norms. For example, six female respondents in Fonogram said that they maintained self respect because they did not go outside of their homestead, thus maintaining *purdah* norms. Whether or not this adherence to *purdah* norms, which contributed centrally to women's oppression (as seen from an outsider's viewpoint), constitutes 'participation in one's own repression' is beyond the scope of the discussion here because of the complexity of the subject and the extensive feminist debate concerning it.[11] But it is worth pointing out that many people in western societies do things to maintain their sense of self-esteem that may in the long term be harmful to them – for example, overworking, drinking large amounts of alcohol, taking drugs, or driving cars dangerously.

Respondents in the three villages were asked if their self respect had gone up or down in the last 10 to 20 years (i.e. during the period of Left Front rule). Replies partly depended on the village context. In Fonogram most respondent households had experienced economic decline. Nineteen of the twenty-two respondents replying said that their self respect had declined, and linked this to their loss of land or labour power, as well as to their shunning by the rich.[12] In Keshipur, where a similar process of economic decline had occurred, partly counteracted by the government development programmes, in eight cases respondents thought that their self respect had declined, and in five cases that it had remained the same.

By contrast in Bithigram fifteen of the nineteen respondent households thought that their self respect had increased. This they linked directly to the role of the CPM and to their receipt of *patta* land. They also linked this to the fact that rather than being seen as criminals and outcastes by the

---

[10] The importance of self respect to the poor in South Asia is also commented on in Agarwal, 1989b: WS59; Jodha, 1989; Chambers, 1988; and BRAC, 1984: 27–8.

[11] This matter is considered by White (1988: 145–6), and Arens and Van Beurden (1977: 62).

[12] Van Schendel (1981: 92) also notes from village Bangladesh that self-respect is closely linked to wealth, but not identical with it.

Mahato farmers, as formerly, these farmers now offered the Lodhas a place to sit in their houses. There was here therefore a similar paradox to the situation of the female respondents in Fonogram who supported *purdah* norms. The same woman who commented on the complexion of the daughters of the rich also said: 'Self respect is more important for us. Ten to fifteen years ago we didn't have any self respect, now farmers tell us to sit in their houses and give us tea.' Several of the other Bithigram respondents spoke in a similar fashion. As some of the other comments quoted here show (for example, the widow in Keshipur quoted above who said that rich people did not even talk to the poor when the latter asked for food), despite their hostility towards the rich, respondents were keen to keep good relations with them. This appeared to be more than pragmatism; respondents wanted to be treated as neighbours and accepted as human beings even by those who they saw as cheating them. Poorest people's priorities may therefore be complex, and they may retain 'multiple identities'.[13]

One final point about poorest people's long-term priorities can be made. Respondents were asked what hopes they had for their children. Of the forty who had children and replied, seven said that they would like to marry off their children well, four said they would like land for their children, and twenty-five said that they wanted to send their children to school to learn how to read and write. Some respondents linked this desire for education for their children to their own powerlessness, for example in the way that they were cheated by shopkeepers or employers because they were illiterate, and others said that if their daughters could read and write they would make a better marriage. Literacy also meant greater self respect. As one man in Bithigram put it: 'I will put my kids into school. If they learn how to read and write they won't have to labour all their lives.' Respondents recognized the difficulties of sending children to school given their own poverty and the income 'working' children brought in, but were still determined that the children should attend school for a better future.

Conclusions

The experience of poverty for the poor was closely linked above all to lack of power. It is this lack of power that I see as the most important organizing feature in their lives, and into which all other attributes of poverty – such as

---

[13] The maintenance by individuals of paradoxical views, and the difference between perceptions and 'reality', are major subjects of study in their own right (see for example the discussions in Dreze and Sen, 1989, and the discussion of 'mental-metricism' in chapters three and five). For a critique of Gramsci's notion of false consciousness, and a discussion of 'multiple identities' see Scott (1985, especially chapter 8).

lack of assets, ill health or isolation, and the need for credit – feed. And in a society where prestige and a good reputation were vital, lack of power meant as well lack of respect from the powerful in the village, which the poor saw as devastating.

My findings show that Thompson's view of the poor and rich as 'mutually bound' can be seen to operate at different levels. The poorest in the study villages did demand what they saw as rights – use of land, CPRs, livestock or credit. When these were denied they demanded them by insulting the rich, and sometimes by force. They were mutually bound in a social sense as well, in that, as social beings, the poorest were concerned with the opinions that the rich held of them, and did not hesitate to express their own opinions about the rich. But the rich were also bound to the poor in that they too wanted to maintain their reputations and prestige, and needed to tie the poor by debt to both gain extra resources and to ensure a compliant labour supply.

There was a large degree of agreement across the three villages and among the different caste, religious and ethnic groups concerning respondents' views on power. Their ritualized replies, often in colloquial Bengali, suggest that such ideas had become embedded in their minds, and these ritualized messages contested the world view of the dominant by saying: 'Poor people help each other. Rich people like to eat fish and throw poor people the bones.' Like CPRs or land, prestige and reputation were a resource to fight for.

The question as to whether the poor in the study villages formed a class is a difficult one. They perhaps met Thompson's requirement that (1986: 9–10): ' . . . .class happens when some men, as a result of common experiences, feel and articulate the identity of their interests as between themselves, and as against other men whose interests are different from (and usually opposed to) theirs.' Respondents did 'articulate the identity of their interests', in that they expressed sympathy with their fellow poor and hostility to the rich. But on the other hand this articulation of their class interests did not go so far as to allow respondents to make a causal connection between their poverty and others' wealth. I hypothesize that if the poorest had made this causal connection, it would have increased their impetus to organization. It was the Lodhas in Bithigram who were nearest to a class, and, as has been noted elsewhere (Tharamangalam, 1986), one of the most important factors contributing to organization and protest is that of ethnic identity. The Lodhas were certainly the most vocal and organized in demanding their rights from their wealthy neighbours, although the poor in Fonogram and Keshipur also found means of voicing their discontent.

As argued throughout this book, the concentration by poverty measurers on nutritional minima and levels of income needed to survive ignores power, the experience of poverty, and poor people as agents who fight for resources and over the ideology of what poverty and wealth are. The historical dimension to this agency and contestation has been discussed in chapters three and four, and it is in the context of this history of 'everyday forms of poor people's survival and resistance', much of it unwritten, that the present findings should be placed.

9   Death comes to poorest households

Nothing that I have written so far should be taken to mean that the poor can get by without outside support. Because I have chosen to focus on strengths of the poor does not mean that I am arguing that their coping strategies can necessarily ensure them a better quality of life. These strategies are often insufficient to ensure survival of some members of the household. I want to look now at what happens when these strategies break down by presenting three case studies of death from poorest households in Fonogram.

Case 1. Death of Asgar

Asgar had not grown up in Fonogram, but had come to live there as he had a distant relative who lived in the village. Rumour had it that Asgar had a colourful past. One of these rumours concerned his smuggling goods from Bangladesh during the Independence War in 1971. There were also rumours that he had married several times, although Asgar said that he had married three times, that his first wife had died during childbirth, and that he had divorced his second wife who lived in Calcutta. In 1987 he lived in Fonogram with his third wife, Surjahan, and their two children, a boy aged about 12 and a girl of 10. Asgar was about 50 in 1987 and Surjahan 35.

Asgar's household was landless, and he made his living by plying a cycle van (basically an elongated three-wheel cycle with some boards of wood attached to the back), taking people to the local doctor or market, or moving housing material or crops. Asgar's son did not go to school, and could often be seen running behind the cycle van pushing it as Asgar cycled, to help it go faster. Surjahan worked in a local tobacco factory owned by a wealthy absentee landowner, where for a ten-hour working day she earned eight rupees. Her employment was sporadic. Theirs was a precarious existence but they managed to get by.

The incident that eventually led to Asgar's death was a complicated one. Asgar was jealous of his neighbour, Habi, who apparently used to come and flirt with Surjahan. So Asgar decided to take revenge. In April 1987 he arranged a liaison between Habi's wife and an outsider who stayed every year in a mango garden in the village owned by Habi's mother, with whom Habi and his wife lived. It was a common practice for traders to purchase the total mango crop from a garden at a set price, and to stay in the gardens to protect the mangoes against theft. News of the liaison got out to the other villagers, and it was deemed outside of the moral norms of the village by some of the more powerful villagers. There are various versions as to what happened next, but the mango trader was waylaid and beaten up on one of his evening visits to Habi's wife, and it seems he told them who had arranged the meetings. Habi fled the village, and his wife was beaten up.

Asgar was then also beaten up badly. Four of his ribs were broken, his house was destroyed, and he was told that he and his family would have to leave the village. He complained bitterly that the *samity* members had persuaded some other villagers to attack him.

Asgar and Surjahan then rented a small hut near to Fonogram on the land of the absentee landlord for whom Surjahan worked. This cost them 25 rupees a month. Asgar was unable to work because of his injuries, and they could not afford a doctor. They were forced to rely on Surjahan's irregular income during the pre-monsoon period. By the end of 1987 Asgar had contracted tuberculosis, probably because of undernutrition, and could hardly walk. They were forced to sell their cycle van in the market for 700 rupees to buy food and medicine. This was much less than it was worth, according to Asgar. They also resorted to taking loans from the local shops and Surjahan's employer. Despite this, Asgar's condition worsened and he succumbed to TB in the summer of 1988.

At one level this case involves a villager who had transgressed the moral boundaries of the village and was punished by the powerful in the village for doing so. But there may have been other elements involved in this death. Asgar was unusual in that he had spent time in Calcutta, and was perceived to have led an unconventional life (for example the rumours about his having married several times). He was also more outspoken on political matters than many other of the poor villagers in Fonogram, and had a clearer knowledge of state politics. In his expulsion from the village there may also have been an attempt to warn other villagers not to move outside of their normal sphere of activity as far as politics were concerned.

Case 2. Death of Moni

Moni was the daughter of Hamedchha, my guide in Fonogram. Hamedchha and his son earned their main source of income through agricultural labouring. Hamedchha also had one other daughter, who was marriedand lived outside the village.

Moni had not had an easy youth. Her household had been in economic decline since at least the 1960s. Hamedchha had inherited about three *bighas* of land, but he had been seriously ill in the mid-70s and was forced to sell and mortgage this land. During this period his wife divorced him, thinking he was going to die, and his children were forced to go around the village begging for *bhater phen* (rice water). Eventually Hamedchha recovered, but the household's land was now controlled by others. By the end of the 1980s, Hamedchha had just a few decimals of land left, all mortgaged either to relatives or other, wealthier villagers.

Moni had been brought up by her father. In 1988, Hamedchha decided it was time for Moni, who was aged about fifteen or sixteen, to get married. He organized the marriage through an acquaintance in the village where his first daughter had been married. Hamedchha could afford little dowry,

187

so the match was with a man from a poor agricultural labourer household. As is the custom, the marriage was arranged by the parents and the potential bride had little say in the matter. Accordingly, Moni left her natal village for her husband's village.

When Moni returned to her father's house for a visit a few months after her marriage it was evident that there was something seriously wrong. Hamedchha told me the details. Moni had become mentally deranged since her marriage. After her return to Fonogram, she began to wander outside of the village and then would get lost, forcing Hamedchha to spend long hours searching for her. Hamedchha went to Moni's husband's house to investigate, and returned saying he had discovered that Moni's husband had a serious disease and he was trying to get her dowry returned. This was too late for Moni. She began visiting a local doctor, but her wanderings around the region continued and she was evidently in a state of severe mental distress about whatever had happened to her at her husband's house. At the beginning of 1989 she took poison and killed herself.

Case 3. Death of an agricultural labourer
Jiar came from a household that relied on his labour for its main source of income. Jiar was married and there was one young daughter as well in the household. He and his family lived in the same compound as his father, but they supplied their own food and cooked from a separate *chula* (hearth). Jiar's father, Anerali, had been married twice. From his first marriage Anerali had four surviving children, all younger than Jiar. Anerali's first wife had died, and he remarried, and from his second marriage two boys and one girl, who were teenagers, lived with him. Anerali owned about two *bihgas* of land, which he farmed himself. Jiar worked on his father's and other villagers' land and his main source of income came from agricultural labouring.

In 1988, the year he died, Jiar was aged about 30. Jiar's health had not been good for some time. He suffered from asthma, and was subject to severe coughing fits. He was undernourished and his body was worn by attempting to work on an empty stomach. Eventually he began spitting blood. His father took him to the local hospital in the winter of 1987 and he was diagnosed as having tuberculosis.

After a few days of taking medicine and drinking milk regularly Jiar's health seemed to improve. He left his house where he had been resting and could move around the village again. Still not strong enough to work, he took a loan from one of the local shops to provide food for himself and his family. The chances were good that he would recover. But slowly his health deteriorated. His father said he had no more money for treatment. So Jiar lay on the verandah of his house all day and night covered in a thin blanket. A wealthy villager, one of the *samity* members, commented that if his own family did not help him then why should outsiders do so. It seemed that

188

Anerali's wife (Jiar's stepmother) refused to let Anerali mortgage their land to buy the medicine and food that Jiar needed. Some villagers said that she was looking to her own children before those of her husband's first wife.

Jiar died in mid-afternoon and his wife's cries could be heard throughout the village. Apart from the grief on the death of her husband, she was now left alone to support her daughter, and Jiar's stepmother's animosity towards her was obvious. A few days after Jiar's body had been washed, laid out in his best clothes, and buried, she was forced to beg for food in the village.

Conclusions

While the cause of death in the final instance in each of these three cases was physical, there were many factors that lead up to death. Grinding poverty and undernutrition were the background to all three case studies, but none of the three deaths was caused by lack of food alone. There were social factors that were as important as physical ones.

In the case of Moni patriarchal structures meant she had no say in her marriage, and this decided her fate. Jiar's death was the result of poverty and illness, but was also due to relations within his household. And in the case of Asgar, being a poor landless worker meant that he was punished for moral misdeeds by the 'middle' farmers in the village which, if he had been richer, might have been ignored. In the cases of the two men it was the main wage earner who died, and their wives and children were left to get by as best they could; isolated from family or other village members their sources for survival were extremely limited. In the case of Moni, apart from being grieved by her family, she became one of the many invisible statistics that make up Indian mortality figures. About a year after her death Hamedchha's son married and took on the role that had formerly been taken by Moni.

Although it may be possible to locate and build on the strengths of the poor, it is clear that at some point in their lives the crises they face may be unsurmountable and, whether they sell assets, draw on mutual support systems or use other strategies, they will be unable to survive without external support. Such crises inevitably involve power relations, whether between poor and rich or women and men.

189

10 Rich people like to eat fish and throw poor people the bones

This book has examined the realities of development and survival for the Indian poorest in three villages of West Bengal. In this last chapter I would like to draw out some general themes and conclusions from the material presented. I will cover three areas: the importance of building on the strengths of the poor and taking into account their experience when formulating development programmes; the importance of understanding how ideologies involved with the construction of the concept of poverty affect policy making; and why people with power need to get involved in development.

Poverty and rural development

This book has highlighted the importance of seeking practical solutions at the village level to the problems of poverty, and has done so by concentrating on the strengths of the poor and the strategies that they use to improve their quality of life. This is in sharp contrast to most studies of poverty, which focus on weaknesses of the poor such as ill health, undernutrition or illiteracy. To achieve its purpose the book has contrasted two differing kinds of development. The first kind involved external intervention in the villages through government administered or funded development projects. In the case of Fonogram village, the West Bengal government had supported an irrigation project which, developed and run by the village élite, caused substantial additional benefits to accrue to those already largely in control of village resources. At the same time, there was some 'trickle down' to the Fonogram poor in terms of increased labour, but while this was significant relative to labourers' incomes, its significance diminished in the eyes of its recipients as they watched their increasingly wealthy neighbours build large brick houses and buy luxury items with their newfound profits. In the case of Bithigram and Keshipur, the government administered land reform programme did relatively better than the Fonogram irrigation project in getting resources to the poor, although the village élite also performed consistently in capturing a considerable share of the benefits. I stressed as well the importance of looking at the qualitative effects of development programmes; in the case of the land reform programme, even a tiny piece of land could provide a psychological boost to a formerly landless household, because it acted as a symbol that the government was working for the poor.

The evidence presented on external interventions was of course only from three villages, but adds to the growing information concerning development projects in India which suggests that external resources, particularly those under government schemes, are mediated by village socio-economic structure, and benefit disproportionately in particular a small élite.

This form of external intervention was contrasted to what I term indigenous rural development, which was analysed in chapters seven and eight. These chapters examined how poorest people themselves negotiated, bargained and struggled with the rich, and manipulated village power structures, to gain access to resources and to maintain or improve their quality of life. Broadly, there were two types of strategies the poor used – firstly, practical and everyday, and secondly, ideological and confrontational. Chapter seven outlined several practical and everyday survival strategies from an informal economy which was operated to a large extent by village women. These strategies had been tried and tested, and either benefited poor and rich, or benefited the poor but not to the detriment of the interests of the rich, and therefore worked within existing power structures. These strategies included use of the depleting but still vital 'common' resource base, management and sale of assets, the borrowing of livestock from the rich, and variations in cooking and eating patterns. A review of relevant studies from South Asia showed that, while in some cases comparative material was scarce, each of these strategies was found to be common to the poor in the region. None of these strategies simply involved the poor accessing a resource; in each case the poor needed to bargain or negotiate with the rich in their villages concerning these resources, which is why I consider gaining access to them a strength of the poor.

When contrasting external and indigenous forms of rural development, it is particularly instructive to look at the comparison between sharerearing of livestock, common throughout India and many other parts of the developing world as a means of redistributing livestock within villages, and the government funded Integrated Rural Development Project which aimed to provide livestock to the Indian poor. That the indigenous system of livestock redistribution worked more effectively than the government intervention in terms of providing assets for the poor should give planners pause for thought. This is particularly true given that the indigenous system has been improved upon by NGOs in the region, which have removed its 'exploitive' elements. Why was the most important anti-poverty programme in India since Independence developed in parallel to, but apparently without recognition of, a 'successful' India-wide system of indigenous resource distribution? This says much about our general ignorance of systems that might be in operation in village India for resource redistribution, as well as the ability of the poor to gain these resources. The increased demand for livestock resulting from IRDP may actually make livestock more scarce and thus damage the indigenous system. The same holds true for the effects of the green revolution. As more land goes into production

191

in an ungoverned fashion, the vital natural resource base that adds significantly to poor households' welfare will become increasingly depleted, making survival for them all the more difficult.

From one perspective, the practical, everyday strategies that I have outlined do little to change the degree of exploitation that the poor face. They may appear as simply a means to gain more resources. But I have argued that such strategies are intricately linked to power conflicts in the villages between poor and rich. Over even what appeared to an outsider to be minor resources such as gleaned grains there was significant conflict. Through this conflict poor and rich continuously negotiated their relative status in the villages; for while the aim of the rich was to keep the poor subordinated, the poor were constantly making demands on the rich. In chapter eight I moved from strategies that involved bargaining and negotiation to analysis of direct confrontation, struggle and ideological conflicts between poor and rich. I examined these conflicts from the perspective of the poor, looking at strategies the poor used to hold their wealthy neighbours to account in their search for respect and resources. Strategies of confrontation ranged from rare open violence of poor against rich to bargaining for wages as a group; ideological conflict, where the poor threw their poverty in the faces of the rich, included such 'weapons of the weak' as gossip, slander, use of humour and storytelling, and theft at night.

Findings at the field level lead me to suggest that a sensible rural development strategy would involve paying much closer attention to areas where the poor fight for respect and resources, and subsequently supporting the negotiating strategies of the poor and the demands that poor women and men make on the state or on local élites. If the main barrier to rural development projects being effective in India is village power structures, and the poor have learnt to manipulate power structures, why not learn from this? The support the West Bengal government gave to the existing ability of the Lodhas in Bithigram to organize is a good example of this, and strengthened the Lodhas' hands as well in other areas of their lives within the village, for example their ability to access the village natural resource base.

In chapters seven and eight I touched briefly on attempts by NGOs and unions in South Asia to support the poor in their struggles and demands on the state and local élites. There have been several recent studies of such activism in India. These include the work of Durno and Mondal (1989), describing the activities of the Socio-Legal Aid Research and Training Centre, based in Calcutta, which has been working since 1983 to provide poor women with knowledge of their rights under the Indian Constitution, as well as to understand the procedures of Indian law. Other examples come in essays in the volume edited by Sen (1990) of local trade union and women's groups. One of the best recent examples of such activism comes from a book by Primila Lewis, *Social Action and the Labouring Poor*, covering the ten years after 1978, and the attempts she and a small group of other activists, affiliated to an NGO, Action India, made to organize and change the lives of farm workers, Harijans and quarry workers at Mehrauli, near to Delhi. Lewis describes in painful detail ten years of difficult and ultimately only partly successful work by her group attempting to organize co-operatives and unions. Because of political contacts and proximity to Delhi, Action India did help the Harijans of Mehrauli to gain some local land, but it would be hard to imagine a similar attempt to organize the poor in rural Bihar achieving even the limited success of Lewis' group. The achievements of the group were therefore at once encouraging and sobering. Encouraging, because with sufficient resources, time and energy it is possible to support the poor in gaining their rights. Sobering because even with years of work, good contacts in Delhi, and a high profile, the gains were relatively small.

Lewis establishes an ideology based on the dual strategy of organizing the poor so that they can claim their rights from the state, and allowing poor people space to 'develop' themselves. As she puts it at the end of her book (1991: 265): 'Among the main lessons we have learned after 10 years of intense involvement in grassroots work is that in the process of 'empowering the people it is essential to allow space for independent initiative, creativity and personal aspirations. Otherwise we become an oppressive rather than a liberating factor.' This realization is in tune with various other contemporary schools of thought that have over the last ten years stressed the importance of including the poor in development which they themselves design and implement.[1]

In terms of rural development, a number of different interventions to support the poor are possible, ranging from such semi-confrontational activities as protecting common property land used by the poor, to supporting direct confrontation by backing agricultural labourer unions. Which strategy should be developed depends both on the individual situation and the wishes of those who will be most involved. The potential risks involved in supporting the poor in claiming their legal rights from the state may be great, especially if activists support organizations of the poor and then leave the poor to face the consequences of their organization. It is clear that only long term commitment is a viable option here. However, all strategies bear some element of risk, because Indian villages are inherently political institutions and any intervention in them is necessarily political. It should also be remembered that the poor may be skilled in the area of negotiation and struggle, and may already be well aware of the consequences of challenging those in power and willing to take the necessary risks of doing so. In addition, intervention in this area is likely to be more effective in states such as West Bengal where the government is sympathetic to the plight of the poor.

---

[1] For a summary differentiating the literature on participation, see Oakley (1991).

Poor people's experience

My second conclusion refers to the importance of taking poor people's experience into account when attempting to understand poverty. I have argued in this book against Sen's concept of 'mental-metricism', which emphasizes that individuals embody a kind of false consciousness where they are unable to understand fully the reality of their circumstances. Instead I have made the case that, like those of anybody else, the comments of the poor must be seen in the context of the environment in which they live and the constraints they face in their everyday lives. The poor in the study villages were illiterate and denied access to information. They themselves realized that knowledge (and education) are closely related to power, that being denied information contributed to their relative powerlessness, and many of them saw education as the hope for their children's future.[2]

Given these circumstances and that they had been isolated by the élite in their villages, one would not expect the poor to be well informed about party politics or wage legislation. Similarly, given the enormous social pressures that they faced, one would also expect some internalization of dominant ideologies and norms, for example the belief expressed by some female respondents in Fonogram that they had more self respect because they abided by *purdah* restrictions.

But to say that the poor have internalized all dominant ideologies and that they are completely subject to 'mental-metricism' or false consciousness would be quite wrong. As Scott (1990; 1985) has pointed out, the 'public transcript' of the oppressed or subordinated presented for everday consumption to powerful outsiders may be quite different from the 'private transcript', or what the oppressed or subordinated person actually feels and believes. One of the problems we face when trying to distinguish public from private transcripts is that the acedemic community has made little effort to explore the private transcripts of the poor. It is generally assumed, as in the concept of 'mental-metricism', or in the writings of authors such as Frankel and the Rudolphs discussed in chapter two, that the poor will believe what they are told to believe.

Conversations with respondents from the three study villages of this book show that the poor have constructed an alternative ideology to the dominant one concerning poor people's abilities. I reiterate two points. Firstly, the poor stressed the importance of self respect, and their need to be accepted as social beings. For them, and I suspect for many other people, respect and social prestige were more important than material factors such as food. This is all the more remarkable given that the 60

---

[2] In this respect the West Bengal literacy campaign goes a long way to meeting the requirements of a development project that poor people want (see Bannerjee, 1992).

respondents in the case study villages lived on the edge of survival. Measurers of poverty should take note of the importance of self respect to the poor, for studies that focus obsessively on single indicators of poverty such as income or nutritional intake are presenting a perspective that radically misrepresents poverty. Secondly, poor people hated the rich in their villages, even as they envied their lifestyles, and even though for the most part they did not connect their own poverty to others' wealth. Insults, theft and other forms of resistance by the poor were the main means of expressing this hatred. Closely connected to this, and perhaps most importantly, they empathized strongly with their fellow poor, and belonged to well developed mutual support networks made up of friends and relatives that were central to their ability to survive.

If the poor people in Fonogram, Bithigram and Keshipur were to rewrite the accounts endlessly produced on poverty from their own perspective, they might sum up their views of power relations in village life as: 'Poor people help each other. Rich people like to eat fish and throw poor people the bones.' From the similar comments made by the poor in each of the study villages, it is possible to construct a raw vision they held of a radically different village society based on mutual respect and support, rather than the society in existence based on what I have termed exploitation. These views may be as problematic and subjective as any other. Their comments on the importance of mutual support among the poor may be symbolic and represent their vision of an ideal village rather than the realities of everyday village life, and these comments must be read in the context of the hardships of their everyday lives. But in all the debates on poverty between erudite scholars, the experience of the poor is rarely taken into account, and because scholars deny the importance of this experience, our understanding of what poverty actually means is weakened.

Poverty, ideology and policy-making

The third conclusion concerns the relation between the ideological construction of poverty and policy-making. Discussions I have held on poverty and anti-poverty projects with farmers, government officials in India and Bangladesh, and aid workers from around the world, have generally returned at some point to the character of the poor. More often than not in these discussions, the poor are characterized as apathetic, ignorant or lazy, and therefore are considered as responsible for their own poverty. Similarly, in every study of poverty, even in studies where the poor are reduced to statistical data sets, there is an implicit or explicit value judgement as to the nature of poor people. The economic literature on poverty measurement deconstructed in chapter two, and which currently dominates discussions of poverty in India, has attempted to delineate the poor as a set of statistics, ignoring all but their number, income levels and nutritional intake. I have suggested that this excessive reduction of the human to the statistical level follows in a tradition of poverty measurement in nineteenth-century Britain where moral divisions among the poor over-lapped with the introduction of 'scientific' measurement. This tradition has viewed the poor as incapable and irresponsible, and therefore accountable for their own poverty; and it has also viewed the poor as passive, but, paradoxically, potentially dangerous if organized by external forces. Such conceptualizations necessarily feed into and direct policy making, because even in our so-called modern society value judgements still determine to a large extent how policy is made. If poverty studies argue that the poor are incapable and need to be lifted, raised or levitated above the poverty line, anti-poverty programmes become blunt instruments which aim to haul the poor to a given income. If poverty studies argue that the poor are dangerous, anti-poverty programmes become instruments of social control. Hence the importance of challenging such representations of the poor, and this has been one of the central aims of this book.

I have drawn on an alternative humanistic tradition to question the sterile economic and élitist analysis that makes up most contemporary analysis of poverty in India. With its roots in people's history, this tradition has viewed the poor as those who can contribute to, form and reform the societies of which they are a part. I have argued that the poor in the case study villages were, for the most part, capable agents, but also that theirs was an agency severely constrained by the socio-economic and political environment in which they found themselves. This discussion of the con-juncture of agency and constraining structure should be situated in a wider and complex debate concerning individual rationality and agency that I want to touch on briefly here.

In the neo-classical economic paradigm, most recently in the well pub-licized writings of Fukuyama (1992), the individual is characterized as a self-maximizing rational agent, a body that moves in a linear fashion to-wards the goal of self improvement and greater economic wealth. One can see the attraction of this kind of theorising, for in this neo-classical para-digm individuals can take control of their own destinies and, given the right circumstances (a major qualification), their potential for movement to-wards the goal of self improvement is virtually unlimited. This view of society has become popular not just in western but in many other societies, and this is why Fukuyama, reversing Marxist doctrine, can write of liberal democracy and the free market, which incorporate this view of the individ-ual, as being the best of all possible political and economic systems. In this reading of society, failure to follow the linear path to self-maximization lies with the individual. So the nineteenth-century immoral poor in Britain *were* seen by social commentators such as Booth and Rowntree as agents, but their agency was of a negative kind which meant that, through their ignorance and apathy, the cause of poverty lay with them. As has been

196

pointed out on numerous occasions, such a view ignores questions of class, relations of power within communities, and the structural constraints that limit the potential of individuals to change their circumstances. Despite this, the attraction of an ideology that concentrates on individual potential should not be underestimated.

One can see in the writings of the authors discussed in chapter three a similar stress on agency, but in their challenge to the neo-classical approach or to economic determinist writing, these authors emphasize the positive agency and capabilities of the poor. Historians such as Thompson and Raphael envision society as being formed by groups or classes working together towards a common cause. But as I argued in chapter three, one of the problems that Marxist and people's history authors have grappled with has been the necessity of delineating the interaction of the agency of subordinated groups and the socio-economic structures that constrain them. If these structural constraints are not carefully outlined, the temptation is to focus exclusively on agency and experience. However, if structural constraints are over-stressed, any agency the poor may have disappears and they become objects in a deterministic machine that crushes them and which they cannot resist or change. The task that serious students of poverty face is thus a complex one. The challenge remains to spend time with the poor focusing on their experience, as well as to analyse how the poor interact with the structural constraints of the society in which they live. But it is essential to meet this challenge if poverty studies are to present both a positive and realistic view of the realities of Indian village life, and inform policy-making with a clear picture of the Indian village.

Despite the shortcomings of his work reviewed in chapter three, E.P. Thompson's concept of the moral economy, with the rich and poor bound in a ring of mutual need and antagonism, was seen to be a useful concept with which to analyse the struggles in the study villages between poor and rich over resources and ideology. In fact, the negotiation and struggles concerning the informal economy in early and mid-nineteenth century rural Britain and contemporary rural West Bengal, struggles for example over gleaned grain and the tethering of stock 'in the lanes' or on common land, revealed a degree of congruence that makes one conjecture about common forms of exploitation and class relations in industrializing societies.

Poverty and public action

I have suggested above that an important intervention in villages in India would be to support the negotiating strategies of the poor and the demands that poor women and men make on the state or on local elites. There is another form of intervention that people in the west can make in their own countries to influence development. This is to become involved with policy-

197

making and advocacy. How politicians and bureaucrats in developed countries make development policy, and the best way to influence this, is not well understood. There have not been, to my knowledge, any studies made of decision making in bilateral development agencies such as the British Overseas Development Administration or the Canadian International Development Agency, although such studies could enhance the ability to influence policy-makers.[3]

But there is every reason to hope that action by the public will be effective in influencing policy. By the public here I mean those in developing and developed countries who are interested in eliminating poverty and famine. A survey of public campaigning on aid in Britain in the 1980s shows that public pressure can influence policy making if it is sufficiently directed (Mitchell, 1991). There does appear to be a consensus emerging at least in some parts of the NGO community in both developing and developed countries that influencing government policy is a development strategy that is worth attempting. This appears to be partly because it seems pointless creating projects for the poor that are subsequently destroyed by government decree. If governments of developed countries, who control the global purse strings and aid budgets, are to make better policies about poverty, then the public in these countries will have to influence them to do so. While it is worthwhile travelling and even working in a developing country to learn more about poverty, much of the real work lies at home. This work involves joining organizations, going on marches, writing to politicians, keeping informed, and giving money. It requires a belief that groups of concerned people can promote change. It requires as well a professed solidarity with the poor and a commitment to work for a better society.

It would be pleasant to be able to come to an optimistic conclusion about poverty and poor people's futures in the villages covered in this book. However, in the ring binding poor and rich, the rich – themselves feeling, thinking and capable agents – have a strong upper hand in their attempts to subordinate the poor. Focusing on poor people's capabilities should not detract from the extraordinary difficulties faced by the poor. The poor people I spoke to in the study villages will probably continue to eke out a living on the margins of tolerable existence, and continue to be insulted, exploited, sick, hungry and angry. Several poorest respondents said, with Shakespearean bleakness, that they had no hope and no future. However, their ability to support each other, their sense of mutual suffering, as well

---

[3] Two recent innovative volumes on aid and policy making, based on interviews with senior policy makers in the World Bank, reveal the complex process by which policy is carried out in the World Bank as well as the negotiation that takes place between World Bank officials and senior politicians and bureaucrats in developing countries (Mosley *et al.*, 1991).

as their sense of humour, which all act as a weapon against the rich and a means of self preservation, may help them through. This book is a testament to their ability not only to get by in appalling conditions, but to do so as warm human beings.

Bibliography

Abbreviations

EPW	Economic and Political Weekly
IDS	Institute of Development Studies, University of Sussex
ILO	International Labour Office
JDS	Journal of Development Studies
JPS	Journal of Peasant Studies
WBSWP	World Bank Staff Working Paper

Abdullah, T. and Zeidenstein, S. (1982) *Village Women of Bangladesh: Prospects for Change* Pergamon Press, Oxford.

Agarwal, A. and Narain, S. (1989) 'Towards Green villages: A strategy for Environmentally-Sound and Participatory Rural Development'. Centre for Science and Environment Delhi.

Agarwal, B. (1989a) 'Social Security and the Family in Rural India'. LSE, University of London, Development Economics Research Programme, Paper no. 21.

Agarwal, B. (1989b) 'Rural Women, Poverty and Natural Resources: Sustenance, Sustainability and Struggle for Change'. *EPW* 24 (43), WS46–65.

Agarwal, B. (1986) 'Women, poverty and agricultural growth in India'. *JPS* 13 (4), 165–220.

Ahluwalia, M. (1986) 'Rural poverty, agricultural production and process: A re-examination'. In Mellor, J. and Desai, G.M. (ed). *Agricultural change and rural poverty: variations on a theme* Oxford University Press, Delhi, 59–75.

Akhter, F., Lily, F. and Karim, N. (1984) *Women's Role in Livestock Production in Bangladesh. An Empirical Investigation* Bangladesh Agricultural Research Council, Dhaka.

Alexander, K. (1989) 'Caste Mobilization and Class Consciousness: The Emergence of Agrarian Movements in Kerala and Tamil Nadu'. In Frankel, F. and Rao, M. (eds) *Dominance and State Power in Modern India: Decline of a Social Order. Volume 1* Oxford University Press, Delhi, 362–414.

Anderson, P. (1980) *Arguments within English Marxism* Verso, London.

Anderson, R., Brass, P., Levy, E. and Morrison B. (eds) (1982) *Science, Politics and the Agricultural Revolution in South Asia* Bowker Publishing Company, Epping.

Arens, J. and van Beurden, J. (1977) *Poor peasants and women in a village in Bangladesh* Third World Publications, Birmingham.

Arnold, D. (1988) *Famine: social crisis and historical change* Basil Blackwell, Oxford.

Arnold, D. (1984) 'Famine in Peasant Consciousness and Peasant Action: Madras 1876–8'. In Guha, R. (ed.) *Subaltern Studies III* Oxford University Press, Delhi, 62–115.

Aronson, N. (1984) 'The making of the U.S. Bureau of Labor Statistics Family Budget Series'. Paper given at the American Sociological Assoc. Meetings, San Antonio, mimeo.

Bandyopadhyay, N. (1983) 'Evaluation of Land Reform Measures in West Bengal: A report'. Centre for Studies in Social Sciences, Calcutta, mimeo.

Bandyopadhyay, N. (1977) 'Causes of sharp increase in agricultural labourers, 1961–1971: A case study of social-existence forms of labour in North Bengal'. *EPW* 12 (52), A111–126.

Bandyopadhyay, S. and Von Eschen, D. (1988) 'Villager Failure to Cooperate: Some Evidence From West Bengal, India'. In Attwood, D. and Bavsikar, B.S. (eds), *Who Shares? Co-operatives and Rural Development* Oxford University Press, Delhi, 112–45.

Bannerjee, S. (1992) 'Uses of Literacy: Total Literacy Campaign in three West Bengal Districts'. *EPW* 27 (9), 445–9.

Bannerjee, S. (1984) *India's Simmering Revolution* Zed Press, London.

BARD (1976) *Exploitation and the rural poor – A working paper on the rural power structure in Bangladesh* Bangladesh Academy for Rural Development, Comilla.

Bardhan, K. (ed.) (1990) *Of Women, Outcastes, Peasants and Rebels. A selection of Bengali Short Stories* University of California Press, Berkeley.

Bardhan, P. (ed.) (1989) *Conversations Between Economists and Anthropologists. Methodological Issues in Measuring Economic Change in Rural India* Oxford University Press, Delhi.

Bardhan, P. (1988) 'Agrarian class formation in India'. In Srinivasan, T.N. and Bardhan P.K. (eds) *Rural poverty in South Asia* Columbia University Press, New York, 501–25.

Bardhan, P. (1973) 'On the incidence of poverty in rural India in the sixties'. *EPW* 8 (4, 5 + 6), 246–54.

Bardhan, P. (1970) 'On the minimum level of living and the rural poor'. *Indian Economic Review* 5 (1), 129–36.

Bardhan, P. and Rudra, A. (1980a) 'Types of labour attachment in agriculture: Results of a survey in West Bengal 1979'. *EPW* 15 (35), 1477–84.

Bardhan, P. and Rudra, A. (1980b) 'Types of labour attachment in agriculture: results of a survey in West Bengal'. *EPW* 15 (45 + 46), 1943–1949.

Bauer, P. (1976, 1st ed. 1971) *Dissent on Development* Weidenfeld and Nicolson, London.

Bayly, C.A. (1988) 'Rallying round the sub–altern'. *JPS* 16 (1), 110–20.

Bayliss-Smith, T. and Wanmali, S. (eds) (1984) *Understanding Green Revolutions. Agrarian change and development planning in South Asia* Cambridge University Press, Cambridge.

Beck, T. (forthcoming) 'Common Property Resource Access by the Poor and Class Conflict in West Bengal'. *EPW* (1994).

Beck, T. (1991a) 'Review article of Dreze, J. and Sen, A. *Hunger and Public Action Disasters* 15 (4), 389–92.

Beck, T. (1991) 'Poverty and Power: Survival of the Poorest in Three Villages of West Bengal, India'. PhD thesis, University of London.

Begum, A. (1985) 'Women and technology in rice processing in Bangladesh'. In *Women in Rice Farming* International Rice Research Institute, Gower, 221–41.

Bhaduri, A. *et al.* (1986) 'Persistence and Polarisation: A Study in the Dynamics of Agrarian Contradiction'. *JPS* 13 (3), 82–9.

Bharati, P. and Basu, A. (1988) 'Uncertainties in food supply, and nutritional deficiencies, in relation to economic conditions in a village population of southern West Bengal, India'. In De Garine, I. and Harrison, G.A. (eds) *Coping with Uncertainty in Food Supply* Oxford Science Publications, Clarendon, Oxford, 418–36.

Bhattacharya, N., Chattopadhyay, M. and Rudra, A. (1987a) 'Changes in level of living in rural West Bengal: private consumption'. *EPW* 22 (28), 1149–50.

Bhattacharya, N., Chattopadhyay, M. and Rudra, A. (1987b) 'Changes in level of living in rural West Bengal: social consumption'. *EPW* 22 (33), 1410–3.

Bhattacharya, N. Chattopadhyay, M. and Rudra, A. (1987c) 'Changes in level of living in rural West Bengal: housing conditions'. *EPW* 22 (36–37), 1559–60.

Bhowmick, P. (1963) The *Lodhas of West Bengal. A Socio-Economic Study* Punthi Pustak, Calcutta.

Biggs, S. and Clay, E.J. (1981) 'Sources of innovation in agricultural technology'. *World Development* 9 (4), 321–36.

Biswas, A. (1981) 'The Decay of Irrigation and Cropping in West Bengal – 1850–1925'. *Cressida Transactions* 1 (1), 74–95.

Blaikie, P., Cameron, J. and Seddon J.D. (1979) *The struggle for basic needs in Nepal* OECD, Paris.

Booth, C. (1969) *Charles Booth's London* Fried, A. and Ellmann P. (eds) Hutchinson, London.

Bosanquet, H. (1898) *Rich and poor* Macmillan, London.

Bose, A. N. and Bhadoria, P. (1987) *Village planning by villagers. The rural people of Midnapore District 1986* Indian Institute of Technology, Kharagpur, Midnapore 721302, and Zilla Parishad, Midnapore.

Bose, P.K. (1985) *Classes and class relations among tribals of Bengal* Ajanta Publications, Delhi.

Bose, P.K. (1984) *Classes in a rural society: A sociological study of some Bengal villages* Ajanta Publications, Delhi.

Bose, S. (1986) *Agrarian Bengal: Economy, Social Structure and Politics 1919–1947* Cambridge University Press, Bombay.

Boyce, J.K. (1987) *Agrarian impasse in Bengal: institutional constraints to technological change* Oxford University Press, Oxford.

BRAC (1986) *The Net. Power structures in ten villages* Bangladesh Rural Advancement Committee, Dhaka.

BRAC (1984) *Peasant Perceptions: Famine, Credit Needs, Sanitation* Bangladesh Rural Advancement Committee, Dhaka.

BRAC (1983) *Who Gets What and Why: Resource Allocation in a Bangladesh Village* Bangladesh Rural Advancement Committee, Dhaka.

Breman, J. (1988) Agribusiness and labour in South Gujarat. Paper given at the Institute of Commonwealth Studies, University of London, mimeo.

Breman, J. (1985a) *Of Peasants, Migrants and Paupers. Rural Labour Circulation and Capitalist Production in West India* Oxford University Press, Delhi.

Breman, J. (1985b) 'Between accumulation and immiseration: the partiality of fieldwork in rural India'. *JPS* 13 (1), 5–35.

Breman, J. (1979) *Patronage and Exploitation: Changing Agrarian Relations in South Gujarat* University of California Press, Berkeley.

Briscoe, J. (1979) 'Energy use and social structure in a Bangladesh village'. *Population and Development Review* (12), 615–41.

Brown, J. (1968) 'Charles Booth and Labour Colonies, 1889–1905'. *The Economic History Review* XXl (2), 349–60.

Bussink, W. *et al.*, (1980) 'Poverty and the development of human resources'. WBSWP 406, World Bank, Washington DC.

Byres, T.J. (1988) 'A Chicago view of the Indian State: An Oriental Grin without an Oriental Cat and Political Economy without Classes'. *Journal of Commonwealth and Comparative Politics* 26 (3), 246–69.

Byres, T. J. (1981) 'The New Technology, Class formation and Class Action in the Indian Countryside'. *JPS* 8 (4), 405–54.

Byres, T. J. (1979) 'Of Neo-Populist Pipe-Dreams: Daedalus in the Third World and the Myth of Urban Bias'. *JPS* 6 (2), 210–44.

Cain, M. (1981) 'Risk and insurance: perspectives on fertility and agrarian change in India and Bangladesh'. *Population and Development Review* 7 (3), 435–74.

Cain, M. (1977) 'The economic activities of children in a village in Bangladesh'. *Population and Development Review* 3 (3), 201–28.

Caldwell, J. *et al.* (1986) 'Periodic high risk as a cause of fertility decline in a rural environment: survival strategies in the 1980–83 South Indian drought'. *Economic Development and Cultural Change* 34 (4), 677–701.

Caplan, P. (1985) *Class and Gender in India: Women and their organizations in a South Indian City* Tavistock Publications, London.

Cashdan, E. (1985) '"Coping with risk": Reciprocity among the Basarwa of Northern Botswana'. *Man* 20 (3), 454–74.

Cassells, C., Wigha, A., Pant, M. and Nabarro D. (1987) 'Coping Strategies of East Nepal Farmers: Can Development Initiatives Help?' Department of International Community Health, Liverpool School of Tropical Medicine, mimeo.

Cecelski, E. (1987) 'Energy and rural women's work: crisis response and policy alternatives'. *International Labour Review* 126 (1), 41–64.

Chadha, G.K. and Bhaumick, S.K. (1992) 'Changing Tenancy Relations in West Bengal. Popular Notions, Grassroot Realities'. *EPW*, 27 (20+21), 1089–98.

Chambers, R. (1989) 'Editorial Introduction: Vulnerability, Coping and Policy'. In *IDS Bulletin*, 20 (2), 1–7.

Chambers, R. (1988) 'Poverty in India: Concepts, Research and Reality'. IDS Discussion Paper, 241.

Chambers, R. (1984) 'Beyond the Green Revolution: a selective essay'. In Bayliss–Smith, T. and Wanmali, S. (eds) *Understanding Green Revolutions. Agrarian change and development planning in South Asia* Cambridge University Press, Cambridge, 362–79.

Chambers, R. (1983) *Rural Development: Putting the Last First* Longman, London.

Chambers, R. (1981) 'Introduction'. In Chambers, R. *et al* . (eds) *Seasonal Dimensions to Rural Development* Frances Pinter, London, 1–8.

Chambers, R. and Leach, M. (1989) 'Trees as Savings and Security for the Rural Poor'. *World Development* 17 (3), 329–42.

Chambers, R., Saxena, N.C. and Shah, S. (1989) *To the hands of the poor. Water and Trees* Intermediate Technology Publications, London.

Chambers, R., Pacey, A. and Thrupp, L. (eds) (1989) *Farmer First: Farmer innovation and agricultural research* Intermediate Technology Publications, London.

Chambers, R., Longhurst R. and Pacey A. (1981) *Seasonal Dimensions to Rural Poverty* Frances Pinter, London.

Chaudhuri, P. (1978) *The Indian Economy: Poverty and Development* London, Crosby, Lockwood and Staples.

Chaudhuri, S. (1980) Study of 'Food for work programme in West Bengal'. A case study in two Panchayat areas in Birbhum District'. Santiniketan, Agro-Economic Research Centre.

Chen, M. (1983) *A Quiet Revolution: women in transition in rural Bangladesh* Salenkman, Cambridge MA.

Chen, M. and Dreze, J. (1992) 'Widows and health in rural north India'. *EPW*, 27, 43+44, WS81–92.

Chen, M. and Dholakia, A. (1986) *Indian Women: A study of their role in the dairy movement* Shakti, Delhi.

Clay, E.J. (1991) 'Famine, Food Insecurity, Poverty and Public Action'. Review of *Hunger and Public Action* and *The Political Economy of Hunger, Development Policy Review*, 9, 307–12.

Cleaver, H. (1982) 'Technology as Political Weaponry'. In Anderson, R. *et al.* (eds) *Science, Politics and the Agricultural Revolution in South Asia* Bowker Publishing Company, Epping, 261–75.

Conroy, C. (1992) 'Trees as Insurance against Contingencies: Case of Panchmahals District, Gujarat'. *EPW* 27 (43+44), 2381–7.

Cookery Annual (1908) *The Cookery Annual for 1908 and Year Book of the Universal Cookery and Food Association* The Food and Cookery Publishing Agency, London.

Cooper, A. (1984) 'Sharecropping and Sharecroppers' Struggles in Bengal, 1930–1950'. D.Phil thesis, University of Sussex, unpublished.

Crow, B. (1984) 'Warning of famine in Bangladesh'. *EPW* 19 (40), 1754–8.

Cruz de Carvalho, E. (1974) '"Traditional" and "Modern" Patterns of Cattle Raising in south-western Angola: A Critical Evaluation of Change from Pastoralism to Ranching'. *The Journal of Developing Areas* 8, 199–226.

Currey, B. (1981) 'The famine syndrome: its definition for relief and rehabilitation'. In Robson, J. (ed.) *Famine, Its Causes, Effects and Management* Gordon and Breach, London, 123–34.

Cutler, P. (1984) 'The Measurement of poverty: A review of attempts to quantify the poor with special reference to India'. *World Development* 12 (11/12), 1119–30.

Cutler, P., Kamal, A., Kennedy, J. and Lily F. (1989) 'Evaluation of Post-Flood Rehabilitation Projects of Four NGOs in Bangladesh'. A study undertaken on behalf of Royal Norwegian Ministry of Development Cooperation, Swedish International Development Agency, and Canadian International Development Agency, mimeo.

Danda, A. and Danda, D. (1971) *Development and Change in Basudha. Study of a West Bengal Village* National Institute of Community Development, Hyderabad.

Dandekar, V.M. (1981) 'On measurement of poverty'. *EPW* 16 (30), 1241–50.

Dandekar, V.M. and Rath N. (1971a) 'Poverty in India l: Dimensions and Trends'. *EPW* 6 (1), 25–48.

Dandekar, V.M. and Rath, N. (1971b) 'Poverty in India 2: Dimensions and Trends'. *EPW* 6 (2), 106–46.

Dasgupta, A. (1981) 'Land and Politics in West Bengal: a sociological study of a multi–caste village'. D.Phil. thesis, University of Sussex, unpublished.

Dasgupta, B. (1984a) 'Sharecropping in West Bengal during the Colonial Period'. *EPW* 19 (13), A2–A8.

Dasgupta, B. (1984b) 'Sharecropping in West Bengal: from Independence to Operation Barga'. *EPW* 19 (26), A85–A96.

Dasgupta, B. (1984c) 'Agricultural labour under colonial, semi-capitalist and capitalist conditions. A case study of West Bengal'. *EPW* 19 (39), A129–A148.

Dasgupta, B. (1980) *The New Agrarian Technology and India* Macmillan, Delhi.

Dasgupta, B. (1975) 'A Typology of Village Socio–Economic Systems from Indian Village Studies'. *EPW* 10 (33–5), 1395–1414.

Dasgupta, M. (1987) 'Informal Security Mechanisms and Population Retention in Rural India'. *Economic Development and Cultural Change* 36 (1), 101–20.

Dasgupta, S. (1985) 'Adivasi Politics in Midnapur, c. 1760–1924'. In Guha, R. (ed.) *Subaltern Studies* 1V, Delhi, Oxford University Press, 101–35.

Davis, M. (1983) *Rank and rivalry: The politics of inequality in rural West Bengal* Cambridge University Press, Cambridge.

Dayal, E. (1989) 'Rural Poverty in India: a Regional Analysis'. *Journal of Rural Studies* 5 (1), 87–98.

De Garine, I. and Harrison, G. (eds) (1988) *Coping with Uncertainty in Food Supply* Oxford Science Publications, Clarendon, Oxford.

Dendy, H. (1895) 'Industrial Residuum'. In Bosanquet B. (ed.) *Aspects of the social problems* Macmillan, London, 82–102.

Dreze, J. (1990) 'Poverty in India and the IRDP Delusion'. *EPW* 25 (39), A95–104.

Dreze, J. (1988a) 'Famine Prevention in India'. Paper presented at the World Institute for Development Economics Research, Helsinki, mimeo.

Dreze, J. (1988b) 'Social insecurity in India: A case study'. Paper for a Workshop on Social Security in Developing Countries, London School of Economics, University of London, mimeo.

Dreze, J. and Sen, A. K. (1989) *Hunger and Public Action* Oxford University Press, Oxford.

Durno, J. and Mandal, M. (1989) 'Legal Rights for Poor Women – SLARTC in India'. In Holloway, R. (ed.) *Doing Development* Earthscan Publications, London.

Eden, F. (ed. and abridged, Rodgers, A.) (1928) *The State of the Poor: A history of the labouring classes in England, with parochial reports* Routledge, London.

Epstein, T.S. *et al.* (1983) *Basic Needs Viewed from Above and Below: the case of Karnataka State, India* OECD, Paris.

Farmer, B.H. (1986) 'Perspectives on the "Green Revolution" in South Asia'. *Modern Asian Studies* 20 (1), 175–99.

Farmer, B.H. (ed.) (1977) *Green Revolution? Technology and Change in Rice-growing Areas of Tamil Nadu and Sri Lanka* Macmillan, London.

Folbre, N. (1986) 'Cleaning house: new perspectives on households and economic development'. *Journal of Development Economics* 22, 5–40.

206

Franke, R. and Chasin (1991) 'Kerala State, India: Radical Reform as Development'. *Monthly Review*, 42 (8), 1–23.

Frankel, F. (1989) 'Introduction'. In Frankel, F. and Rao, M. (eds) *Dominance and State Power in Modern India: Decline of a Social Order* Oxford University Press, Delhi, 1–20.

Frankel, F. (1978) *India's Political Economy – 1947–1977* Princeton University Press, Princeton.

Frankel, F. (1971) *India's Green Revolution* Princeton University Press, Princeton.

Franklin, N.N. (1967) 'The Concept and Measurement of "Minimum Living Standards"'. *International Labour Review* 95 (January–June), 271–98.

Freeman, J. (1979) *Untouchable: An Indian Life History* Stanford University Press, Stanford.

Frye, N. (1947) *Fearful Symmetry: A study of William Blake* Princeton University Press, Princeton.

Fukuyama, F. (1992) *The End of History and the Last Man* The Free Press, New York.

Gaiha, R. (1988) 'On measuring the risk of poverty in rural India'. In Srinivasan T.N. and Bardhan P. (eds), *Rural poverty in South Asia* Columbia University Press, New York, 219–61.

Gaiha, R. (1987) 'Inequality, earnings and participation among the poor in rural India'. *JDS* 23 (4), 491–508.

Gaiha, R. and Kazmi, N.A. (1981) 'Aspects of poverty in rural India'. *Economics and Planning* 17 (2–3), 74–112.

Ghatak, M. (1985) 'Study of rural landless employment guarantee programme in Purulia and Bankura districts'. Calcutta, CRESSIDA, mimeo.

Ghatak, M. (no date) 'Development of women and children in rural areas (DWCRA) of Bankura and Purulia districts; an evaluation'. Calcutta, CRESSIDA, mimeo.

Ghatak, M. (1983) 'Peasant mobilisation in Bengal'. *CRESSIDA Transactions*, Calcutta, 3 (1), 104–142.

Ghose, A.K. (1983) 'Agrarian reform in West Bengal: objectives, achievements and limitations'. In Ghose, A.K. (ed.), *Agrarian reform in developing countries* Croom Helm, London.

Ghosh, T.K. (1986) *Operation Barga and Land Reforms (An Indian Experiment)* B.R. Publishing Corporation, Delhi.

Giddens, A. (1987) *Social Theory and Modern Sociology* Polity Press, Cambridge.

Giddens, A. (1986) *The Constitution of Society* University of California Press, Berkeley.

Glaser, M. (1988) 'Land Tenancy and Shallow Tubewell Irrigation: Alternative Trajectories of Agrarian Change in Bangladesh'. *Journal of Social Studies* 45, 51–67.

Government of India (1985) *Seventh Five Year Plan 1985–1990* Planning Commission, Government of India, Delhi.

Government of India (1981) *Sixth Five Year Plan 1980–1984* Planning Commission, Government of India, Delhi.

Government of India (1973) 'Draft Five Year Plan 1974–1979'. Planning Commission, Government of India, Delhi.

Government of India (1945a) 'Famine Inquiry Commission. Report on Bengal'. Government of India, Delhi.

Government of India (1945b) 'Famine Inquiry Commission. Final Report'. Government of India, Delhi.

Government of India (1928) 'Report of the Royal Commission on Agriculture in India'. Cmd. 3132, HMSO, London.

Government of West Bengal (1986) 'Left Front Government in West Bengal. Nine years'. Department of Information and Cultural Affairs, Government of West Bengal, Calcutta.

Greeley, M. (1987) *Postharvest losses, technology and employment: The case of rice in Bangladesh* Westview, Colorado.

Greeley, M. and Huq, A.K. (1980) 'Rice in Bangladesh: An empirical analysis of farm–level food losses in five post–production operations'. Bangladesh Institute of Development Studies, Dhaka, mimeo.

Greenough, P. (1982) *Prosperity and Misery in Modern Bengal: The Famine of 1943–1944* Oxford University Press, New York.

Grossman, L. (1984) *Peasants, subsistence ecology and development in the highlands of Papua New Guinea* Princeton University Press, Princeton.

Guha, R. (ed.) (1982–1989) *Subaltern Studies 1–6* Oxford University Press, Delhi.

Guha, R. (1986) *Elementary Aspects of Peasant Insurgency in Colonial India* Oxford University Press, Oxford.

Guha, Ranajit (1989) *The Unquiet Woods: Ecological Change and Peasant Resistance in the Himalaya* Oxford University Press, Delhi.

Hammond J. L. and Hammond B. (1948) *The village labourer* Guild Books, Liverpool.

Harari, D. and Garcia–Bouza, J. (1982) *Social Conflict and Development: Basic needs and survival strategies in four national settings* OECD, Paris.

Harriss, B. (1990a) 'The Intra-Family Distribution of Hunger in South Asia.' In Dreze, J. and Sen, A. (eds) *The Political Economy of Hunger. Volume 1, Entitlement and Well-Being* Oxford University Press, Oxford.

Harriss, B. (1990b) 'Anti-Female Discrimination in Nutrients Sharing'. *EPW* 25 (3), 179.

Harriss, B. (1987) 'Poverty in India: Micro Level Evidence'. First draft of a paper for workshop on Poverty in India, Queen Elizabeth House, University of Oxford, mimeo.

Harriss, B. (1986) 'The Intra-Family Distribution of Hunger in South Asia'. Paper for WIDER Project on Hunger and Poverty, Seminar on food strategies, Helsinki, mimeo.

Harriss, B. (1982) 'Food Systems and Society: The System of Circulation of Rice in West Bengal'. *CRESSIDA Transactions* 2 (1 + 2), Calcutta, 158–250.

Harriss, J. (1987) 'Capitalism and Peasant Production: The Green Revolution in India'. In Shanin, T. (ed.) *Peasants and peasant societies* Basil Blackwell, Oxford, 227–45.

Harriss, J. (1984) 'The political economy of rice in a Bengal District: or "What happened to Semi-Feudalism in Birbhum"'. University of East Anglia Discussion Paper 134.

Harriss, J. (1977) 'Bias in Perception of Agrarian Change in India'. In Farmer B.H. (ed.) *Green Revolution? Technology and Change in Rice-growing Areas of Tamil Nadu and Sri Lanka* Macmillan, London, 30–6.

Hartmann B. and Boyce J. (1983) *A Quiet Violence: view from a Bangladesh village* Zed, London.

Hashmi, S. (1989) 'NGO's in Bangladesh'. Paper given at SOAS, University of London, mimeo.

Heyer, J. (1989) 'Landless Agricultural Labourers' Asset Strategies'. *IDS Bulletin*, 20 (2), 33–40.

Hill, C. (1975) *The World Turned Upside Down: Radical Ideas During the English Revolution* Penguin, Harmondsworth.

Hill, P. (1986) *Development Economics on Trial* Cambridge University Press, Cambridge.

Himmelfarb, G. (1985) *The Idea of Poverty. England in the Early Industrial Age* Faber and Faber, London.

Hobsbawm, E.J. (1975) *The Age of Capital: 1848–1875* Weidenfeld and Nicolson, London.

Hossain, M. (1989) *Green Revolution in Bangladesh. Impact on Growth and Distribution of Income* University Press Limited, Dhaka.

Hossain, M. (1987) *The assault that failed: A profile of absolute poverty in six villages of Bangladesh* UNRISD, Geneva.

Howes, M. (1985) *Whose Water? An Investigation of the Consequences of Alternative Approaches to the Small-Scale Irrigation in Bangladesh* BIDS, Dhaka.

Howes, M. and Jabbar, M. (1986) 'Rural fuel shortages in Bangladesh: the evidence from four villages'. IDS Discussion Paper 213, University of Sussex.

Hufton, O. (1974) *The poor of eighteenth century France, 1750–1789* Oxford University Press, Oxford.

Hunter, R. (1912) *Poverty* Macmillan, London.

IDS (1989) 'Vulnerability: How the Poor Cope'. *IDS Bulletin* 20 (2).

IDS (1986) 'Seasonality and Poverty'. *IDS Bulletin* 17 (3).

IDS (1979) 'Whose knowledge counts?' *IDS Bulletin* 10 (2).

Inter-departmental Committee (1904) 'Inter-departmental Committee on physical deterioration'. Report Cd. 2175, House of Commons Sessional Papers XXXll, HMSO, London.

Jackson, P. and Smith, S. (1984) *Exploring Social Geography* Allen and Unwin, London.

Jansen, E. (1989) 'Processes of Polarization and the Breaking Up of Patron–Client Relationships in Rural Bangladesh'. *Journal of Social Studies* (42), 52–63.

Jansen, E. (1986) *Rural Bangladesh: Competition for Scarce Resources* University Press Limited, Dhaka.

Jeffery, P., Jeffery R. and Lyon, A. (1989) *Labour Pains and Labour Power: Women and Childbearing in India* Zed Books, London.

Jeffery, R., Jeffery, P. and Lyon, A. (1989a) 'Taking Dung-Work Seriously: Women's Work and Rural Development in North India'. *EPW* 24 (17), 32–6.

Jensen, K. (1986) 'Survival Strategies of the Rural Poor in Bangladesh'. Danida, Asiatisk Plads, 2, Copenhagen K, Denmark 1448, mimeo.

Jodha, N.S. (1990) 'Rural Common Property Resources: Contributions and Crisis'. *EPW* 25 (26), A65–A78.

Jodha, N.S. (1989) 'Social Science Research on Rural Change: Some Gaps'. In Bardhan, P.K. (ed.) *Conversations Between Economists and Anthropologists. Methodological Issues in Measuring Economic Change in Rural India* Oxford University Press, Delhi, 174–99.

Jodha, N.S. (1986) 'Common Property Resources and Rural Poor in Dry Regions of India'. *EPW* 21 (27), 1169–81.

Jodha, N.S. (1978) 'Effectiveness of farmers' adjustment to risk'. *EPW* 12 (26), A38–48.

Jodha, N.S. (1975) 'Famine and famine policies: some empirical evidence'. *EPW* 9 (41), 1609–23.

Johnston, R.J. (1989) 'Philosophy, Ideology and Geography'. In Gregory, D. and Walford, R. (eds) *Horizons in human geography* Macmillan, London.

Jones, S. and Ahamad, C.S. (1985) 'The impact of water sector projects on income distribution and employment'. Technical Report no. 23. Ministry of Water Development and Flood Control, Government of Bangladesh, Dhaka.

Jose, A.V. (1988) 'Agricultural Wages in India'. *EPW* 23 (26), A46–58.

Jose, A.V. (1984) 'Poverty and income distribution: the case of West Bengal'. In Khan, A. R. and Lee, E. (eds.), *Poverty in Rural Asia* ILO–ARTEP, Bangkok 137–63.

Joshi, B. (ed.) (1986) *Untouchable! Voices of the Dalit Liberation Movement* Zed Press and Minority Rights Group, London.

Katona-Apte, J. (1988) 'Coping strategies of destitute women in Bangladesh'. *Food and Nutrition Bulletin* 10 (3), 42–7.

Kaye, H. (1984) *The British Marxist Historians* Polity, Cambridge.

Kaye, H. and McClelland, K. (eds) (1990) *E.P. Thompson: Critical Perspectives* Polity Press, Cambridge.

Kelly, K. (1985) *Agricultural revolution in a third world economy. A nineteenth century Indian case study* Discovery, Delhi.

Khan, M.A. (1961) *Selections from Bengal Government Records on Wahhabi Trials (1863–1870)* Asiatic Society of Pakistan Publications, Dhaka.

Khasnabis, R. and Chakraborty, J. (1982) 'Tenancy, credit and agrarian backwardness: Results of a field study'. *EPW* 17 (11), A21 – A 32.

Kitteringham, J. (1982) 'Country work girls in nineteenth-century England'. In Samuel, R. (ed.) *People's History and Socialist Theory* Routledge and Kegan Paul, London, 73–138.

Kishwar, M. and Vanita, R. (1984) *In Search of Answers* Zed Books, London.

Kobayashi, A. and Mackenzie, S. (eds) (1989) *Remaking Human Geography* Unwin Hyman, Boston.

Kohli, A. (1990) *Democracy and Discontent: India's growing crisis of governability* Cambridge University Press, Cambridge.

Kohli, A. (1987) *The state and poverty in India* Cambridge University Press, Cambridge.

Kothari, R. (1988) 'Political economy of the Indian state: The Rudolph thesis'. *Contributions to Indian Sociology* 22 (2), 272–8.

Kurien, C.T. (1982) 'Economics and analysis of levels of living – some methodological problems'. In Rao, B.S. and Deshpande, V.N. (eds.) *Poverty: an interdisciplinary approach* Somaiya, Delhi, 245–51.

Kynch, J. (1990) 'Agricultural Wage Rates in West Bengal and their Trends over Time'. Centre for Development Studies, University College of Swansea, mimeo.

Kynch, J. and Sen, A.K. (1983) 'Indian women: well being and survival'. *Cambridge Journal of Economics* 7 (3/4), 363–80.

Lakdawala, D. (1988) 'Planning for Minimum Needs'. In Srinivasan, T.N. and Bardhan, P. K. (eds.) *Rural poverty in South Asia* Columbia University Press, New York, 389–401.

Leakey, C. (1986) 'Biomass, Man and Seasonality in the Tropics'. *IDS Bulletin*, 17 (3), 36–43.

Levy, E. (1982) The Responsibility of the Scientific and Technological Enterprise in Technology Transfers. In R. Anderson *et al.* (eds.) *Science, Politics and the Agricultural Revolution in South Asia* Bowker Publishing Company, Epping, 277–97.

211

Lewis, J.P. (1988) *Strengthening the Poor: What Have We Learned?* Transaction Books, New Brunswick.

Lewis, O. (1966) *La Vida* Random House, New York.

Lewis, P. (1991) *Social Action and the Labouring Poor* Vistaar Publications, Delhi.

Ley, D. (1989) 'Fragmentation, coherence, and limits to theory in human geography'. In Kobayashi, A. and Mackenzie, S. (eds.) *Remaking Human Geography* Unwin Hyman, Boston, 227–244.

Lieten, G. (1990) 'Depeasantisation Discontinued: Land Reforms in West Bengal'. *EPW*, 25 (40), 2264–71.

Lieten, G. (1988) 'Panchayat Leaders in a West Bengal District'. *EPW* , 23 (40), 2069–73.

Lieten, G. and Nieuwenhuys, O. (1989) 'Introduction: Survival and Emancipation'. In Lieten, G., Nieuwenhuys, O. and Schenk–Sandbergen, L. (1989) *Women, Migrants and Tribals. Survival Strategies in Asia* Manohar, Delhi, 1–18.

Lipton, M. with Longhurst, R. (1989) *New seeds and poor people* Unwin Hyman, London.

Lipton, M. (1985) 'Land assets and rural poverty'. WBSWP 744, World Bank, Washington DC.

Lipton, M. (1983a) 'Poverty, undernutrition and hunger.' WBSWP 597, World Bank, Washington DC.

Lipton, M. (1983b) 'Labor and poverty.' WBSWP 616, World Bank, Washington DC.

Lipton, M. (1983c) 'Demography and poverty.' WBSWP 623, World Bank, Washington DC.

Lipton, M. and Toye, J. (1990) *Does Aid Work in India?* Routledge, London.

Lis, C. and Soly, H. (1979) *Poverty and capitalism in pre-industrial Europe* Harvester Press, Brighton.

London, J. (1903) *The People of the Abyss* Isbister and Company, London.

Longhurst, R. (1986) 'Household Food Strategies in Response to Seasonality and Famine'. IDS Bulletin, 17 (3), 27–35.

Malhotra, K.C. and Gadgil, M. (1988) 'Coping with uncertainty in food supply: case studies among the pastoral and non-pastoral nomads of western India'. In de Garine, I. and Harrison, G.A. (eds) *Coping with Uncertainty in Food Supply* Oxford Science Publications, Clarendon, Oxford, 379–404.

Mallick, R. (1992) 'Agrarian Reform in West Bengal: the End of an Illusion'. *World Development*, 20 (5), 735–50.

Mallick, R. (1988) 'West Bengal Government Policy 1977–1983'. PhD thesis, University of Cambridge, unpublished.

Mayoux. L. (1988) 'Not a panacea but part of the solution: handicraft development for women in West Bengal'. Report presented to Visvabharati University, Santiniketan and ODA, London, mimeo.

Mayoux, L. (1982) 'Women's work and economic power in the family: A study of two villages in West Bengal'. PhD, University of Cambridge, unpublished.

Mellor, J. (1976) *The new economics of growth: A strategy for India and the developing world* Cornell University Press, Ithaca.

Mencher, J. (1980) 'On Being an Untouchable in India: A Materialist Perspective'. In Ross, Eric (ed.) *Beyond the Myths of Cultural Materialism* Academic Press, New York.

Mencher, J. (1975) 'Viewing hierachy from the bottom up'. In Beteille A. and Madan T.N. (eds.) *Encounter and experience: Personal accounts of fieldwork* Vikas, Delhi, 114–30.

Mennell, S. (1985) *All manners of food. Eating and taste in England and France from the Middle Ages to the Present* Basil Blackwell, Oxford.

Midgley, J. (1986) 'Community participation: history, concepts, and controversies'. In Midgley, J. *et al., Community Participation, Social Development and the State* Methuen, London, 13–44.

Miller, R. and Kale, P. (1972) 'The Burden on the Head is Always There'. In J. Michael Mahar (ed.) *Untouchables in Contemporary India* University Of Arizona Press, Tuscon.

Minhas, B.S. (1974) 'Rural poverty, land redistribution and development strategy: facts'. In Srinivasan and Bardhan (eds) *Poverty and income distribution in India* Statistical Publishing Society, Calcutta, 252–63.

Mitchell, J. (1991) 'Public campaigning on overseas aid in the 1980s'. In Bose, A. and Burnell, P. (eds) *Britain's overseas aid since 1979* Manchester University Press, Manchester.

Mitra, A. (1953) *An account of land management in West Bengal, 1870–1950* West Bengal Government Press, Calcutta.

Moffat, (1979) *An Untouchable Community in South India* Princeton University Press, Princeton.

Moore, Barrington (1987) *Social origins of dictatorship and democracy* Peregrine, Harmondsworth.

Morgan, D.H. (1982) 'The place of harvesters in nineteenth–century village life'. In Samuel, R. (ed.), *Village Life and Labour* Routledge and Kegan Paul, London, 27–72.

Morris, B. (1982) *Forest Traders. A Socio-Economic Study of the Hill Pandaram* Athlone Press, New Jersey.

Morris, N.D. and Mcalpin, M. (1979) *Measuring the condition of the world's poor. The Physical Quality of Life Index* Pergamon, New York.

Mosley, P, Harrigan, J. and Toye, J. (1991) *Aid and Power: The World Bank and Policy Based Lending* Routledge, London.

Mukherjee, M. (1988) 'Peasant Resistance and Peasant Consciousness in Colonial India: "Subalterns" and Beyond.' *EPW* 23 (41), 2109–20.

213

Nesmith, C. A. (1990) 'People and trees: gender relations and participation in social forestry in West Bengal, India'. PhD, Department of Geography, University of Cambridge, unpublished.

Nossiter, T.J. (1988) *Marxist State Government in India: Politics, Economy and Society* Pinter, London.

O'Hanlon, R. (1988) 'Recovering the Subject. Subaltern Studies and the Histories of Resistance in Colonial South Asia'. *Modern Asian Studies* 22 (1), 189–224.

O'Malley, L.S.S. (1914) *Bengal District Gazetteers: 24 Parganas* Bengal Secretariat Book Depot, Calcutta.

O'Malley, L.S.S. (1911) *Bengal District Gazetteers: Midnapore* Bengal Secretariat Book Depot, Calcutta.

Oakley, P. (1991) 'The concept of participation in development'. *Landscape and Urban Planning*, 115–22.

Oasa, E. (1987) 'The political economy of international agricultural research: a review of the CGIAR's response to criticisms of the "Green Revolution"'. In B. Glaeser (ed.) *The Green Revolution revisited. Critique and alternatives* Allen and Unwin, London, 13–55.

OFI (1991) 'Common Property Resource Management in India'. Oxford Forestry Institute, University of Oxford, Tropical Forestry Papers 24.

Omvedt, G. (1977) 'Revolutionary Music of India'. *JPS* 4 (3), 243–57.

Orwell, G. (1981) *Down and Out in Paris and London* Penguin, Harmondsworth.

Palmer–Jones, R. (1989) 'Water Management and Irrigation Issues in West Bengal'. Report for the Ford Foundation, New Delhi, mimeo.

Pant, P. (1974) 'Perspective of development:1961–1976. Implications for planning for a minimum level of living'. In Srinivasan, T.N. and Bardhan P.K. (eds) *Poverty and income distribution in India* Statistical Publishing Society, Calcutta, 9–38.

Platteau, J.P. (1988) 'Traditional Systems of Social Security and Hunger Insurance: Some Lessons from the Evidence Pertaining to Third World Societies'. LSE, University of London, Development Economics Research Programme, paper no. 15.

Prahladachar, M. (1983) 'Income distribution effects of the green revolution in India: a review of empirical evidence'. *World Development* 11 (11), 927–44.

Proshika (1991) 'Proshika/ODI case study paper on livestock and social forestry'. Paper presented at the Asia Regional Workshop: 'NGOs, Natural Resources Management and Linkages with the Public Sector.' Hyderabad, India, mimeo.

Proshika (1990) *Annual Activity Report, July 1989 – June 1990'*. Dhaka, mimeo.

Rahaman, M. (1981) 'The causes and effects of famine in the rural population'. In Robson, J. (ed.) *Famine: its causes and management* Gordon and Breach, London, 135–138.

Rahmato, D. (1988) 'Peasant survival strategies'. Institute for Relief and Development, Food for the Hungry International, Geneva.

Ranade, S. (1988) 'On Estimating and Explaining Rural Poverty'. *EPW* 23 (16), 805–8.

Rao, B.S. and Deshpande, V. N. (eds) (1982) *Poverty: an interdisciplinary approach* Somaiya, Delhi.

Rao Bhanoji V. (1981) 'Measurement of deprivation and poverty based on the proportion spent on food'. *World Development* 9 (4), 337–53.

Rao, V.K.R.V. (1982) *Food, nutrition and poverty* Harvester Press, Brighton.

Rao, V.M. and Vivekananda, M. (1981) 'The poor as a social stratum: some economic criteria for studying poverty'. *EPW* 17 (27), 1007–12.

Rath. N. (1985) '"Garibi Hatao": Can IRDP do it?' *EPW* 19 (6), 238–46.

Ray, R. (1979) *Change in Bengal agrarian society c. 1760–1850* Manohar, Delhi.

Reeves, M. P. (1979) *Round about a pound a week* Virago, London.

Rein, M. (1970) 'Problems in the Definition and Measurement of Poverty'. In Townsend, P. (ed) *The concept of poverty, working paper on methods and lifestyles of the poor in different countries* Heinemann, London, 46–63.

Richards, P. (1987) 'Indigenous Approaches to Rural Development: The agrarian populist tradition in West Africa'. Department of Anthropology, University College, University of London, mimeo.

Richards, P. (1986) *Coping with hunger: hazard and experiment in an African rice-farming system* Allen and Unwin, London.

Richards, P. (1985) *Indigenous Agricultural Revolution: Ecology and food production in West Africa* Hutchinson, London.

Rogers, P., Lydon P. and Seckler, D. (1989) 'Eastern Waters Study: Strategies to manage flood and drought in the Ganges–Brahmaputra Basin'. Irrigation support project for Asia and the Near East, Arlington, Virginia.

Rohner, R. and Chaki–Sircar, M. (1988) *Women and Children in a Bengali Village* University Press of New England, Hanover.

Rowntree, B.S. (1922) *Poverty, a study of town life* Longmans, Green and Company, London.

Rowntree, B.S. (1913) *How the labourer lives* Longman, London.

Rowntree, B.S. (1941) *Poverty and progress. A second social survey of York* Longman, London.

Rowntree, B.S. and Lavers, G. P. (1951) *Poverty and the welfare state. A third social survey of York dealing only with economic questions* Longman, London.

Rowntree, J. and Sherwell, A. (1899) *The temperance problem and social reform* Hodder and Stoughton, London.

Roy, S. (1992) 'Forest Protection Committees in West Bengal'. *EPW* 27 (29), 1528–30.

Rudolph, L. and Rudolph, S. (1987) *In pursuit of Lakshmi: The political economy of the Indian State* University of Chicago Press, Chicago.

Rudra, A. (1985) 'Agrarian Policies of Left Front Government in West Bengal'. *EPW* 20 (23), 1015–6.

Rudra, A. (1981a) 'One step forward, two steps backward'. *EPW* 16 (25–26), A61–8.

Rudra, A. (1981b) The basic needs concept and its implementation in Indian Development policy. ILO–ARTEP, Geneva.

Rudra, A. (1974) 'Minimum level of living – A statistical explanation'. In Srinivasan, T. and Bardhan, P.K. (eds), *Poverty and income distribution in India* Statistical Publishing Society, Calcutta, 281–90.

Sadeque, S. (1990) 'Capture fisheries and other common property resources in the flood plains of Bangladesh'. Paper presented at the 2nd workshop of European Network of Bangladesh Studies, Bath.

Sagar, D. (1988) 'Rural Poverty in India: An Evaluation of the Integrated Rural Development Programme in Uttar Pradesh and Bihar'. M.Phil. Thesis, Department of Land Economy, University of Cambridge, unpublished.

Said, E. (1978) *Orientalism* Routledge, London.

Saith, A. (1990) 'Development Strategies and the Rural Poor'. *JDS* 17 (2), 171–244.

Samuel, R. (ed.) (1982) *Village Life and Labour* London, Routledge and Kegan Paul.

Samuel, R. (1982a) 'Village Labour'. In Samuel, R. (ed.), *Village Life and Labour* London, Routledge and Kegan Paul, 3–26.

Samuel, R. (1981) 'People's history'. In Samuel, R. (ed.) *People's History and Socialist Theory* Routledge and Kegan Paul, London, xix–xxxiii.

Samuel, R. (1980) 'On the methods of History Workshop: A reply'. *History Workshop Journal* 9, 162–76.

Samuel, R. and Stedman Jones, G. (eds) (1982) *Culture, ideology and politics* Routledge and Kegan Paul, London.

Sarkar, T. (1987) *Bengal 1928–1934. The Politics of Protest* Oxford University Press, Delhi.

Sastry, S.A.R. (1980) 'Poverty: concepts and measurement'. *Indian Journal of Economics* 61, 1 (240), 67–82.

Sayer, A. (1989) 'On the dialogue between humanism and historical materialism in geography'. In Kobayashi, A. and Mackenzie, S. (eds.) *Remaking Human Geography* Unwin Hyman, Boston, 206–26.

Schaffer, B. (1985) 'Policy Makers Have Their Needs Too: Irish Itinerants and the Culture of Poverty'. In Wood, G. (ed.) *Labelling in development policy: Essays in honour of Bernard Schaffer* Sage, London, 33–66.

Schmink, M. (1984) 'Household Economic Strategies: Review and Research Agenda'. *Latin American Research Review* 19 (3), 87–101.

Scott, J.C. (1990) *Domination and the Arts of Resistance: Hidden Transcripts* Yale University Press, New Haven.

Scott, J.C. (1985) *Weapons of the weak: Everyday forms of peasant resistance in Southeast Asia* Yale University Press, New Haven.

Scott, J.C. (1976) *The Moral Economy of the Peasant. Rebellion and Subsistence in Southeast Asia* Yale University Press, New Haven.

Seabright, P. (1988) 'Identifying Investment Opportunities for the Poor: Evidence from the livestock market in South India'. University of Cambridge, Department of Applied Economics, mimeo.

Seavoy, R.E. (1986) *Famine in peasant societies* Greenwood, New York.

Selbourne, D. (1980) 'On the methods of History Workshop'. *History Workshop Journal* 9, 150–161.

Sen, A.K. (1990) 'Gender and Cooperative Conflicts'. In Tinker, I. (ed.), *Persistent inequalities: Women and world development* Oxford University Press, Oxford, 123–49.

Sen, A.K. (1985) *Commodities and capabilities* North Holland, Amsterdam.

Sen, A.K. (1983) 'Poor relatively speaking'. *Oxford Economic Papers* 35, 153–169.

Sen, A.K. (1982) *Poverty and famines: An essay on entitlement and deprivation* Clarendon Press, Oxford.

Sen, A.K. (1976) 'Poverty: An ordinal approach to measurement'. *Econometrica* 14 (2), 219–31.

Sen. A.K. (1974) 'Poverty, inequality and unemployment: some conceptual issues in measurement'. In Srinivasan, T.N. and Bardhan, P.K. (eds.) *Poverty and income distribution in India* Statistical Publishing Society, Calcutta, 67–82.

Sen, I. (ed.) (1990) *A Space within the Struggle: Women's Participation in People's Movements* Kali for Women, Delhi.

Sengupta, S. (1981) 'West Bengal land reforms and the agrarian scene'. *EPW* 16 (25–26), A69–75.

Sengupta, S. and Associates (1991) 'Rural Economy and Poverty in West Bengal and the Public Policy Interventions'. Santiniketan, Visva–Bharati University, mimeo.

Sengupta, S. with Ghosh, M. G. (1978) 'State intervention in the vulnerable food economy of India and the problem of the rural poor'. Paper for workshop on problems of public distribution of foodgrain in Eastern India, mimeo.

Sewell, W. (1990) 'How Classes are Made: Critical Reflections on E.P. Thompson's Theory of Working-class Formation'. In Kaye, H. and McClelland, K. (eds) *E.P. Thompson: Critical Perspectives* Polity Press, Cambridge, 50–77.

Shah, T. (1987) 'Gains from Social Forestry: Lessons from West Bengal'. Paper given at a workshop on 'Commons, Wastelands, Trees and the Poor: Finding the Right Fit', IDS, University of Sussex.

Siddiqui, K. (1982) *The political economy of rural poverty in Bangladesh* National Institute of Local Government, Dhaka.

Singh, K. and Bhattacharjee, S. (1991) 'Privatization of Common Pool Resources of Land. A Case Study of West Bengal'. Anand, Institute of Rural Management, Case Study 6.

Singh, T. (1989) 'Agriculture and rural poverty: issues re-examined'. *Marga* 10 (1), 17–36.

Snell, K. (1985) *Annals of the Labouring Poor. Social Change and Agrarian England, 1660–1990* Cambridge University Press, Cambridge.

Soyer, A. (1855) *A Shilling Cookery for the People: embracing an entirely new system of plain cookery and domestic economy* Routledge, London.

Srinivasan, T.N. and Bardhan P.K. (eds) (1988) *Rural poverty in South Asia* Columbia University Press, New York.

Srinivasan, T.N. and Bardhan, P.K. (eds) (1974) *Poverty and income distribution in India* Statistical Publishing Society, Calcutta.

Stokes, E. (1959) *English utilitarianism and India* Oxford University Press, Delhi.

Stree Shakti Sanghatana (1989) *'We Were Making History'. Life Stories of Women in the Telangana People's Struggle* Zed Press, London.

Sukhatme, P.V. (1981) 'On measurement of poverty'. *EPW* 16 (33), 1928–35.

Sundaram, K., and Tendulkar S.D. (1983) 'Poverty in mid-term appraisal'. *EPW* 16 (45/6), 1928–35.

Swaminathan, M. (1990) Village Level Implementation of IRDP. Comparison of West Bengal and Tamil Nadu'. *EPW*, March 31.

Swift, J. (1981) 'Labour and Subsistence in a Pastoral Economy'. In Chambers, R. *et al.* (eds) *Seasonal Dimensions to Rural Poverty* Frances Pinter, London, 80–7.

Taylor, D. (1992) 'Development from within and survival in rural Africa: A synthesis of theory and practice'. In Taylor, D. and Mackenzie, F. (eds) *Development from Within: Survival in Rural Africa* London, Routledge, 214–58.

Thakur, D.S. (1985) 'A Survey of Literature on Rural Poverty in India'. *Margin* April, 32–49.

Tharamangalam, J. (1986) 'Indian Peasant Uprisings: Myth and Reality'. *JPS* 13 (3), 116–34.

Tharamangalam, J. (1981) *Agrarian Class Conflict. The Political Mobilization of Agricultural Labourers in Kuttanad, South India* University of British Columbia Press, Vancouver.

Thompson, E.P. (1991) *Customs in Common* Merlin Press, London.

Thompson, E.P. (1990) *Whigs and Hunters: The origins of the Black Act* Penguin, Harmondsworth.

Thompson, E.P. (1986) *The making of the English working class* Penguin, Harmondsworth.

Thompson, E.P. (1978) *The Poverty of Theory and other essays* Merlin Press, London.

Thompson, E.P. (1978a) 'Eighteenth-century English society: class struggle without class'. *Social History* 3 (2), 133–65.

Thompson, E.P. (1977) 'Folklore, anthropology and social history'. *The Indian Historical Review* 3 (82), 247–66.

Thompson, E.P. (1971) 'The Moral Economy of the English Crowd in the Eighteenth Century'. *Past and Present* 50, 76–136.

Thompson, E.P. and Yeow E. (eds) (1971) *The Unknown Mayhew: Selections from the 'Morning Chronicle', 1849–50* Merlin, London.

Thompson, F. (1983) *Lark Rise to Candleford* Penguin, Harmondsworth.

Tindall, H.D. (1983) *Vegetables in the Tropics* Macmillan, London.

Toulmin, C. (1986) 'Access to Food, Dry Season Strategies and Household Size amongst the Bambara of Central Mali'. *IDS Bulletin*, 17 (3), 58–66.

Torry, W. (1986) 'Drought and the Government–Village Emergency Food Distribution System in India'. *Human Organization* 45 (1), 11–23.

Townsend P. (1979) *Poverty in the United Kingdom. A survey of household resources and standards of living* Penguin, Harmondsworth.

Townsend, P. (1970) 'Measures of Income and Expenditure as Criteria of Poverty'. In Townsend P. (ed.) *The concept of poverty, working paper on methods and lifestyles of the poor in different countries* Heinemann, London, 100–12.

Tressell, R. (1914) *The ragged trousered philanthropists* Grant Richards Limited, London.

Tura Institute (1981) 'A study on policies and programmes for the eradication of rural poverty in selected districts of Thailand'. Thai University Research Association, Bangkok.

Vaidyanathan, A. (1974) 'Some aspects of inequalities in living standards in rural India'. In Srinivasan, T.N. and Bardhan, P.K. (eds) *Poverty and income distribution in India* Statistical Publishing Society, Calcutta, 215–41.

Van Schendel, W. (1989) 'Self-Rescue and Survival: The Rural Poor in Bangladesh'. In Lieten G. *et al.* (eds) *Women, Migrants and Tribals. Survival Strategies in Asia* Manohar, Delhi, 159–83.

Van Schendel, W. (1981) *Peasant Mobility: The Odds of Life in Rural Bangladesh* Van Gorcum, Assen.

Van Schendel, W. and Faraizi, A.H. (1984) *Rural Labourers in Bengal 1880–1980* Rotterdam, Comparative Asian Studies Programme, Erasmus University.

Veit-Wilson, J. (1986) 'Paradigms of poverty: A rehabilitation of B.S. Rowntree'. *Journal of Social Policy* 15 (1), 69–99.

Wade, R. (1988) *Village Republics: Economic conditions for collective action in south India* Cambridge University Press, Cambridge.

Wade, R. (1973) 'A culture of poverty'. *IDS Bulletin* 1 (1), 4–30.

Watts, M. (1983) *Silent violence: Food, famine and peasantry in Northern Nigeria* University of California Press, Berkeley.

Webster, N. (1989) 'Agrarian Relations in Burdwan District, West Bengal. From the Economics of the Green Revolution to the Politics of Panchayati Raj'. Copenhagen, Centre for Development Research, Working Paper 89.2.

Westergaard, K. (1986) 'People's Participation, Local Government and Rural Development: The case of West Bengal, India'. Copenhagen, Report no. 8, Centre for Development Research.

Wheeler, E. (1985) 'To feed or to educate: Labelling in Targeted Nutrition Intervention'. In Wood, G. (ed.) *Labelling in development policy: Essays in honour of Bernard Schaffer* Sage, London, 133–41.

Wheeler, E. and Abdullah, M. (1988) 'Food allocation with the family: response to fluctuating food supply and food needs'. In de Garine, I. and Harrison, G. (eds) *Coping with Uncertainty in Food Supply* Oxford Science Publications, Clarendon, Oxford, 437–51.

White, C. (1986) 'Food Shortages and Seasonality in WoDaaBe Communities in Niger'. *IDS Bulletin*, 17 (3), 19–26.

White, S. (1991) 'Evaluating the Impact of NGOs in Rural Poverty Alleviation. Bangladesh Country Study'. ODI Working Paper 50, London.

White, S. (1988) 'In the teeth of the crocodile: class and gender in rural Bangladesh'. PhD. thesis, University of Bath, unpublished.

Williams, R. (1989) *Keywords* Fontana Press, London.

Wood, C. (1981) 'Structural Changes and Household Strategies: A Conceptual Framework for the Study of Rural Migration'. *Human Organization* 40 (4), 338–44.

Wood, G. (ed.) (1985a) *Labelling in development policy: Essays in honour of Bernard Schaffer* Sage, London.

Wood, G. (1985b) 'The Politics of Development Policy Labelling'. In Wood, G. (ed.) *Labelling in development policy: Essays in honour of Bernard Schaffer* Sage, London, 5–31.

Wood, G. (1985c) 'Targets strike back – Rural Works Claimants in Bangladesh'. In Wood (ed.) *Labelling in development policy: Essays in honour of Bernard Schaffer* Sage, London, 109–131.

Wood, G. (1984) 'Provision of irrigation services by the landless – an approach to agrarian reform in Bangladesh'. *Agricultural Administration* 17, 55–80.

Wood, G. and Palmer-Jones, R. (1991) *The Water Sellers: A Cooperative Venture by the Rural Poor* Intermediate Technology Publications, London.

Yun Heung–gil (1989) *The House of Twilight* Readers International, London.

Yunus, M. (ed.) (1984) *Jorimon of Beltoil village and Others: in search of a future* Grameen Bank, Dhaka.